TRADITION
AND
INNOVATION

D1526768

Proforma Emery

DATE DUE

SUNY Series in Modern Jewish Literature and Culture
Sarah Blacher Cohen, Editor

TRADITION
AND
INNOVATION

Reflections
on Latin American
Jewish Writing

EDITED BY

Robert DiAntonio and Nora Glickman

STATE UNIVERSITY OF NEW YORK PRESS

Published by
State University of New York Press, Albany

For information, address State University of New York Press,
State University Plaza, Albany, N.Y., 12246

Production by Cathleen Collins
Marketing by Theresa A. Swierzowski

Library of Congress Cataloging in Publication Data

Tradition and innovation : reflections on Latin American Jewish
   writing / edited by Robert DiAntonio, Nora Glickman.
      p.   cm. -- (SUNY series in modern Jewish literature and
   culture)
      ISBN 0-7914-1509-0. -- ISBN 0-7914-1510-4 (pbk.)
      1. Latin American literature--Jewish authors--History and
   criticism.   2. Latin American literature--20th century--History and
   criticism.   3. Jews in literature.   I. DiAntonio, Robert E., 1941-   .
   II. Glickman, Nora.   III. Series.
   PQ7081.A1T73   1993
   860.9'98'089924--dc20   92-25845
                                                              CIP

10 9 8 7 6 5 4 3 2 1

Contents

Introduction I

ROBERT DiANTONIO

OVER THE PAST DECADES the literary marketplace has been greatly enriched by a new wave of Latin American fiction. Masterworks by Jorge Luis Borges, Mario Vargas Llosa, Jorge Amado, Manuel Puig, and Gabriel García Márquez attest to the validity of this statement. While these Latin American writers are familiar to most English-speaking readers, Jewish Latin American authors have also played an important role in this literary renaissance. They have been able to offer a distinctive socioliterary perspective, as Jews generally have occupied positions of marginality within the dominant Catholic nations of the Americas. This has given them an opportunity to analyze both their own experience and the greater reality of their respective countries.

Presently, Jewish writers like Brazil's Moacyr Scliar and Clarice Lispector, Peru's Isaac Goldemberg and Argentina's Gerardo Mario Goloboff are beginning to acquire an international readership with successful and well-received translations. Lispector has long been considered one of the world's premier fiction writers; however, few critics to date are aware of her Jewish heritage, and even fewer have considered the influence that that heritage has exercised on her writing. Jewish authors constitute an important part of the Latin American literary community as their works are widely read and discussed. Though not yet at a level of recognition as that of Scliar or Lispector, many other writers are beginning to receive intense international attention—authors like Costa Rica's Samuel Rovinski, Cuba's José Kozer, and Argentina's Marcos Aguinis. However, other fine Latin American Jewish authors are still unknown outside the Portuguese- and Spanish-speaking worlds. It is the intention of this book to correct this anomaly as the following studies turn the attention of the English-speaking reader to the state of Jewish thought

1

and letters in Latin America, highlighting a unique vision of Jewish culture and history.

An important aspect of this general analysis will be an effort to underscore the contributions of women authors to this field, writers like Sabina Berman, Angelina Muñiz, Margo Glanz, Esther Seligson, and Manuela Fingeret. Women in observant Jewish societies held a secondary role to that of men—especially with regard to scholarship—and the book intends to explore what effect the openness of the Latin American experience has had on this present generation of authors. The studies present the tension of the contemporary Latin American Jewish female as both incorporating and rejecting the images that have been impressed upon her for generations. These authors' writings question the traditionalism of the woman's place in modern society, exploring eternal existential questions within a contemporary sociohistorical system that has been, at best, indifferent to them. In essence, their works reflect upon the role of the contemporary woman within two male-dominated societies: the traditional Jewish world and the sociopolitical actuality of present day Latin America.

These authors have placed in sharp focus the conflict that arises between their Jewish heritage and their female identity. In the Western Hemisphere, estranged from the orthodoxies of a more formalized Judaism, these writers explore the varying ways that Judaic traditions both enhance and diminish the condition of being female. They analyze the role of the Latin American Jewish female and her feelings of dual marginality.

I

These studies also explore Jewish life in communities that are little known in either the Jewish or non-Jewish world, communities unique within the Diaspora experience. The book places in sharp relief the diversity of these Jewish communities: the *gaúchos* of Rio Grande do Sul; the beachfront Copacabana communities of Rio de Janeiro; "Barrio Once," an Argentinian Hester Street; and the Caribbean atmosphere of the dwindling Jewish population of Havana. The history of Jewish immigration to Latin America has been marked by both violent anti-Semitic clashes like Argentina's "Semana trágica" and relatively unencumbered settlement in countries like Mexico and Chile.

The long Jewish historical presence in the Americas has been a fascinatingly complex experience. It comprises the exotic world of Marano and Converso adventures; Jewish settlers, slave traders, and wealthy sugar barons drawn to the religious freedom of the Dutch colonies of Brazil's tropical Northeast; Sephardic colonies from North Africa and the Levant freely moving about the Caribbean basin; and the massive immigration that accompanied Baron de Hirsh's funding of agrarian communities on the Argentine and Brazilian pampa.

The variegated backdrop that forms the underpinnings of the following studies has been detailed by scholars like Jacob Beller, Judith Laikin Elkin, and Arnold Wiznitzer.[1] This history includes incidents like the ill-fated voyage of the *S. S. St. Louis*, the so-called "Voyage of the Damned," and, surprisingly, includes unlikely heroes like the Dominican dictator Rafael Trujillo. Among the world's nations—including the United States and Canada—only Trujillo showed a willingness to offer refuge to 100,000 Jews trapped in Nazi Germany. While the rest of the world turned a deaf ear to the plight of East European Jewry, Rafael Trujillo planned to establish a Jewish settlement in the Sasua province of his country. This strange addendum to Holocaust historiography leaves one not quite sure if Trujillo's motives were purely humanitarian or if he, as Howard Sachar has suggested, wished to cull favor with what he perceived as the "Jewish-controlled press in the United States"[2] to help "sanitize"[3] his regime. After the Holocaust, survivors found their way to almost all of the Latin American nations, with the vast majority settling in Mexico, Argentina, and Brazil.

The establishment of the state of Israel in 1948 inspired many Latin American Jews to make *aliyah*, to immigrate to the Holy Land. During times of extreme political and financial turbulence, immigration to Israel and other lands such as France and the United States, created immigrant communities that produced a rich Latin American literature in exile.

Contemporary Middle Eastern politics also has had a strong effect on immigration. During the Sinai Campaign in 1956 thousands of Jews—mainly Sephardim—were placed in detention camps in Egypt. After establishing one of the oldest and most illustrious Jewish communities in the history of the Diaspora, Jews were ordered to leave the country and within a matter of weeks 15,000 were admitted to Brazil and 9,000 to

---

1. See Jacob Beller, *Jews in Latin America* (New York: Jonathan David, 1969); Judith Laikin Elkin, *Jews of the Latin American Republics* (Chapel Hill: The University of North Carolina Press, 1980); and Arnold Wiznitzer, *Jews in Colonial Brazil* (Morningside Heights, NY: Columbia University Press, 1960).

2. Howard Sachar, *Diaspora: An Inquiry into the Contemporary Jewish World* (New York: Harper & Row, 1985), 238.

3. Sachar, 238.

Argentina. Some would eventually earn a living in areas like São Paulo's Bom Retiro alongside Syrian, Lebanese, and Palestinian immigrants. In Rio de Janeiro there even was formed an Arab-Jewish business association.

In general terms the large Jewish communities of Argentina and Brazil are predominately secular. Although newer communities of small sects of ultra-orthodox groups, Chabad, are making inroads, the vast majority of Jewish Latin Americans group together more for social than religious reasons, attending local sporting and social centers, the Hebraica, or the Macabi.

II

The half-million Jews living in Latin America have passed through periods of difficulties as their position between marginal status and the mainstream has not been maintained without conflict. The concept of marginality entails a balance that a person must sustain between the culture and religion of one's ancestors and the desire to assimilate into a new, non-Jewish, way of life. Writer and critic Saúl Sosnowski observes that this literature is born "of the encounter between ancient Jewish culture and the New World."[4] He affirms that it is "also concerned with writing the living history of a recent past that has certain repercussions for the millenial history of the Jews. Latin American history—in its particular national configurations—and Jewish history intersect to celebrate their commonalities."[5]

Since there exists a strong interrelationship between the social history of a people and their literature, it must be kept in mind that Jewish assimilation in Latin America was not always easily accomplished and the resulting tension was often the cause of a dynamic surge of literary activity. The immigrant generation with its strong Yiddish storytelling background was generally bound to a realistic presentation of the difficulties of life in the "New World," while this present generation of Jewish writers parallels the more universal literary currents of our time.

The Jewish writer in Latin America is and always has been torn between conflicting loyalties. From this tension is born their dynamic and insightful literature, a literature that enriches the mainstream of modern Latin American fiction as it underscores the unique and multifaceted nature of Judaic literary history.

---

4. Saúl Sosnowski, "Latin American Jewish Literature: On Ethnic and National Boundries," *Folio*, No 17, (September 1987), 1.

5. Sosnowski, 4.

Within the dominant non-Jewish cultures of Latin America, Jewish life has flourished in many aspects, but seems to have diminished with respect to the maintenance of religious fervor. In multi-ethnic cities like Rio de Janeiro, Buenos Aires, and São Paulo, there is a sense of alienation as many aspects of Jewish culture seem to be quickly eroding. Nachman Spiegel, commenting on Elkin and Merkx's *The Jewish Presence in Latin America*, concludes that, "Jews have been more of a tolerated intrusion than a welcome inclusion. . . . Very little, however, indicates any broad or lasting changes are in the offing. Irreconcilable differences are likely to survive between Jewish and National identities."[6] He goes on to state that, "Jews there seem far more prepared to flee from Judaism than leave the good life, however shaky, that generations of hard work and difficult adaption have earned."[7] This tension that results from being cut off from one's roots gives rise to themes that will be traced through the works of various authors.

III

In very general terms, and excluding specific epochs, the present-day post-immigrant generations now seem to be comfortable within the confines of the larger culture. Within the broad canopy of Jewish literature, there exists a wide spectrum of writings. There are authors who may only make passing reference to their ethnic heritage and others—many of whom are non-observant—who create literary works that examine ethnocentrism: the resonance of their families' *Yiddishkeit* traditions or the shards of their Sephardic background.

In general most Jewish immigrants left worlds of poverty, oppression, and persecution, worlds where a strong sense of community and appreciation for scholarship were forged, for a New World where tensions existed, but not to the same degree. The insular world of the Jews in Latin America opened up and, often within a single generation, intermarriage, commercial interests, radicalism, and apathy left traditions and religion relegated only to the yearly observance of the High Holidays.

The passage from marginality to mainstream was achieved with only limited conflict, especially for a people whose history has been marred with long periods of repression and ghettoization, a people whose faith and unity have sustained them for centuries.

---

6. Nachman Spiegal, "Tolerated in a Precarious Environment," a review of *The Jewish Experience in Latin America*, ed. Elkin and Merkx. In *The Jerusalem Post* 10 (February 1990); 16.
7. Spiegal, 16.

Within the umbrella themes of cultural identity and cultural persistence are explored the conflicts born of the immigrant experience, the subject of intermarriage, the spector of the Holocaust, the Inquisition as a reality and a metaphor for present-day oppression, Zionism and Israel reflected in literature, the "Goldene Medine," the expanded Diaspora (Latin American Jewish writers in exile again), the influence of Yiddishists and *Yiddishkeit* on Latin America fiction, and the Jewish woman's perspective.

While the theme of the immigrant experience seems to have run its course, the newer issues of the Holocaust and the literature of exile in Paris, Tel Aviv, and New York are presently being written. This writing revitalizes and broadens the scope of the Latin American literary perspective as individual writers attempt to define and analyze their Jewish identity, creating a literary expression that is linked to the history of all people.

IV

Literature is a highly personal and imaginative method for exploring the problems of Jewish cultural identity. Any analysis of this Jewish writing begins with the assumption that Jewish literature, like Jewish culture and religion itself, is marked by extreme diversity. In religious and academic circles the discussion long has persisted as to exactly what it is that defines Jewish writing. Judeo-Latin American writing is not an easily defined concept and is a term that is almost impossible to pin down. Mark Schechner points out in his essay "Jewish Writers," that "Neither 'Jewish writer' nor 'Jewish fiction' is an obvious or self-justifying subdivision of literature, any more than Jewishness itself is now a self-evident cultural identity. . .(However) it is not unreasonable to invoke 'the Jewish writer' as a convenient shorthand for a feature of the literary census that we want to examine but are not yet prepared to define."[8] Bearing in mind this cautionary note, a study of Jewish writing in Latin America merits consideration from a socioliterary perspective. An analysis of the role of minorities in any culture is a critical approach whose validity contributes to a broader understanding of existing literary forms.

This is a literature whose history dates back to the time of European "discovery," in fact, some say to Columbus's arrival.[9] Jews and crypto-Jews

---

8. Mark Schechner, "Jewish Writers," *The Harvard Guide to Contemporary American Writing*, ed. Daniel Hoffman (Cambridge: Belknap Press, 1979), 191.

9. See Salvador de Madariaga, *Christopher Columbus* (New York: Ungar, 1967).

have played a significant role in the development of Latin American literary history. Thus, this book begins with the simple recognition of the immensity of the topic to be undertaken. We have chosen relevant thematic, sociopolitical and aesthetic issues that will help define and narrow the vastness of this writing. In the space that this book affords us, we hope to shed new light on these issues, while suggesting directions for future studies.

To better understand the intense diversity of the Jewish historical consciousness in Latin America, we are studying the writing of a broad spectrum of authors. As Argentina, Brazil, and Mexico received the vast majority of immigrants, we have had to weight our studies to reflect this fact. It is also well to remember that each author's sense of "Jewishness" and his or her use of Judaism itself as a literary theme inevitably underlies that author's world view. All of these writers touch upon a sense of continuity with Judaic history; all are affected to a greater or lesser degree by a "Jewish presence" in their writing.

In their fiction these authors stress a sense of community with all women and men: the Judaic moral code of *mentschlekeit*. Many attempt directly to explain the Jewish situation, while others, like Clarice Lispector, create an aesthetically universal art. However, even Lispector's writing is forged by a strong undercurrent of traditional Judaic symbology.

V

Latin Americans now consider this flourishing of Jewish writing an integral component of the contemporary narrative scene. It is both marginal writing that is closely drawn from the Diaspora experience itself and an expression that stems from contemporary Latin American life. Each collaborator, in stressing her or his particular critical approach in the field of literature, also emphasizes the sociopolitical dimension of this vibrant body of writing. With their varied backgrounds and differing approaches to literature, our contributors have presented and analyzed this writing for both the specialist and the general reader.

Again, the following studies are seeking to introduce an important group of writers to an English-speaking audience and to analyze their treatment of literary themes related to Jewish life in the Americas. We hope that our studies will go beyond the strictly literary and bring to light the unique nature of the Latin American Jewish experience. Contemporary Jewish writing is flourishing worldwide, and this book focuses attention on the Spanish and Portuguese component of this literary renaissance.

Tradition and Innovation is an attempt to illuminate the literature that the *Am ha-Sefer*, People of the Book, have written of diasporic life in the New World. It provides the reader with a series of critical articles on the major movements, concerns, and writers of this dynamic literature. Taken in its totality, the book serves as both a general introduction to the subject of Jewish writing in Latin America and a useful aid in disseminating and understanding these works and writers for students and scholars in the fields of Judaic, Spanish American, Brazilian, and comparative literature.

Introduction II:
The Authors Speak For Themselves

NORA GLICKMAN

THE SEVENTEEN ESSAYS that compose this book analyze the work of a selected number of contemporary Latin American Jewish writers. Some deal with a particular aspect of their fiction, others treat the entire *oeuvre*. In order to present a more comprehensive picture of these writings, I have asked each of the authors represented in the essays that follow to provide a brief answer to two questions:[1]

1. What does it mean to you to be a Jewish writer in your country?
2. How is Judaism expressed in your own writing?

My purpose in asking these questions was to gain insight into the authors' views of the world. The answers I received are as diverse and individualistic as the authors themselves; and yet, beyond their particular styles, there are some common ideas and themes that give coherence and unity to their responses.

All these writers share a tradition of multiple exiles and migrations, and all are fully acculturated in the countries where they live. Thus, many of them have double or even multiple identifications, which might extend to being a Latin American, a Jew, a woman, a fighter against oppression, and so forth.

These multiple identifications can be both exciting and frustrating, leading one to be pulled in different directions. Ricardo Feierstein, an Argentine novelist, uses the word *mestizo* to refer to the dichotomy which the people of his generation suffer when attempting to bridge the past with the future generations. Manuela Fingueret, an Argentine writer,

---

1. Clarice Lispector (Brazil) and Jacobo Fijman (Argentina), who are the subject of two essays, are deceased.

speaks of a movement of oscillation—like a pendulum—between the ties to an ancestral past and an attachment to the local lifestyles of her native country. And Ariel Dorfman expresses the desire for a homeland and for a sense of belonging: he observed that the experience of uprootedness from one's native land, coupled with the subsequent return to one's country, may result in the fear of not fitting in anywhere anymore. All these writers have an awareness of sharing in the unique experience of living on the fringes of history, alienated and alone.

The sense of cultural estrangement is sharpened for writers living outside their native countries, who have chosen to continue writing in their mother tongue. Gerardo Mario Goloboff, an Argentine who resides in France, sees these writers' multiple foreignness as part of a common tradition of permanent exile, of added up diasporas.

Coming from countries with a dominant Catholic majority, the reception of their work is a matter of importance to these minority writers. Samuel Rovinski is concerned with the way he is perceived by others. He is made to feel proud for his ability to reproduce the most typical speech of the Costa Rican native, although he is a stranger in his own land because of his foreign-sounding surname. For Moacyr Scliar, being a writer in Brazil presents a paradox. His writing presents an enigma to Brazilian readers who have a stereotypical image of the Jew. Scliar's characters do not fit that image, as they are not real people; they are hybrids. And this is precisely what Scliar and the rest of the writers represented here seek to demonstrate: that they have created a space between different worlds, the Latin American and the Jewish, the Indian and the biblical, the secular and the religious, the rational and the mystical. That space is the realm of the writer and his or her imagination.

Some of the authors welcome the different sources of inspiration for their fiction and especially express their debt to the richness of their tradition: Luisa Futoransky, for example, blends the vein of Jewish humor with magical realism, and deals in this particular way with injustice and oppression. Moacyr Scliar, looking at Brazilian history through Jewish eyes, focuses on discovering the Jewish condition as it appears in the "New World."

A number of writers reject any sort of categorization, as they point out that a search into one's identity in itself could be construed as discriminatory. José Kozer asserts that he writes not because he belongs to a certain group, gender, nation, or color, but rather in spite of belonging to all of them. Similarly, Luisa Futoransky resents being singled out for the uniqueness of her condition as a Jew, just as she opposes being singled out as an Argentine, a writer, or a woman. And yet, in response to the stated pressure to define herself, she turns her resentment into an advantage by capitalizing on her distinctiveness. The case of Angelina Muñiz is similar. Rather than assuming her Mexican, Sephardic and Ashkenazic origins as "a schizophrenic burden," she welcomes these as a source of satisfaction and as yet another distinctive trait of her "typical" multiple Jewish background. Mexican novelist Esther Seligson, who characterizes her writing as deriving from a "double source/spring," searches there for "the roots of the human condition, the Universal Being, beyond all particulars."[2]

Some of the writers attest that, while they lacked a formal Jewish education—or, as in the case of Margo Glanz, the Judaism of their childhoods was of a folkloric nature, sensually alive in ritual and practice, yet detached from written theology and history—still they find in their adult lives that they have adopted a Jewish consciousness that is present in their texts. For writers like Toker, Gutman and Scliar, a sense of being Jewish was nurtured by the Bible and by works of Jewish authors, such as Sholem Aleichem, Kafka, and Babel, which were important to their intellectual and artistic development. A number of them recognize the power the Holocaust played in awakening an awareness of their Jewish identity.

Some of these authors express their Jewishness consciously and directly. In the writings of the Mexican Angelina Muñiz, for example, Jewish symbols, motifs, and themes are always deliberately present. In the prose of Gerardo M. Goloboff, Jewishness is an essence that can be perceived in his depictions of reality, history, and language. José Kozer notes the Jewish tonalities in his poetry, but Judaism is mainly manifest in his choice of major themes, like the Bible, the Kabbalah, the rabbinical tradition. And Samuel Rovinski, from Costa Rica, contends that Jewishness simply cannot be denied—it is expressed consciously or unconsciously because it is inherent to one's cultural background.

Frequently, Jewish consciousness entails a political commitment. Ariel Dorfman's main concern is to inscribe his literature into a philosophy of political liberation. Manuela Fingueret, in response to the violations she witnessed under the Argentine military rule in the late seventies, sees writing as an act of defiance, as another way of opposing authoritarianism. And Argentine dramatist Ricardo Halac draws his lessons from his own experience of persecution and intolerance and links it, in his plays, to that

---

2. See interview with Esther Seligson, p. 58 of this book.

of the Jewish past—the Spanish Inquisition and the expulsion of the Jews from Spain in 1492.

In translating the responses of these sixteen writers, I have attempted to preserve as much of the original style as possible. This sometimes meant sacrificing English idioms in order to convey the rhetorical embellishments that typify Latin American literature.

MARCOS AGUINIS, Argentina
Translated by Nora Glickman

I am tempted to respond with questions. What is specifically Jewish about it? How could I know? Is it perceived in the themes, the language, the form, or the context? The residual and irritating Jewish custom of answering with questions!. . .What is interesting about this often repeated fact are its motivations. I will point out some because—whether I want to accept it or not—they are articulated in my life and in my literature.

To answer with another question, in some way, is to disobey—to rebel. Jewish history is filled with vigorous rebellions, many of epic proportions. It is filled with rebellions that enrich anecdotes and nourish humor. There is also a secret rebellion, quite stubborn, that colors the grey periods of submission.

To answer with questions implies a rejection of dogmas, an adherence to a certain kind of skepticism. The truth is not as clear nor as apprehensible as it seems to be. It evades man. The Talmudic texts prove this awareness: they are a perpetual torrent of questions that lead to further questions and to conflicting opinions. This is also why the Talmud was fanatically burnt for centuries.

To answer this way is a gesture of personal dignity, of proving an equivalent dialogue. It is not a vertical, but rather it is a horizontal link. It is a fluid process, of going back and forth. This binds the relationship; it crumbles the thin wall. To answer with another question helps one to distend. It often helps to smile.

On the other hand, it is a cheap antidote to pathological narcissism. When you answer with a question you say: "I don't know," or "I am not omnipotent." Dangerous omnipotence is wisely displaced towards the unteachable, towards God. It implies a frequent juggling of modesty that helps one to survive, especially during difficult times.

It occurs to me that answering with a question is a gregarious feature, because it links and sustains the union. It is like a melody that escapes the fading of the final chord. It keeps the interlocutors united in the suspense of an unfinished dialogue.

Finally, intelligence and mystery. Both infinite. The more they continue to grow, the more the potential for growth.

I will stop here. I am changing the course of my writing.

And now I will go on. I went on a roundabout way to point out some roots, some influences; I might add certain obsessions: a visceral rejection of an attachment to justice, a solidarity with the weak, a respect for people, a love of life. In order to avoid confusion I will add that I don't consider myself a saint. Moreover, I recognize that I admire the prophets—their way of acting, their way of speaking.

With all this in mind, am I answering the question?

And if I really answer it, am I not contradicting the initial paragraphs? It wouldn't bother me. It's just another Jewish feature.

SABINA BERMAN, Mexico
Translated by Nora Glickman

What does it mean to be a Jewish writer in Mexico?

Each person is a unique hybrid, not reproducible, of her or his circumstances. To be a Jew has meant, historically, having a sharpened consciousness of partaking of at least two destinies. I am Mexican and I am Jewish, and I am Jewish-Mexican and Mexican-Jewish. I am Mexican by decision and following many years of studying what it is to be Mexican; I am also Jewish by choice and by faith.

As to the question regarding the Jewish presence in my literature, I believe that if I have affected in any way the Mexican readers of my work, it is by impressing upon them that Mexico is a country formed by a Catholic *mestizo* majority, and various minorities—the indigenous minority and the descendants of immigrants who arrived in Mexico during this century. Such has not been a conscious decision, but a natural consequence of my particular condition.

ARIEL DORFMAN, Chile

For many years I did not feel while I was writing that my Jewish identity was in any way at the forefront of what I was trying to express, perhaps because being Jewish has—at least seemingly—not been particularly important in my life. This may have been due to the fact that my parents were not (and are still not) practicing Jews, or that I never had the chance to become part of any stable Jewsih community due to my own peculiar history of exiles and migrations (born in Argentina, left for the States at age two, went to Chile at age twelve, forced into exile twenty years later, lived in France, Holland, and presently the U.S., still struggling with ways of going back). The truth is that I always consider myself a Chilean and Latin American writer above all, profoundly interested in the ways in which my literature might inscribe itself in the efforts of the people in my adopted country and in my native continent to achieve liberation and consciousness.

Although I am aware that such a desire—to assimilate and to belong—is a radically Jewish experience, I did not, at least in the surface of my mind, live it as such. The main Jewish character who managed to slip his way into my fiction, David Wiseman in *The Last Song of Manuel Sendero*, considers that the foundational experience of his life was the moment the people of Chile elected Salvador Allende as President on September 4, 1970—the coming out of exile of those oppressed and marginalized serving as a metaphor for his own coming home. David is not quite my alter ego, as some critics have suggested, but his words in that context do have a strong autobiographical resonance. If that dream of David's (and mine) of fusing with a people and a revolution had turned out the way we expected, who knows what my literature would be like. What followed were years of wandering. Instead of a sense of belonging, an exploration of a living, immediate community that I had chosen as my own, my life burned with a fierce longing to be back where I though that things would have once again a meaning, an order, a center. It is possible that this experience of distance and rejection, of desire for a homeland, has helped me to understand what could well be termed the Jewish component of my fundamental obsessions. My many returns to Chile in these years—some in my imagination, some with this body of mine getting off and on places—have revealed to me that I do not quite fit in the country I had constructed for myself in exile, that perhaps I never did fit there—or anywhere.

Is this Jewish? Is the ethical strain that stubbornly crisscrosses my literature another product? Once you start asking questions of this sort, it can be endless: Is it a coincidence that my first novel starts with a Jewish detective in Auschwitz trying to find out who is killing the prisoners before they can be gassed? Is the presence of a man without a face and without an identity who steals features from others (in my novel *Mascara*) a Latin American version of Kafka, as several reviewers have written, or is there a more penetrating and recondite relationship with a culture of alienation that both Kafka and I belong to by virtue of our birth and the looks that others give us? Is *The Last Song of Manuel Sendero* a book imbued with messianic figures, its meditation over the sacrifice of sons by fathers, its search for a common humanity (and story) we can all tell? Is my obsession with the "disappeared" only to be understood from a Chilean or Third World perspective, or is it fueled by another sort of mourning and sadness, another sort of struggle to remain and appear and be heard?

If the answers to these questions reveal Jewish themes and passions behind my work, I would not be surprised. That still would not change why I write, and for whom I write, nor would it situate in a different context the reasons why I write or deny the specific place my work has in Latin American culture that is, after all, a hybrid woven from so many cultures and traditions.

RICHARDO FEIERSTEIN, Argentina
Translated by Nora Glickman

Jewish writers born in this part of the world share two characteristics: a cultural *mestizaje* and an unevenness with history. I am a product of both.

I am a cultural *mestizo*:[1] A bi-frontal being, with two heads oriented simultaneously to both the Jewish and the Latin American consciousness; to the birth of Israel and to the feats of American liberation; to the European Holocaust and the genocide that resulted from the Argentinean military dictatorship. I am in the fringes of history: I was born at a strange moment, amidst the coughs of Hiroshima and the take-off of the electronic and the computerized era. I remained in the middle. A generation of the wilderness: neither a slave in Egypt, nor an inhabitant of the land of milk and honey. Condemned to wander, as in the biblical parable, amidst half-realized dreams. Ours—the youthful sixties—were years of hope and of an alluring uprootedness.

I was born in Latin America. I was not part of that European Judaism that saturates the senses: of the magic of Yiddish, of rabbis riding donkeys, of the *heder* rod, of the taste of herring. I was too late for that date with history.

I belong to the first native generation in Argentina. I love my country, whose idiomatic and vital codes—those of my childhood—are my "portable" land. The landscape of my port-city neighborhood is the substance of which my dreams are woven.

Although I have a limited historical memory and received a traditional religious upbringing, my Jewish condition deepened at that time. My

---

1. Ethnic, and by extension, cultural mixture.

mestizo identity included a familiarity with River-Plate slang as well as a passion for soccer, up to the years that I lived in Israel. There I expressed myself in Hebrew, at a Kibbutz in the Golan Heights.

Jewish and human components appear together in my literature in variable proportions. They share a temporal asymmetry: the more alive the Jewish element, the less I write about it, and vice versa. There are stages for action and others for reflection: what they have in common is their intensity.

Whatever one writes is autobiographical. The difference—as Andre Malraux points out—is that the writer believes he can turn his experience into destiny. I have displayed in four consecutive novels—*Entre la izquierda y la pared* (Between the Left and the Wall), *El caramelo descompuesto* (The Broken down Candy), *Escala uno en cincuenta* (Scale of One to Fifty), and *Mestizo*—the Jewish and historic saga of my generation.

The theoretical journey begins in the sixties in Latin America. It travels through the Israeli experience, then it re-enters Argentina in the era of the Argentinean military dictatorship and the return to democracy in 1983. The dichotomy about being a Jew and a Latin American is critical to those of us who live in a continent that is also *mestizo*, where we attempt through our fiction to bridge past generations with future ones.

In my novels I have attempted to build the character as well as his identity. The graphic synthesis concludes with the design of a tree: the roots, trunk, branches and fruits nurture a continuously enriching landscape. Each one transmits his essence to the other, and reinforces the central idea that each narrator, each reader builds his own tree with his life.

The difference lies in embodying the search for identity through the body itself. The Jewish and American condition "built" through daily actions and through being engaged with reality. It isn't passed on through blood or religion. Existence determines consciousness.

The English translation of my stories and poems is entitled *We, the Generation of the Wilderness* (Ford & Brown Publishers, Boston, 1989). This area of my literature includes essays and journalistic articles, which are not limited to Jewish matters, but integrate them as essential components of my writing.

MANUELA FINGUERET, Argentina
Translated by Nora Glickman

How does the Jewish element appear in your literature?

In my personal history, Judaism is part of certain zones of marginality, which constitute an expressive memory that lives within me. When I attempt to recreate my sense of difference in my writings, it sometimes causes me pain and sometimes pleasure. According to the circumstances in which my expressive voices develop, Judaism will appear either explicitly or tangentially as one of the masks that compose my identity.

Although I may perceive writing as a permanent construction, all the elements that form the kaleidoscope of myself, including Judaism, are the result of constant reinterpretation, which I attempt both in my poetry and in my prose.

I am a link in the history of a people that is forever writing a book. In this unending time, my literature is permeated by real and imaginary dreams.

What does it mean to you to be an Argentine-Jewish writer?

The term "Jewish-Argentine" only emphasizes this oscillating feeling, in which my Judaism is the product on the one hand of the people of Buenos Aires and on the other of my Argentine identity, which is given substance by the ancestral histories that make me who I am.

For me it also meant a way of opposing authoritarianism and death at a moment in which diversity was a dangerous and clandestine activity under the governing dictatorship. Since the return of democracy, the understanding of this indissoluble link between the nature of being Jewish and Argentinean is an essential task in a country that is still struggling to grow as a nation.

It is not a task I am forced to accomplish. I simply believe that this current that flows and feeds off itself keeps alive the wandering word—a vital expression of the lights and the shadows that run through me.

LUISA FUTORANSKY, Argentina, France
Translated by Nora Glickman

What does it mean to you to be an Argentinean-Jewish writer residing in France?

I will tell you of an experience I had during a recent congress, where one of the topics of discussion was one's experience of liberation, writing in a language other than one's native tongue. After reviewing my resume and those of the other Jewish participants, the organizers of the conference identified us solely as Jews, while the faith of the other members was not singled out. This event occurred during the Persian Gulf war. I felt compelled to confront the organizers. I had been singled out as a Jew.

It bothers me that we still categorize ourselves according to our origin, our profession, our faith, our nationality. Our work should speak for itself. If I am to call myself anything in my work, that is my choice; that others should do so disturbs me. Such an act reduces me to a label. I have encountered this behavior for nearly fifty years and convinced myself that it enriches my writing. I capitalize on such feeling in my work.

How do Jewish elements appear in your literature?

We should consider other distinctions: in my case, there are many elements to my identity. I come from a periphery: I was born in the village of Santos Lugares (Holy Places) at the periphery of a large metropolis, Buenos Aires, and I moved to another Holy Place—Jerusalem, the terrible, the celestial. My comings and goings seem to be between Holy Places. Some days I would like to follow the path of exile of my grandparents and of my own exile as well. I have moved from Jerusalem to China to Japan, and now reside in France.

To be a Jew was always to be other. It lay in our gestures, our daily routines, our tastes that persisted—even if Argentinean nutrition drowned us in opulence when we were children—in memories of our singing, our living, our fears, our games of hide and seek. We Jews have another way of experiencing fear, which contributes to the mosaic of our lives. And all this constitutes our personal palette—the archetype of our memory. What's essentially Jewish colors our palette. I am me and all of this as well.

MARGO GLANTZ, Mexico
Translated by Nora Glickman

These kinds of questions leave me perplexed. I tend to look for the answer in others: almost always turning to Walter Benjamin, the writer I admire the most. Like myself—*toute proportion gard*ée—but under very different circumstances, he was born, according to Gershon Sholem, in a golden ghetto. Only mine was the golden *"churrigueresco"*[1] of a Jesuit church, while his belonged to a humanistic Europe where culture unified men and sought to put an end to exile. Nazism ungilded Benjamin's ghetto and defined mine: I began to feel Jewish when, back in 1944, I watched in a newscast at a local cinema how some young girls identical to me were taken—numb, what other way?—to a concentration camp.

This strangeness had antecedents, but they were mainly anecdotal: I had felt it violently in 1939, during a pseudo-pogrom——of a size proportionate to an underdeveloped country—in which my father was almost lynched by a band of local fascists. Much earlier, my consciousness of Judaism, which was comparative, would awaken during Wise King's day: the children of my neighborhood opened their toys simply because

---

1. Exaggerated baroque, following the style of Churriguera, a Spanish architect.

they were Christian. The marvelous Easter Saturdays of my childhood gave me a very disquieting feeling: the great papier maché Judases burnt with much noise, were the living image of those evil ones who had crucified Christ; in the middle, a delicious image, my trashy Christianity at the hairy hands of a priest, like in my dreams of King Kong; and then the sumptuous breakfasts that an aristocratic lady prepared to celebrate my first communion, with masses of white leather, very pure wax candles, tamales, chocolate, and pirate editions of the martyrs of Christianity. To even things up, there were traditional festivities: Pessach, above all, and Chanukah, in which my uncle, the baker, would give us a real silver peso; the false fasts of Yom Kippur and a fascination and complex obsession with the Kol Nindre sounds, or the tenor-like voice of my father singing Ukrainian songs while my mother served a delicious dish of gefilte fish.

To be Jewish-Mexican was, by all appearances, a natural thing, but of a folkloric nature. Its dimensions were outlined with some precision in my book: *The Genealogies*. There I outlined an adventure into the interior of a woman waiting to produce three of my main attributes: the feminine one, and my double identity. Curiously, my genealogic adventure had, as it should have had, sequels. Several texts of this kind have been published in Mexico since 1981, the year in which I published mine: they are by women, some are also by Jewish women.

Under these conditions the word integration sounds, at the least, equivocal. The feeling of exile, which is typical of the Jew, has followed me just the same—whether it is an exile from God, from the Promised Land or from oneself—as was the case with Walter Benjamin. But the needle is tenuous, weak, almost sweet, a little coarse. The integration produced *avant la lettre* and by *interposita persona*, in the immigrants' ship in which my parents travelled. My mother tells me of her experience: I understand that since her exit from Russia she protected herself against exile through a slow process of finding her roots in my father. Now that he is dead, she has territorialized him definitively. He, or rather his voice, had the effect of launching, and with extreme unction, a Yiddish poet; he turned Russian into the language of exile and of love, and communicated with the other world, that of his chosen country, in Spanish. We, his daughters, born in Mexico, assumed his design and stayed anchored in the third language, sprinkling it with hebraisms, like the chicanos who speak English truffled with mexicanisms.

Don't think I have an Oedipus complex. It is rather a portable, messianic sense, discolored and very precarious. That messianism, which does not dare confess its ambiguity, opposes, in a literal sense, the complacency of having become territorialized, with certain reticence, in a minor literature:[2] the Mexican.

GERARDO MARIO GOLOBOFF, Argentina, France
Translated by Nora Glickman

What does it mean to be a Jewish writer in France today?

I suppose my case must seem somewhat atypical, since I am not a French Jewish writer who resides in France, but a Latin American—an Argentine, to be precise—and that entails an additional dimension of trans-territoriality and of estrangement.

As I view my situation in terms of double or multiple foreignness, I have to acknowledge that the primary thing for me was exile, having to leave my native land, and being unable to return. I became, through an unforeseen turn of events, a sort of zombie who wanders around cities and unknown streets and sidewalks, amidst unfamiliar people and histories, carrying within him another history, other peoples and other streets.

Before leaving Argentina I had started, somewhat belatedly, to acknowledge my Jewish condition and to accept it in all its complexity. But during those years, Argentina's social and political problems were so pressing and so pervasive that they imposed themselves on me with a weight of their own, creating boundaries and a prioritization of concerns. Given this, I realize that these realities, and quite probably my own immaturity, which was also part of reality, must have intervened in the development of my Jewish identity.

In France, on the other hand, I learned everything slowly, painfully, but also more calmly, with a space, and with direction. I also experienced similarities, affinities, origins with other beings, whose blood was mingled with mine; who over the centuries were driven from their houses and their lands, who were forced to wander, like myself, through foreign places, and probably in worse circumstances than my own. How could I fail to recognize myself in them—an insignificant carrier of a trait that marked our common essence? In treasuring my own language and in hearing another that sounded, if not strange, foreign to me, how could I not rediscover the tremors of those lips that whispered only in Yiddish the truths that were closest to my own heart?

---

2. "Minor" in the sense that Deleuze and Guattari use the term, when they speak of Kafka: "A minor literature is not the literature of a minor language, but rather the literature that a minority produces within a major language."

I believe that all that is, more or less, what it means to me to be an Argentinean writer and a Jew in France: someone who adds up diasporas and who interweaves stories in his original Castilian to which he adds, I don't know in what order nor to what degree but I guess very intensely, the languages resulting from exile.

How do you integrate the Jewish element in your literature?

The Jewish element is not an addition or an adjective that should be pointed out or underlined. It is a substantive way of being and feeling reality, history, my own personal history, the life and death of loved ones, love, friendship, the whole world. And naturally, the word and the writing, the book, all that is what verbal imagination (and Jewish verbal imagination) have contributed to human culture. That's why I make an effort so that what's Jewish in my writing should not be present, or that it is only slightly present. It should not appear in my literature through idioms, words or anecdotes, but rather in the most interior possible way; like an essence, like writing itself.

I would like to believe that Jewishness is felt and sensed in my literature at each instance. It is a world in which what's Jewish is present, secretly present, which is how everything that is really important should, in my estimation, manifest its existence in a work of art. To say, to speak, to name, to number is, in the final analysis, an easy habit. To work with silence and with sensations, with the spaces that the voice and the word leave behind, seems to me more adventurous and more risky. But it's what makes working with language and writing all the more fascinating.

DANIEL GUTMAN, Argentina
Translated by Nora Glickman

How is Jewishness reflected in your literature?

The influence of Jewish heritage on my literature up to this date has been weak. I lack a Jewish education; I didn't come from a home which kept the traditions and rituals of the Jewish calendar. Nor did I, as a child, hear my elders speak Yiddish or Hebrew. Neither have I preserved on my own the thousand-year-old yearning to return to the Promised Land.

Coming from Argentina, where a laicism of agnostic character has always prevailed—barely tainted by some family dinners on the occasion of Rosh Hashanah or Pesach—I did not feel my connection with Jewish people until adolescence, when I discovered Jewish writers.

Through the reading of poetry I arrived at Ibn Gabirol, Heine, and the King of the Psalms. Through fiction I met Kafka and Proust, Bashevis Singer and Amos Oz, Cynthia Ozick and Saul Bellow. And thanks to my excursions as a reader through the gardens of philosophy and linguistics, psychology and anthropology, I came to Freud and Maimonides, Josephus Flavius and Marcuse, Baruch Spinoza and Bergson.

I admired all of them, and many others, long before knowing that we belonged to the same people. And thanks to the influence of their work I began to take a growing interest in the history of the Jewish people and what it means to be a part of it. That is why I often say that my Judaism is more a task of my present and my future than a gift from my past.

With "Erosion," a long poem published in 1989, I attempted a Jewish theme for the first time. I have several writing projects that will continue along those lines, and I hope to be able to turn a dream I had in Florence many years ago into a novel, as prefiguring a fantastic story about the prophet Elijah.

What does it mean to you to be a Jewish-Argentine writer?

A writer, a Jew, an Argentine—these three words refer to three possible identities: Each one presents a challenge, a project implying the step from adjectivity to substantivity. These are identities in process, activities of becoming that never achieve a state of being. Thus, there is no conclusive definition for any of these identities, and nobody can finally assert what it means to be a writer, a Jew, and an Argentine. The task of forging a human identity is the art of maintaining unity while avoiding rigidity and stagnation.

Therefore there are various ways of being a writer, a Jew, an Argentine. These are not crystallized identities but rather identities in progress; their greatest yearning is to find definitions and to throw their light and darkness on new, unedited speculation and propositions. Finally, I can only speak of my particular way of being an Argentine Jewish writer, in terms that may not work for others.

If, on the one hand, I feel as a Jewish writer protected by a vision of reality that consecrates the verb as being the texture of the world, and which understands the world as an event of verbal nature, as an Argentine writer I consider myself the beneficiary of my Hispanic heritage and of the great Latin American creations; that is why I carry on an internal dialogue between these two traditions, by my choices of style, theme, and vocabulary.

My identity as a writer, a Jew, and an Argentine flows as a dialogue among those three fields of the human experience. I have often felt—and illustrious examples testify I am not the only one—the temptation to eliminate one or other of these three great tributaries. This is understandable, since a dialogue is easier when only two partake of it.

The third presents a threat of exclusion to the other two, and if one is excluded, its jealous resentment is bound to increase. But I have always resisted, and will continue to resist the temptation to suppress a problem when it is not fully understood. I leave to my writing the responsibility for giving testimony about the development of that dialogue. I am also prepared to have my books judged as proof of the maturity of this difficult process of communication. Let my poems and my novels answer for me, and let justice be tempered with mercy.

RICARDO HALAC, Argentina
Translated by Nora Glickman

In what way does your Jewish origin appear in your work?

The reading of the Bible, which I was encouraged to pursue since I was a child, leads me above all to a philosophical answer; I feel a need to fight against injustice, just as the great prophets teach us. Arthur Miller, one of my mentors, fought an unrelenting battle against injustice, especially in his early works. The criticism of social inequality that appears in my last work of Open Theatre, entitled "Ruido de Rotas Cadenas" (The Clamor of Broken Chains), can be traced back to my first production "Soledad para cuatro" (Solitude for Four), where I defend the controversial idea that there is no true love between a couple when their love is built on abundance on one side and deficiency on the other. The analysis of intolerance and religious persecution in "La cabala y la cruz" (The Kabbalah and the Cross), and the denunciation of "the dirty war" crimes in "Lejana tierra prometida" (Far Away Promised Land)—which was the first Argentinean work to open even under the military regime and the first to include a reference to the Mothers of the Plaza de Mayo—further exemplify the iron-like morality in which I was brought up.

But this philosophical answer doesn't take us very far. Other cultures have demanded a similar sacrifice from the artist. "It can be costly to defend a just cause," Sophocles warned. "The artist should not side with those who make power, but rather with those who suffer from power," Camus said. I believe that a review of my daily past could provide you with a richer answer.

If we accept, as Sartre says, that "we are what we make of what other people do to us," then what is fundamental—what made me into the person I am—is how I was treated as a child, and the situation that led my parents to be so overprotective and worrying. I was an overprotected child, held very tightly to my mother's bosom; she had come from very far away—Syria. I saw the insecurity with which my father walks on this land—he also was an immigrant from Damascus. I heard strange languages spoken in my successive houses in Buenos Aires—Arabic and French. The first was the intimate language of my parents; the second was used when they did not want those who were present to know what they were saying. My father had financial difficulties. He admired immigrants who had made money (which I thought loathsome). And then there was his love for culture, in spite of all his confusion. I remember the crisis my father went through while riding in a tram—I am sitting next to him when he opens "La Prensa" and discovers, at the end of the Second World War, the existence of concentration camps, which makes him tell me, while crying, a phrase that will ring over and over in my head the rest of my life: "You have to be ready my son. We Jews will soon have to leave this place and shall always live with the possibility of having to be on the move again and again." In addition, the establishment of the State of Israel in 1949 changed the traditional image of the Jew—gradually in my parents, and decidedly in my whole generation. The image of the Jew—bent over in prayer, the aquiline nose, the usurer—gave way to the new image that comes from the Middle East: a Jew who loves to work the land, but who can also be an implacable soldier.

All this reinforces and explains the 'atmosphere' in which my works have developed: some relations between mother and son, and with others, which I leave the readers to infer (namely, what I made and what "they made of me"). However, one should not overlook a deep and primordial integration into Argentine reality (present throughout my plays), which I believe provides the basis for my writing: My knowledge of man, and my real link with culture.

JOSÉ KOZER, Cuba, U.S.

How does Jewishness appear in your work?

Desire and immediacy propel my writing. This writing, always in the form of poems, is jumpy, shifty, unfaithful. I have but one allegiance: poetry. This poetry seems to have but one allegiance: memory, revulsive, springing forth through present stimulation. Such stimulation is varied, changing, perhaps whimsical and superficial, perhaps superfluous, as I may be superfluous and disposable, and so my poetry.

Yet, in spite of oscillation and constant displacement, in spite of shifting structures and references, I seem to favor certain themes: the family, a voracious need for totality, a spiritual quest, a Cuban identity which is solid and dubious, a preference for elegant poverty, a need for the narrative in poetry, a search for the moral and rabbinical self, a desire to reach a transcendental and transfigurative space, a will to tranquility, the exploration of Oriental philosophy (Confucianism and Zen Buddhism, Taoism) and, last but not least (on the contrary), the Jewish reference, the exploration (through poetry) of my Jewish self, its dolorous and odorous way of manifesting itself, in continuity and oblivion.

In continuity, for the Jew in me is always there, a constant, a permanent affliction, a wound. A wound? Look, the Jew has received a command. And under such burden he labors, acts, errs, struggles, cries. Poetry is my command. At one point, rather early, I must have reacted to the command that the Jew receives (and hears, as a voice from above) by making poetry my vessel, a vessel where the Order, and a chaotic sense of order, is poured. What is poured is, in part, not only referentially but, above all spiritually Jewish. A moral sense, a deep sense of the poverty of self, an awesome regard for the Mighty and for all that is above (and, of course, its perversion: the Below); a need for words, to express, explore, attempt. What is particularly Jewish about this? Nothing is particularly Jewish about this. It's just that I happen to be Jewish and thus the manifestation has in me, in my poetry, that particular and specific tone, hurt (festering), obsession and referential material (the Bible, the rabbinical tradition, Kabbalah; and certain gestures, certain tonalities in the writing: the versicles, for instance) that makes a Jew precisely that—a Jew, an ineffable concept.

In oblivion, also. For I am Jewish and my work conveys it, as something natural, perhaps not very important, perhaps so simple and synthetic that it "almost" doesn't exist. And so I forget. I forget that I am Cuban or Jewish or an old monk whose fate was to live in the world, wishing not to have to participate.

What does it mean to be a Cuban Jewish writer living in the United States?

1. Not much. Another way of dealing with one's death through some sort of a device called creativity, poetry.

2. I see no significance in national, racial, religious, sexual identity in terms of intimacy and the ultimate. I see no greater gain in the institutionalizing of identity. Moreover, it is in detriment of creativity, poetry, to put too much weight on this business of identity.

3. To put it differently, I am what I am (whatever that may be or mean, if anything at all) in spite of being writer, poet, Cuban, Jewish, living in this country. Which does not mean that I am not a writer, poet (perhaps), Cuban (for sure), Jewish (for sure) living in the USA (perhaps). I don't want to sound facetious, nor do I want to deal with this issue tautologically, say in a negative or positive sense, but I do want to stress that this business

of being of a certain species, gender, number, group, nation, or pigment has become so overly and overtly stressed that we are all being shortchanged and taken for a ride by critics, professors, bureaucrats, and politicians.

4. Or rather: I do not write, after all, because I am Cuban or because that Cuban is combined chemically with a Jew, and because the combination became uprooted at one point and moved to a place called the United States; the city being New York; the borough, Queens; the neighborhood, Forest Hills (used to be very Jewish). I write because I do not know where I am, where (or why) I live, who talks to me or instead of me, to what purpose the Voice, and all those voices inside me, in twelve different tongues, ten different tribes, four different seasons, seven different stations of the Cross, five different holy books, and God knows how many sutras.

5. Someday I will write a beautiful and heartfelt poem about being a Cuban Jew writing and living in the United States.

6. Will it be a slip of the tongue?

ANGELINA MUÑIZ, Mexico

Jewish motifs in my literature:

Jewish motifs have always been a feature of my work, since my first book, *Morada interior.* I am especially attracted by conflictual situations, such as relations between Christianity and Judaism, mysticism and heresy, the pure and the impure. Some of my characters are cabbalists, alchemists, monks or nuns in search of a divine experience from a very worldly point of view. Even if they attain the *unio mistica*, their personal emotional involvement is such that they can be considered as holy sinners. They usually have historical roots, but are not closely bound by them. Some of my fiction is biographical, providing a reinterpretation of the lives of real people.

The holocaust theme appears in a few of my short stories, as in the books: *Huerto cerrado, huerto sellado* and in *De magias y prodigios*. A symbolic and figurative approach permits me to break with traditional genres and, once again, to utilize history as a kind of rupture with general norms.

My relationship with Judaism is chiefly concerned with exile, which is my inspiration in life as in literature. As a child of exile by my double origins (Spanish Civil War, and *Marrano* tradition in my mother's family), it is this special circumstance that drives my creative work. In fact, all my characters are a product of exile: they are all in search of undiscovered worlds.

But themes and forms are not so important to me as the use of language, which is the key to my work. As a kind of cabbalist, I attempt to find new meanings through my use of words, phrases, rhythm and punctuation. I try to blend genders and to break rules, maintaining throughout an overall harmony. That is why I make no distinction between my poetry and my prose.

Being a Jewish-Mexican writer:
In fact, I have no nationality as a writer. Due to my complex origins, I appear in anthologies, in dictionaries and in histories of literature as Spanish, Mexican, Spanish Mexican, Jewish, but never as French (although I was born in Provence). I have recently been included in anthologies as a woman writer, which has been, perhaps, a kind of nationality.

From everything I have said, mine is a very typical Jewish background, which instead of being a schizophrenic burden, is a great source of satisfaction.

SAMUEL ROVINSKI, Costa Rica
Translated by Nora Glickman

What does it mean to you to be a Jewish writer in Costa Rica?
I was born in San José, the capital of Costa Rica, in 1932. I hardly speak any language other than Spanish, my mother tongue, the language spoken in my neighborhood, with which I express not only my childhood memories but also my knowledge of my homeland. So much so that some of my works are studied in schools and universities, as the literary expression of being Costa Rican.

The play "Las fisgonas de Paso Ancho" (The Buffoons of Paso Ancho) marks the beginning of national popular theatre in Costa Rica, and has been published and staged uninterruptedly since 1971.

The novel *Ceremonia de casta* (Kindred Ceremony) offers vignettes of San José during the first seventy years of the century and focuses on the experiences of one family, representative of the coffee producing Costa Rican oligarchy.

The people who know my work respect me and place me among the most prominent Costa Rican writers, but when the time of praise comes, they make me feel a stranger in my own land. I would rather be less distinguished and have more of a sense of belonging in my world.

Why should they admire my great knowledge of popular speech, or of my characters, and the way they think and act, when they don't see me as one of "them"?

Why do they have to question my surname, and trace my origin? Are we two separate beings, my surname and I?

Should I resent it, when there is no malice in the questioning, just a naive attitude? Or should I accept that, indeed, there is a difference? The fact is that I continue writing, with the same spirit as thirty years ago, when I began my profession. It is a vital imperative that has a will of its own.

I have convinced myself that the problem of difference, on account of being Jewish, is also other people's problem.

How does Jewish identity appear in your literature?

The Jewish element in my writing appears mostly in my fictionalized autobiography, *Cuarto creciente* (Fourth Crescent), in the collection of stories *Cuentos judíos de mi tierra* (Jewish Stories of My Land) and in the play *La víspera del sábado* (Sabbath's Eve). It is not obvious in the dialogue itself, but the characters, the themes, the expressions, the messages, and some words in Yiddish and in Hebrew, do correspond to Jewish experiences in Costa Rica.

What is Jewish about the rest of my work? Possibly a particular view of the world, a moralistic background, and a conception of individual and social justice.

After all, the emotions and the ideas I acquired in the midst of a Jewish family closely linked to the Costs Rican Jewish community must have had an influence on the development of my values and on my particular social and philosophical attitudes.

Now, as I am aware that this possible influence on my literature is inherent in my own cultural identity, and therefore expressed in an unconscious manner, it is not my place nor should it be to bring it to the surface and make it conscious.

Moreover, is it so important or necessary to know it?

MOACYR SCLIAR, Brazil
Translated by Nora Glickman

What does it mean to be a Jewish Brazilian writer?

This is a difficult question; there are not too many of us, so I don't have many opportunities to discuss this question. In any event, sometimes I think of myself as a Jewish writer who, by chance (our Wandering People!) was born in Brazil. At other times, I see myself as a Brazilian writer who happens to belong to a very special group, with a very special history and tradition. It is, more or less, the old question of the chicken and the egg: which came first?

The result is that to my readers I am an enigma. Many Brazilians have stereotypes about Jews, so, for them my books come as a surprise: "I never imagined that Jews could be like the characters you portray." Nor did I. The characters I deal with are not real Jews (nor real Brazilians; or for that matter, real people. . .). They are kind of hybrids. Centaurs. (By the way, *gaúchos*, the people of Rio Grande do Sul where I was born, are called the "centaurs of the pampas," because they are cowboys, cattle-raisers.) But in them I see the synthesis of two rich cultures, Jewish and Brazilian. *Ningun* and samba. Stories of the Bible and Indian legends. The ethical impulse of the Old Testament finds an appropriate object in the injustice that has so long visited the poor of South America.

Is it difficult to belong to two worlds? Yes. But then, between these two worlds lies a wonderful space for a writer. A space teeming with mysteries, waiting to be discovered.

How do I integrate the Jewish condition into my literature? First, historically. Jews are witnesses to history. They came to Brazil with the Portuguese discoverers, as *Marranos* or New Christians; they were the first entrepreneurs, doctors, writers, poets. More recently, they came from Eastern Europe, to the lands provided for them by the Jewish Colonization Association, or to the towns, as peddlers, workers, shopkeepers. So I try to see Brazilian history through Jewish eyes, and I also try to discover the Jewish condition as it appears in this new (and strange) world.

Secondly, through the Jewish literary tradition: the Bible, the Sephardic poets, Scholem Aleichem, I.L. Peretz, Franz Kafka, Isaac Babel. . .

Thirdly, through Jewish humor. Ours is a people that laughs at itself. Laughter, to the Jews, is a kind of protection against despair. I think that Jewish humor blends in a wonderful way with magical realism, so characteristic of Latin American writers. In both cases, we are dealing with injustice and oppression. Military governments were, in Latin America, the heirs of the Inquisition which persecuted the Jews.

The Jewish condition is yet another very important component in the literatures of our Latin American countries.

ESTHER SELIGSON, Mexico

Translated by Nora Glickman

What does it mean to you to be a Mexican-Jewish writer? How does "Jewishness" appear in your literature?

I would rephrase both questions and reduce them to one: "What does it mean to you to be a writer, and in what way do Mexican and Jewish elements appear in your literature?"

Ever since I can remember, to write and to read were for me inseparable acts of a search for belonging and of continuity—quite ruthless, to be sure, from adolescence until I managed to assume freely my Jewish condition in the meeting with my spiritual roots (Ashkenazi as much as Sephardic), some ten years ago. Consequently, my sociohistorical context—as a Mexican—acquired reality.

Thus my writing, today, springs from a double source—temporal in its Judaism, spacial in the Mexican culture—in whose waters I search for the sources of the human condition, of the Universal Being, beyond all particularism.

ELIAHU TOKER, Argentina

Translated by Nora Glickman

Some critics have observed that a substantial part of my poetry is imbued with an intense Jewish atmosphere that is not always implicit.

A certain underground river, they say, runs through most of my poetry, carrying to the attentive reader a life of Jewish experience, which is strongest when less manifest. I believe this subterranean current stems from the source that nurtures my words and from the concerns that feed it.

Most important is the Yiddish language. Although I was born in Buenos Aires, Yiddish was my first language; it was the mother tongue that impregnated my secret childhood memories, which in turn, impregnated it. But Yiddish was not just the language of my childhood: during my adolescence, when Spanish was established as my major language, the discovery of modern Yiddish poetry was one of my first links with *the Poetry*, and to translate it to Spanish was one of the first literary challenges.

Next in importance, *the Bible*. My adolescence was a time for great poetic revelations. I was then studying at the "Hebrew Teachers Seminary" and I discovered the voices of the prophets—Isaiah, Amos, Ezekiel, Micheas—who, in the same way as I read and enjoyed Genesis, Job, The Song of Songs, and other biblical texts in Hebrew, provided me with a permanent lesson in poetry, commitment, and expressive synthesis.

The third major influence on my writing is my interest in *origins*, in the *past*, in *memory*. Perhaps in reaction to a Jewish and Argentine-Jewish tendency to deny and forget our own past, my parents, their relatives and their native towns in Eastern Europe are prominent in my poetry.

Finally, I am concerned with the strange place in which I find myself as a *Jew, an Argentine, and a secular man* who is pulled by these various forces that make me into what I am: living while observing the connections and interactions among these different parts within me.

My mission as an Argentine-Jewish writer is a commitment to which I became dedicated well before I realized that I was doing it. It began when I became a translator into Spanish and an anthologizer of Yiddish poetry and of biblical, Talmudic, and historical texts, for a group of Argentine authors committed to their Jewish condition. It was a task that finally took on an institutional character, through a series of half-yearly encounters with Latin American Jewish writers.

To summarize, to be an Argentine-Jewish writer means for me the challenge of discovering and expressing what is Jewish in the Argentine condition, and what is Argentine in the Jewish condition, all of it viewed through a Jewish secular lens. And furthermore, to include something no less important or simpler to understand, which is the place of Israel in the world and in my own thinking—a lifelong endeavor.

I

Jewish Latin American Writers and Collective Memory

LEONARDO SENKMAN

UNTIL RECENTLY, LITERATURE WRITTEN by Jews in Latin America has not dealt with the subject of collective memory.[1] There is something paradoxical in this statement. The children of those Old World chroniclers who immigrated to Latin America chose to become known in their respective national literatures by their preoccupation with the present and the future, almost never for the past. The most talented among them focused upon the genre of the American Utopia, many being in the vanguard of this movement. In the Promised Land of the "New World", having survived pogroms, these immigrant Jewish writers have been the creators of Utopian visions. It is not surprising that it was Jews who pioneered the American Utopia; this space-other, refuge, and land of asylum for Europe's persecuted, America became *terram utonicam* in the imagination the Jewish emigrants who dreamed of finding a new possibility, a *novum* latent in the reality of another place.[2] Just as the utopian island of Brazil was the alternative ideal envisioned by the anarchist colonies in the state of Paraná, for Jewish peasants who arrived at the agricultural colonies of the Jewish Colonization Association (JCA) in Argentina, Uruguay, and Brazil, the promised land became the archetype of utopian space. From Alberto Gerchunoff's *Los gauchos judíos* (1910) and *Madre América* by Max Dickman (1934) to Stefan Zweig's *País de*

---

1. This article forms part of a book in progress on *Memory and Jewish Writing in Latin America*. Some fragments were read at the Third International Congress of Jewish Latin American Writers organized by *Shalom* and by the International Association of Spanish and Portugese language Jewish Writers in São Paolo, August 1990.

2. See a new approach to the use of utopia in literature in Fernando Ainsa's *Necesidad de la utopía* (Montevideo and Buenos Aires: Nordan Guion Tupac, 1990).

futuro, (1941) the focus is the land of the future, and not the memory of the past.[3]

One generation later, Jewish writers concerned about social, political, and cultural upheavals in their own countries replaced the theme of these utopian dreams with one of social reality. The need to accept responsibility for one's country, with all its dense contradiction, refers to the country neither as new place of refuge nor as a mythicized promised land. These themes characterized the work of Judeo-Argentine writers like Bernardo Verbitzky, David Viñas, Pedro Orgambide, Humberto Constantini, and Andres Rivera. The loss of this reality as a result of experiencing the trauma of exile and violence decimated an entire generation in Southern Cone nations, Argentina, Uruguay and Chile. It left these nations transformed beyond recognition to Jewish writers, and sent them back to search for their religious and cultural origins. It is possible to establish a correlation between, on the one hand, the deconstruction of national identity—the substance of many Jewish writers during the forties, fifties, and sixties— and the lack of interest they had in expressing the conflicts between their Jewish and Latin American identities. This fissure takes place as the writers find themselves surviving in nations that are transformed into something unrecognizable. They incorporate the anguish of death into their work, sensing that something very personal has been broken. Among the ruptures and the debris emerge the writer's courage to see in themselves a *Galut*-like interior as banishment. For these writers, calling forth memory has become a way to mark the disenchantment that has uprooted them as citizens, but which simultaneously permitted them, as writers, to also be Jews. This is, in fact, autobiographical literature—a rediscovery of family histories.

The majority of these writers investigate memory as an act of individual and collective identity. They share the trait of *anamnesis*, which is the effort of remembering by one who has forgotten for a long time, as Yosef Haim Yerushalmi mentions in his incisive reflections on the crisis of forgetting.[4]

What is the discourse of memory in Latin American Jewish writers' works? Who have they forgotten? Is the knowledge erased from the conscience of their fictional characters? Of what substance is oblivion made in their novels and stories?

---

3. See my analysis on the role of the land in Gerchunoff's literary strategy in Leonardo Senkman, *La identidad judía en la literatura argentina*, (Buenos Aires: Pardés 1983), chapters 1 and 2.

4. Yosef Haim Yerushalmi, *Zakhor: Jewish History and Jewish Memory*, (London and Seattle Shocken,) 1982.

Several books written during the 1980s respond to these questions, texts written by authors living in Argentina (Ricardo Feierstein, Humberto Constantini, Pedro Orgambide, Antonio Brailovsky, Sergio Chejfec,) Brazil (Moacyr Scliar,) Spain (Mario Staz, Marcos Ricardo Barnatan, Arnoldo Liberman,) France (Alicia Dujovne Ortiz, Gerardo Mario Goloboff, Ana Bronfman Vasquez) the United States (Isaac Goldemberg, Mario Szichman,) Mexico (Margo Glantz, Angelina Muñiz, Esther Seligson, Gloria Gervitz) and Venezuela (Isaac Chocron, Elisa Lerner, Alicia Freilich.)[5]

This study focuses upon two representative Jewish authors, Moacyr Scliar of Brazil and Margo Glantz of Mexico. Notwithstanding the varied causes behind the crises of forgetting that give birth to each of these authors' texts, they are unified by a shared and irresistible need to remember.

Rafael Mendes, the protagonist of Moacyr Scliar's novel, *The Strange Nation of Rafael Mendes*[6], can free himself from the crisis of forgetting that is depressing him only through a dramatic twist in his professional and private life, when he unexpectedly discovers the language of his father. This brings him to an encounter with his forgotten family history. A businessman suffering financial difficulties and anguishing over the disappearance of his daughter, Rafael is completely ignorant of his past, and never suspects being the twelfth descendant of an illustrious family

---

5. See Ricardo Feierstein's trilogy, *Sinfonía Inocente*, (I: *Entre la izquierda y la pared*, Buenos Aires, 1983; II: *El caramelo descompuesto*, Buenos Aires, 1979; III: *Escala uno en cincuenta*, Buenos Aires, 1984). See parts of Humberto Constantini's last and unfinished novel, *Rapsodia de Raquel Liberman* (unpublished) in *Noaj*, II, 2, Jerusalem, 1988, 76–82. Pedro Orgambide called his trilogy "Novels of Memory": *El arrabal del mundo*, (Buenos Aires, 1983), *Hacer la América* (Buenos Aries, 1984), and *Pura memoria* (Buenos Aires, 1984). Antonio Brailovsky, *Identidad*, Buenos Aires, 1980). Sergio Chejfec, *Lenta biografía*, Buenos Aires 1990. Moacyr Scliar, *A Estranha Nacão de Rafael Mendes*, Porto Alegre, 1983. Mario Satz, *Sol*, Barcelona, 1976 and *Luna*, Barcelona, 1978. Marcos Ricardo Barnatan, *El laberinto de Sión*, 1971, *Barcelona 1973 and Una mirada al principio*, Raíces, Madrid, I, 1 (1986), 43–45. Arnoldo Liberman, *Las inquisiciones de la nostalgia*, Madrid, 1988 and *Grietas como templos: Biografía de una identidad*, Madrid, 1984, and *La fascinación de la mentira*, Madrid 1986. Gerardo Mario Goloboff, *Criador de Palomas*, Buenos Aires, 1985; *La luna que cae*, Barcelona 1988; and *El soñador de Smith*, Barcelona 1990; Ana Vasquez Bronfman, *La maldición de Ulises: exilio latinoamericano*, Paris, 1988. Alicia Dujovne Ortiz, *L'Arbre de la Gitane*, (French,) Paris, 1991. Isaac Goldenberg, *La vida a plazos de Jacobo Lerner*, Hanover, 1979. Mario Szichman, *Los judíos del mar dulce*, Buenos Aires, 1971; *La segunda fundacion de Buenos Aires*, unpublished, and *Botín de guerra*, unpublished. Margo Glantz, *Las genealogías*, Mexico, 1981. Angelina Muniz, *Huerto cerrado. huerto sellado*, Mexico, 1985, and *Morada interior*, Mexico, 1972. Gloria Gervitz, *Yiskor*, (poems) Mexico, 1987, and *Migraciones* Mexico, 1991. Esther Seligson, *La morada en el tiempo*, Mexico 1981. Isaac Chocrón, *Rómpase en caso de inciendo*, Caracas, 1975 and *Clipper*, (play) Caracas, 1987. Elisa Lerner, *Mi vida con mamá*, (play) Caracas, 1980. Alicia Freilich *Clapper*, Caracas 1987.

6. Moacyr Scliar: *La extraña nación de Rafael Mendes*, (Barcelona: Sirce, 1988). Hereafter all quotations are taken from this Spanish version.

expelled from Spain and Portugal. This new birth of Rafael Mendes takes place dramatically as he reads some paternal manuscripts secretly transferred to his safekeeping by Samarkand, the genealogist and magician. From the old teacher's hands the son receives the "First and Second Notebook of the New Christian" written by his father. The son confines himself to his study until he has finished reading the Mendes family chronicles. Here we have the true subject of Rafael's forgetting: a family history that goes back to the mythical origins of Jonah, to Habakuk ben Tov, a member of the Essene sect of the Dead Sea, to Moses ben Maimon, the Jewish philosopher from Córdoba, and to Almoravide and Saladin. Rafael regains his identity in the most Jewish of ways, acquiring knowledge by reading a text. From this moment on, he knows he is equal to the profound meaning inherent in the transmission of this genealogical knowledge, so as to prevent collective history from being forgotten. This paternal legacy was written, however, paradoxically: as a family chronicle where the details of the mythical genealogies are the least important element. What most anguished the father was the fact that his son would not know how to decipher the sign of his roving, skeptical ancestors, a perplexed people who, having inhabited the four corners of the earth, were nevertheless incapable of finding serenity—anywhere.

Maimonides' *More Nevuhim*, or *Guide to the Perplexed*, becomes emblematic of the Mendes family's ancestry. Expelled from the Iberian peninsula, they survive the crossing to the "New World," there discovering a place where they could survive through apostasy, cleverness, and simulation. *Ahasverius's* curse will accompany the Mendeses as the mark of the Wandering Jew, a fugitive of Palestine, Egypt, Spain, and Portugal before arriving, finally, in Brazil. In the tropical lands of America, the tenth descendant of the Mendes family recovers the collective memory of his people once he discovers the family genealogy. This recovery of a glorious and dramatic past does not reveal family nobility, because from the earliest moments of the discovery and the conquest of America the presence of the Mendes New Christians conceals the mestizo condition both in colonial and in independent Brazil.

The first Rafael Mendes in the New World was Columbus's cartographer; the second one was a victim of the Inquisition, the third Rafael Mendes had himself baptized a Catholic to obtain the right to survive in a continent declared *Judenrein* by the Spanish and Lusitanian crowns. The fourth Rafael lived as a free man in Dutch Recife and enjoyed the friendship of the painter Franz Post; the fifth Mendes was involved in Maranhão's uprising against the Portuguese occupation. The sixth escaped and was taken prisoner by black fugitive slaves. Later, after the end of the slave republic under the leadership of Zambi de Palmares, another Rafael Mendes found refuge in Rio de Janeiro. In Brazil's northeast the Mendeses come to know the sugar trade, gold mining in Minas Gerais, and the commercialization of mineral wealth in Rio. They live through the war of the Andrajos and meet General Garibaldi. And after years of this exodus, the Mendeses finally know happiness and well-being when they put down roots in Rio Grande do Sul—in Santa Catarina and in Paraná—becoming wealthy through their business in rural property.

In this narrative of the recuperation of personal identity through coming to know one's collective memory, one of the most moving moments is when Rafael, enlisting in Garibaldi's expedition, disobeys the legendary Italian revolutionary's orders and, responding to his reprimand, says that he was only searching for his father, "that man of the Nation." "Being of the Nation" was a saying folklorically repeated in his family, but Rafael Mendes is ignorant of its most profound meaning. The narrator says, "He sings without knowing that it is that Ladino lullaby: 'Duerme, duerme mi angelico/ Hijico chico de tu Nación' " (252). (Sleep, sleep my little angel/ Small child of your Nation.) The entire history of the Mendeses is a false one, reflecting an ignorance of their past, repeated by the lullabies, which is the past of belonging to the *Nation*. The Hispano-Portuguese nation was shaped by dispersals and escapes, by simulation and by flight, and was remembered by the crypto-Jews through very strong bonds among family members scattered over Calvinist Amsterdam, Lutheran Hamburg, Anglican London, Catholic Ferrara, Bayona, Burdeos, and the Luso-Hispanic empire in the "New World."[7] The narrator says that "Rafael Mendes knows that he is of the Nation, but of Judaism he knows almost nothing" (214). This ignorance, or camouflaged forgetting, is transformed into knowledge thanks to a recuperated collective identity, at the same moment that the twelfth Mendes, descendant of the nation, decides in 1973 to put an end to the escapes and the mockery. This is an act both of memory and of conscience, because he does not want to continue escaping as his ancestors have. Rafael Mendes desires to live out his newly discovered Judeo-Brazilian identity, without the perplexity of the marrano. The dream with which Rafael Mendes concludes helps him to recover the double collective memory of the nation and serves as a metaphor for the

---

7. For more about this historical and ethnic concept of the Hispano-Portuguese nation, see Yosef Kaplan, *From Christianity to Judaism: The Story of Isaac Orobio de Castro*, Oxford University Press, 1989. See also Anita Novinsky's comprehensive study *Cristão Novos en Bahía*, São Paolo, 1972, and Jose Antonio Gonsalves de Mello, *Gente da nação: judeus residentes no Brasil holandés, 1630–1654*, Instituto Arqueológico, Histórico, e Geográfico Pernambucano, Recife, 1979. Scliar himself explains the subject somewhat in his essay "A condição judaica," Ed. Marc Chagall Institute, 42, Porto Alegre, 1985, 40–42,

founding document of his new civic and ethical identity, the meaning of which extends even "between the branches of the Tree of Life" ("entre las ramas del Arbol de la Vida") (342).[8]

Margo Glantz's *Las genealogías*[9] shares with *The Strange Nation of Rafael Mendes*, and with the Argentine Ricardo Feierstein's *Mestizo*,[10] the necessity of jolting family memory to unfold the history of one's ancestors and to trace the itinerary of one's exiles, travels, migrations, and resettlements in the "New World." But this wandering is accomplished with a conscious awareness of the branches, the trunk, and the extremities of the family tree, and in the full consciousness of Glantz's ethnic and cultural past. These memories do not emerge from a crisis of forgetting as in Scliar's novel, and even less from a violent amnesia. The tone of these reminiscences is jocular and filled with a humor that reveals the significance of her Jewish-Mexican identity. And although the narrator of these genealogies confesses to some temptations by Christianity during her adolescence in a homogenous, Catholic city, she knows perfectly well that she is Jewish and the daughter of the respected Yiddish poet Jacobo Glantz, a man connected to the cultural centers of his people in the United States, Europe, and in Israel. Deeply integrated into Mexican cultural life, this book is narrated through the voices of her parents, grandparents, uncles, aunts, and cousins. It straightforwardly creates a story using the collective voice of a filial memory turning into fictional discourse. To that end it does not need to use the metaphorical imagery of lineage to re-signify the perplexity of Scliar's Mendes family, nor does it attempt to fictionalize life-histories as a way of reconstructing, from scratch, the identity of a victim of amnesia. Testimonial discourse in Glantz's text is masked by a fictional character who narrates the stories told to her by her parents, her father Nucia (Jacobo Glantz) and her mother Lucia. Imperceptibly the voice slides from third person narrative to the first person. She is expressing a knowledge incorporated since time immemorial, perhaps since before birth.

The narrator of *Las genealogías* not only knows what her parents remember and what they have forgotten; she is also familiar with the time in which what happened took place. This sensation of a lengthy time is

---

8. See Albert von Brunn's study of Scliar's novel in his book *Die seltsame nation des Moacyr Scliar: Judisches Epos in Brasilien*, Frankfurt am Main, 1990, 97–110, and for a historical approach to the novel see David Schidlowsky, *Historische Roman und Judische Geschichte: "A Estranha Nação de Rafael Mendes" von Moacyr Scliar*, M.A. dissertation presented to the Freien Universitat Berlin, Berlin, 1990.

9. Margo Glantz, *Las genealogías*, Martin Casillas Editores: Mexico, 1981. Hereafter all quotations are taken from this edition.

10. I have written a full-length study of this novel which will appear at a later date.

"gelatinous, contracted, and inclined to be summed up in one topic with multiple variations and *codenza*," the narrator says. "It coincides with the life of my parents and with the repetitive conversations from which suddenly a spark bursts, illuminating some event neglected by the ideal chronology that history wants to make us swallow." (". . .gelatinoso, contraído, y dispuesto a resumirse en un tema con múltiples variaciones y codenza. Coincide con la vida de mis padres y con las conversaciones repetitivas de lo que sale de repente una chispa que ilumina algún evento descuidado por la cronología ideal que la historia nos quiere hacer tragar") (p. 42).

The testimonial fiction of *Las genealogías* ignites itself with these illuminating sparks and confers an aesthetic standing to these stories recounted to us in the intonation of *maises*—popular Yiddish tales. For this reason the stories do not need to be identified contextually, nor do they need a story structure organized around a central semantic focus that absorbs other parts of the seventy-one chapters of the book.

It does not matter that the narrator knows neither Hebrew nor Yiddish; these are the languages that organize the melodic substance of her unconscious; nor does it matter that she does not know how to celebrate the Sabbath or how to observe the dietary laws. Her Judaism was nursed at home with Jewish Russian parents and secular poets who bequeathed her the hidden movements of a language written from right to left, one which modulates the tones of her Spanish language. The narrator defends certain paradigmatic Jewish objects in her house: a *shofar*, a *menorah* for nine candles. She does not feel that her identity is degraded by the Judeo-Mexican cultural mixture (*mestizaje*) that has come together in her workroom: an antique candelabrum from Jerusalem next to a few popular icons, replicas of pre-Hispanic idols along with a votive offering, the monsters of Michoacan among which one can find Christ's passion with his devils.

This memorable Jewish narrative voice is capable of identifying every Warsaw shoemaker and every child from the *heder* accompanying a bearded old man from Wolonin; Glantz startles herself by seeing the image of her *zeide* Osher and her paternal uncle and aunt, Moishe Haim and Ilushe, while she continues to light the Christmas tree in her Mexican house.

What does matter is the narrator's disposition to confess without shame that "everything is mine, and you should know, nevertheless, that it is not." ("Todo es mío, y sepa, sin embargo, que no lo es.") What matters, too, is that she says "I appear Jewish and I don't," and that to understand this profound contradiction she has decided to jolt her family's memory and write down her genealogies. The first family genealogy brings out her pride in being the daughter of the Yiddish poet Jacobo Glantz and granddaughter of prosperous and respected Ashkenazis from the Ukrainian Steppes of Bielorussia and Podolia. Her maternal grandparents lived in areas of beetroot plantations crossed by rivers where they fished for sweet-water carp. Later *zeide* moved to Odessa where he was able to join an import/export firm. The narrator's mother tells her of the elite secondary school education she received in a prestigious *gimnasium*, and evokes the various occasions in which she met the great poet Haim Nachman Bialik and his colleague Rovnitzki. For his part, the father remembers his antecedents—rough agriculturalists from the rural colony of Kricog Rog—his longing to be able to study in the *heder*, and the pride of having participated in a self-defense group along with Jewish students who wanted to repel the hooligan gangs' attacks, which decimated the Jewish peasants.

The daughter's narrative voice transforms her father's youthful Russian memories; Jacobo Glantz's pride at having participated in literary bohemia during the Russian Revolution becomes in her narrative both an inheritance and her lost family lineage. The friendships and encounters with well-known figures who are mentioned (Lunacharski, Radek, Babel) not only constitute the paternal artistic lineage that his daughter inherits from the best Jewish cultural tradition of the Russian revolution, but also represents the credentials with which the immigrant Jacobo Glantz became a welcome member of the cultural bohemia in Mexico. He frequented literary cafés and the artistic soirées of muralists such as Siqueiros, Rivera, Orozco, and writers like Gonzalez, Martínez and Mariano Azuela. The facial similarity between Glantz (unmistakable because of his small, pointy beard) and Leon Trotzky was something more than the visible pretext for fascists from the Mexican nationalist group *Camisas Doradas* to attempt to lynch the Yiddish poet in 1939 (122–123). Glantz contained in his personality and in his work a trait insufferable to Mexican anti-Semites: he was the vessel of the great Judeo-Russian revolutionary tradition at the time that a pluralistic, Jewish cultural project was being initiated, a project repulsive to Mexican nationalism.[11] It was inevitable that the narrator, in order to be able to write *Las genealogías*, found it necessary

---

11. For a historical account of the fascist organization called *Camisas Doradas* and their attempt to lynch Jacobo Glantz, see Alicia Gojman Backal, "Minorías, estado, y movimientos nacionalistas de la clase media en México: Liga anti-China y Anti-Judía." In *Judaica Latinoamericana*, Amilat, Jerusalem, (1988), 174–191.

to shift to the European landscapes recalled by her parents.[12] Margo Glantz wrote her book in Mexico, Leningrad and Odessa. Here is the other dimension of this novel of memory: She takes the opposite path of the one her parents took when they immigrated to America. To the majority of immigrant Jews, an Eastern-European past is confusing and cruel, because their villages were buried and their loved ones disappeared,[13]

In contrast, for Glantz this pilgrimage to her origins constitutes not only a trip to times past, but also a test of her knowledge of that Steppe geography, the familiar coast of the Black Sea that was recalled in her Mexican home, a cartographical game of luck with the memory of the land of her Russian ancestors, her "motherland" (229). The narrator is less interested in the hazardous fortunes of her relatives and in the crises of values and mores transmitted from generation to generation all the way to America, than she is in the pleasure of conjuring up her uncles, aunts, and cousins from all branches of this family dispersed the world over— those who were murdered in the Holocaust as well as those who immigrated to Philadelphia. Her mother's high-school friends also appear in these conjurings: neighbours from Moldavanka, the Jewish neighborhood where Leibl, the gang king, kept both the Jews and the police of Odessa under constant threat, much as Isaac Babel described in his tales (236).

The topography of immigrant memory in Mexico traces the outlines of the urban locations in the "New World," where the Jewish colony in Mexico established its residence and population: the street of Jesus María la Corregidora, Tacubo Soledad, Mesones, Regina; old colonial houses with extremely high ceilings; huge patios overgrown with flowers; pushcarts belonging to vendors selling socks, bread, soap, and ties; and the permanent presence of the "Merced's" Market, "La Lagunilla," and its beggars. The genealogies of Mexican artists and writers who frequented Carmel, the restaurant where they were served tasty Ashkenazi dishes made by the narrator's mother, are not absent from this urban landscape. There they ate *varenikes* and *borsht*, strudel and blintzes, dishes for which exiled Russian prince Dolgornki had a weakness (162).

This investigation of both the visible and the hidden elements of family memory unfolds a geography that is separated by oceans and seas and

---

12. The topography of Russian Jewish immigrant memory has been analyzed well in José Itzigsohn, *Tras las huellas de Ashkenaz*, Buenos Aires, 1989, 291–314.
13. See the series of oral histories and testimonies of Jewish immigrants to Argentina in Sara Itzigsohn, Ricardo Feierstein, Isidoro Niborsky, Leonardo Senkman (eds.), *Inmigración y marginalidid*, Buenos Aires, 1985.

is written by a narrator who cedes the words of her story to her parents. The author accepts from the beginning that her book of life histories will be spoken in the voices of her ancestors. It follows, therefore, that the Spanish of this daughter of immigrants is the jubilant celebrant of memory, and the language of *Las genealogías* is spiced with her father's Yiddish and Russian—despite the fact that the narrator confesses to barely understanding the colloquial Yiddish of meals and scoldings (185). Also in the adventurousness of her language does this sort of Judeo-Mexican Telémaco seem to walk in the inverted footsteps of the paternal Ulysses. When "all of a sudden Jacobo writes poems and begins to dream them in Spanish" ("de repente Jacobo escribe poemas y empieza a soñarlos en español") (169). Margo herself dreams in Yiddish about those Hispanic texts in which she writes about Jacobo's intellectual coexistence with North American Jewish poets (including Bashevis and Yehuda Singer, Leivik, Opatoschu, and Niger). It is the same with the culinary art of her mother who prepares "Mexican stews Kosher-style" in her restaurant, Carmel (160). We can imagine that she dreams in Yiddish the autobiographical story of her adolescent temptations by Christianity[14] (217–220). There is no doubt that the parodic allusions to the "mixed" relationships of her romantic life come alive in the Yiddish of her father's condemnation (148). Perhaps this linguistic disagreement between father and daughter creates the most moving utterance of the book, when Glantz confesses that memory "comes back to itself and maybe this can also be said about forgetting" ("Se porta a sí misma y quizás esto se aplique también a los olvidos" (171). One of the "forgettings" told in the book is the story of the daughter incapable of satisfying the father's desire that she translate into Spanish his long Yiddish poem—a poem inspired by Columbus (146). More conflicted, even, is the occasion when her father writes another epic poem in Yiddish, *Nisayon* (Attempt) dedicated to me when I betrayed my people." It was translated in the fifties with *Songs of Absence and of Return*. There I appear as the black sheep, and later maybe also as the Prodigal Daughter," (" 'Prueba,' dedicado a mí cuando traicioné al pueblo. Fue traducido por los '50 con *Cantares de ausencia y de retorno*. Allí aparezco como oveja negra luego quizá, también como Hija Pródiga") (147).

Glantz's collective memory is recovered in untiring trips through time and space, the purpose of which is to evoke her origins, her ancestors, and the languages of her dreams and nightmares. The narrative voice

---

14. See about Margo Glantz's temptation with Christianity in her short story "Blanca Navidad," *La Jornada*, México, (December 24, 1988).

of *Las genealogías* in the end is uniquely Mexican, not only because it contains allusions to Columbus (her love of adventure) but also because the book was published in weekly segments in the magazine *Unomasuno* (13). For the first time in Mexican literature, a descendant of Russian immigrants has the courage to confess[15] to the reading public at large that her love for trips "and expeditions abroad is always a sign of explorers and as always and for a change I am Columbus, who just like my grandfather Osher or my grandfather Mikhail, presides over the navigations" (". . . y expediciones tierra afuera es siempre una marca de descubridores y como siempre y por variar soy Colón, quien al igual de mi abuelo Osher o mi abuelo Mikhail, preside a las navegaciones") (229). In addition to the profound significance of the genealogies that Glantz takes upon herself publicly in a cultural environment that only accepts the prestige of a noble European lineage, we have the testimonial vocation of the writer who, sincerely and with humor, shows an equal interest in embarking upon internal investigations inside the land of Mexico, as she does in writing with pride about her Jewish heritage.[16]

(Translated by Noga Tarnopolsky).

---

15. Jorge Aguilar Mora wrote about the difficulties Mexican authors face talking about intimacy; "en México hablar de las formas que adopta nuestra vida es una impudicia que no se tolera o que no se perdona. . .La intimidad no es de uso corriente en una sociedad católica donde los secretos se trasmiten en el confesorio, y es de uso menos corriente en una sociedad que se sigue viendo a sí misma como un pequeño clan o una estrecha familia. . ." See "Primero una novela y al final un ensayo" in *Hispanoamérica*, no. 50, 3.

16. Interview with Margo Glantz, São Paolo, August 1990. Forthcoming, to be published in *Noaj*.

2

Resonances of the Yiddishkeit Tradition in the Contemporary Brazilian Narrative

ROBERT DiANTONIO

Of what other language can it be said that it died a sudden and definite death, in a given decade, on a given piece of soil?

Cynthia Ozick[1]

Brazil HAS LONG BEEN A SAFE haven for both European and North African Jews. Jewish immigrants have undergone a relatively unencumbered passage from marginality into the mainstream. In *Diaspora: An Inquiry into the Contemporary Jewish World*, Howard M. Sachar concludes that Brazil's "cultural life has been as widely influenced by the Jewish leaven as in any Western land, from the conductor of the national symphony orchestra to directors of state academies and institutes to deans of universities."[2] A devotion to Jewish cultural values rarely has been complicated by the anti-Semitic attitudes of the government nor by the prejudices of the people, but rather by the extreme openness of one of the world's preeminent multi-ethnic countries. Sociologically, the nationalism of the Brazilian myth of state places great value on the assimilationist aspect of its culture.

Sachar cites Benno Milnitzky, president of the Confederation of Jewish Communities, on the Brazilianization of the Jewish experience: "I don't mind that Brazilian society is open...Heaven forbid. I *do* mind that the

1. Cynthia Ozick, "Envy, or Yiddish in America," *The Pagan Rabbi and Other Stories* (New York: Schocken Books; 1979), 42.
2. Howard M. Sachar, *Diaspora: An Inquiry into the Contemporary Jewish World* (New York: Harper & Row; 1985), 259.

openness of society here has undermined our Jewish integrity."[3] Raúl Doctorchick, a B'nai B'rith officer from Recife, is quoted, lamenting, "What will happen to our children in this Jewish cultural wilderness?"[4]

Within the dominant Catholic culture, Jews had to struggle with the issues of identity, acculturation, and assimilation. The passage from marginality to the mainstream with its ever-increasing secularization of Jewish life has spawned a new generation of writers who reflect upon the fading world of their ancestors, a world whose traditions and values are embodied in the term *Yiddishkeit*. Irving Howe has defined *Yiddishkeit* as "that phase of Jewish history during the past two centuries which is marked by the prevalence of Yiddish as the language of the east European Jews and by the growth among them of a culture resting mainly on that language."[5] Bonnie K. Lyons adds that the *Yiddishkeit* tradition is comprised of a "readiness to live for ideals beyond the clamor of self... and a persuasion that human existence is a deeply serious matter for which all of us are finally accountable."[6]

An exploration of the *Yiddishkeit* tradition forms part of a worldwide literary phenomena. Writers as diverse as South African born Antony Sher, Israel's David Grossman, and Americans Jerome Badanes and Cynthia Ozick are exploring contemporary Jewish life by reexamining and, in a sense, mythologizing the culture of their forebearers. They share a nostalgia—but not a sweetened vision of Judaism of writers like I.L. Peretz—for values that the diaspora and the Holocaust have diminished. Their works attempt to recover the shards of Jewish myths, traditions, and values long since past and to use them to enrich the present.

In reflecting upon their heritage, Jewish Brazilian writers are creating a body of fiction that is singular within both Judaic culture in general and the Latin American literary experience in particular. While Yiddish was once the affective bond that held together Brazil's immigrant generation, it also was viewed by that generation as a distancing factor that kept it from entering the mainstream. Today fully acculturated Jewish Brazilians look upon the vanishing *Yiddishkeit* world as a source of ethnic pride and a rich font for the current literary imagination. Contemporary writers are as quick to embrace the Yiddish world as an earlier generation was to shed it. In a strong sense, the Judeo-Brazilian narrative[7] is helping to define

---

3. Sachar, 264.
4. Sachar, 262.
5. Irving Howe, *World of our Fathers* (New York: Touchstone Books, 1976) 16.
6. Bonnie K. Lyons, "American-Jewish Fiction Since 1945" *Handbook of American-Jewish Literature* ed. Lewis Fried (New York: Greenwood, 1988) 66.
7. See Sander L. Gilman, "Jewish Writers and German Letters." *The Jewish Quarterly Review*, LXXVII, Nos. 2–3, 1987. With regard to the problem of definitions and the ambiguities that

the very nature of what some critics are referring to as the Brazilian Boom.[8] A critical consideration of the *Yiddishkeit* tradition within the contemporary Brazilian narrative is to be the central focus of the following study.

I

In Brazil the present resurgence of interest in Judaic fiction is an analogous situation to the emergence of interest during the 1960s in writers like Joseph Heller, Philip Roth, and Saul Bellow, at a time in North American literary history when the fictional character of the Jew took on everyman/everywoman proportions for a nation. Today the Brazilian reading public is embracing a fiction, an expression of a segment of Brazilian life, that reflects the essence of Yiddish culture, a culture whose roots run deep in the mythologies, folklore, and mindset of the *alter-haim*, the old country.

Surprisingly, there still exists a strong and influential nucleus of books written directly in Yiddish. There are excellent works like I. Z. Raizman's *Lebens In Shturm* (1965: *Stormy Lives*), Hersh Schwartz's *Haim, Grin-Goldene* (1960: *Green-Golden Home*) and Meir Kutchinski's *Nusakh Brazil* (1963: *The Brazil Version*). These works fictionalize an important era in their country's social history. They attempt to analyze the profound conflict of values that face Jewish immigrants by placing in high relief their exploitation, confusion, and the reactions to an unpredictable environment. Raizman's book deals specifically with an ugly historical incident that has become a frequent narrative motif in much of recent Jewish writing. It portrays the white slave trade at the turn of the century when young Jewish women were lured to the "New World" by promises of marriage only to be forcefully impressed into prostitution by members of the Jewish underworld, the *Zewi Migdal*.

Kutchinski's book belongs to this same realistic genre and deals with the problems of cultural adjustment. Sol Liptzin, a noted Yiddishist,

---

they engender—What is Jewish writing? Can one be called a Jewish writer?—I cite Gilman, "A Jewish writer is one labeled as a Jew who responds to this labeling in that medium, literature, which has the greatest salience for a Jew and a writer," 120. Also see William Peterson, William Novak, and Philip Gleason, *Concepts of Ethnicity* (Cambridge, MA: Harvard Univ. Press, 1982). Of particular significance for this study is the contention that "assimilation however fast or slow, is a one-way process proved to be quite mistaken," p. 17. See their discussion of "third generation nationalism," a motivation and mind set that reflects much of the writing under consideration.

8. See chapter eight of Robert DiAntonio, *Brazilian Fiction: Aspects and Evolution of Contemporary Narrative* (Fayetteville and London: The University of Arkansas Press, 1989).

synthesizes the thematic significance of Kutchinski's stories.[9] "*Nusakh Brazil* pointed out that for newcomers who had to wander with pack on back, unfamiliar with the language of their customers, and in constant fear of tax collectors and licensing officials, book learning and devotion to intellectual avocations proved a hindrance. Nevertheless, even in the remotest hamlets such individuals were to be found who kept the sparks of Jewish culture, morals and group responsibility glimmering.[1]

The first book in Portuguese to deal with Jewish issues and achieve national notoriety was Samuel Rawet's *Contos do imigrante*, (*Immigrant Tales*), 1956. Rawet is a vastly underrated presence in the history of Brazilian fiction. Dealing strongly with the immigrant experience in this collection, he mirrors the themes and concerns of the aforementioned Yiddishists. In a later short story collection, *O terreno de uma polegada quadrada*, (*A Square Inch of Land*), 1969, (long before Cynthia Ozick's "Puttermesser and Xanthippe") he creates a work that integrates elements of Judaic folklore into a contemporary metafictional narrative, creating one of the classics of Brazilian literature of the fantastic, "Johny Golem." Johny Golem is the contemporary embodiment of Rabbi Judah Löw's "man of clay," a thematic motif directly drawn from the font of Rabbinic mysteries.

The 1969 novel *As seis pontas da estrela* (*The Six Points of the Star*) by Zevi Ghivelder won a special mention of the national Walmap Prize for outstanding writing. Ghivelder's book is a compendium of character types, a literary recreation of sociohistorical issues and thematic concerns. Taken in its totality, it comprises the recent history of Rio de Janeiro's Jewish community. It is a typological study, an explanation of the values and diversity of the Jewish population. The work analyzes the lifestyle, traditions, and even a loss and resurgence of religious consciousness among immigrants from the 1930s to the late 1960s. It considers the various ways that these immigrants were able to survive in the new land.

The book opens with the newcomers—*grine*—gathered together in a rooming house talking incessantly about *klapn clientéle*, calling on clients, and having good *parnússe*, future prospects for supporting their families. Yiddish, those who speak it and when it is employed, becomes an important component of this work.

Written in 1969 at the height of Brazil's ultranationalistic *ditadura*, Ghevelder may have been writing an *apologia pro vita sua* to deal with the perceptions of certain anti-Semitic Brazilians that the Jews—who were on

---

9. See Sol Liptzin, *A History of Yiddish Literature* (Middle Village, NY: Jonathan David, Publishers, 1972.) as Liptzin's text provided much of the information on the Brazilian Yiddishists.

10. Liptzin, 402.

the very voyage of discovery of Pedro Alvares Cabral in 1500—were bound to international political movements. The work focuses on the character of a *kleyne menschele*, an ordinary man, Favel Aterman, who in the *shtetl* community of Bessarabia was little respected for his intelligence or knowledge. However, here in the "New World", Aterman is shown to possess the ability to move from a wandering peddler to a store owner, to a man who cuts corners, bends rules, and succeeds as an entrepreneur during the war. Favel Aterman becomes a community leader in deference to his wealth. However, in a moment of *t'shuva*, a time of decision, Aterman gives of himself tirelessly and opens up his business to provide shelter for recent Holocaust victims.

T'shuva, a cornerstone of the *Yiddishkeit* tradition, is defined by Lyons as: "The idea of turning to God or to the right path that is connected with the Jewish conception of human redemption and underlies both the intrinsic hopefulness about humankind and the longing for messianic salvation which universal *t'shuva* will help bring about."[11] Also in regard to the motif of *t'shuva*, Sol Liptzen characterizes the corpus of Brazilian Yiddish fiction created by Rosa Palatnik, including works like *Beim Geroish Fun Atlantic* (*Along the Atlantic*), 1957, and *Geklibene Dertzehlungen*, (*Selected Tales*), 1966, as being built "around a moment of truth in the life of Jews apparently successfully integrated."[12] Her stories turn on that moment when characters realize "that in the pursuit of wealth precious Jewish values were tossed aside."[13]

Ghivelder's character, Favel Aterman, attains what was denied to him in Bessarabia, *kúvet*, the respect and love he could only find in the "New World." He successfully becomes a *mensch*, a uniquely Yiddish term implying a good, admirable, and loved human being. He has succeeded in his struggle to embody the ideals of *menschlechkeit*, the Jewish ethical code of behavoir based on a strong humanitarian ethos.

One of the book's most moving passages occurs when the entire Jewish community of Rio de Janeiro, after welcoming the Holocaust survivors, holds a symbolic burial for those who died under the Nazis by burying bars of soap recovered from the concentration camp at Auschwitz. Through this symbolic act, the leaders of the community tried to convey to government officials the fact that Brazil should immediately open its doors to other survivors. "Nunca, em vinte anos de construída, a sinagoga ficara tão repleta... Na manhã de domingo, cada judeu ia levar à sepultura um

---

11. Lyons, 69.
12. Liptzin, 403
13. Liptzin, 403

pedaço de seus pais, de parentes e amigos, um pedaço de sí mesmos."
("Never, in 20 years since its construction, had the synagogue been so
filled...On Sunday morning, each Jew was going to carry to be buried
a piece of his parents, of relatives and friends, a piece of his very self.")[14]

T'shuva also plays an important role in Moacyr Scliar's fiction. Scliar
is one of Brazil's most highly respected authors and is fast becoming the
literary voice of its 150,000 member Jewish community. His book, *A estranha
nação de Rafael Mendes* (*The Strange Nation of Rafael Mendes*), 1983, is an
amalgam of historical fact, mysticism, and illusion. Mendes, a successful
businessman who suddenly learns that both his private life and company's
future are in crisis, becomes aware of the existence of a series of
genealogical notebooks in which he discovers he is Jewish. Scliar's novel
presents a paradigmatic symbol, Rafael Mendes himself, the acculturated
Brazilian Jew, totally cut off from his roots, his community, and his God.
In a sense, Scliar's book revives that shared historical and communal spirit
and returns Mendes to his status as a *jüdische menschen*. Mendes has been
cut off from the code of *menschlechkeit*. Mendes is made aware of the fact
that he is the descendant of Portuguese *Marranos* who were forced to affirm
Christianity in 1497 when the entire Jewish community was converted en
masse. Through the notebooks Moacyr Scliar traces the history of Rafael's
ancestors, a Sephardic lineage that dates back centuries. All these Rafael
Mendeses are part of the "nation," and most tried to maintain their ties
to their religion even in the worst of times.

At the work's conclusion in a powerful moment *t'shuva*, of communion
with his nation[15], Mendes finds the courage to avail himsel of the Jewish
moral imperative. Although alienated most of his life from his heritage,
in a time of true crisis and of moral decision he falls back on that heritage
as a solution to his ethical dilemma."Dura alguns minutos, esta titânica
luta de vontade... mas, prestes a desistir, faz um derradeiro esforço—e
consegue... De repente dá-se conta: todos têm a face que ha' pouco viu
no espelho todos são ele, ele é todos. Agora entende os Cadernos do
Cristão-Novo; é o legado que o pai deixou—disso não mais tem dúvida—a
ele." ("It lasts for several minutes...but when he is about to give up, he
makes one last effort—and he succeeds...Suddenly he realizes: All of
them have the face he saw in the mirror a while ago: all of them are him,

14. Zevi Ghivelder, *As seis pontas da estrela* (Rio de Janeiro: Bloch, 1969), 132–33. Unless
otherwise indicated, this and all other translations are my own. However, every effort has
been made to use a previously published translation.
15. While Scliar, whose background is Ashkenazi, explores Brazil's Sephardic history in
this novel, this moment of moral decision strongly reflects the author's Eastern European
heritage.

he is all of them. Now he understands the *Notebooks of the New Christian;* they are his father's legacy to him—Rafael is no longer beset by doubts.")[16]

Moacyr Scliar's many other novels are suffused with *Yiddishkeit.* In *Os voluntários,* (*The Volunteers*), 1980, the character of Benjamin is portrayed as the quintessential *luftmensch,* the man who exists on air, the dreamer, for whom prosaic reality has little meaning. The *luftmensch,* like the *kleyne menschele,* is a common figure throughout Yiddish fiction, a beloved member of Eastern European society. The entire book turns on the obsessive and religiously symbolic goal of reaching Jerusalem. "Era dessas pessoas que querem morar na cidade que nunca viram, casar com a mulher que não conheceram, ler o livro que não foi escrito—manja o tipo? Benjamin queria Jerusalém." ("He was one of those people who yearn to live in a city they've never seen, to marry a woman they've never met, to read a book that has never been written. You know the type, don't you? Benjamin yearned for Jerusalem.")[17]

In *O exército de um homem só,* (*The One Man Army*), 1983, Mayer Grinzberg is another idealistic dreamer. After failing in his youthful vision to build a humanistic utopia, a New World Birobidjan, he lives out his days in the stultifying ambience of a Porto Alegre rooming house. Scliar's *luftmenschen* suffer the prosaic existence of all mortals, but their dreams form part of a lineage dating back to characters like Sholem Aleichem's "Menachem Mendel" and most recently, Henner Rosenbach in Andre Kaminski's international best-seller, *Nächstes Jahn in Jerusalem,* 1986, (*Next Year in Jerusalem*).

In an interview with Regina Igel, Scliar tells of his varied roles as physician, historian, and writer. As a doctor of medicine he did a residency at a local Jewish nursing home. There the idea for one of his best known novels was conceived while treating an old woman who "used to tell very interesting episodes of her life."[18] In his work (*O ciclo das águas*), (*The Water Cycle*), 1976, Scliar recasts an intriguing tale of Jewish white slavery within a postmodern literary perspective. He artfully blends the journey of Esther Markowitz from the pious daughter of a village *mohel* to the owner of one of Porto Alegre's most elegant houses of prostitution. Esther is able to maintain a semblance of her Jewishness even within difficult personal

---

16. Moacyr Scliar, *A estranha nação de Rafael Mendes* (Porto Alegre: L&PM, 1983), 284–85. The work was published in English as *The Strange Nation of Rafael Mendes,* trans. Eloah F. Giacomelli (New York: Harmony Books, 1988), 306.

17. Moacyr Scliar, *Os voluntários* (Porto Alegre: L&PM, 1980) 27. The work was published in English as *The Volunteers,* trans. Eloah F. Giacomelli (New York: Ballantine, 1988), 15.

18. Regina Igel, "Jewish Components in Brazilian Literature: Moacyr Scliar," *Folio,* no. 17. (Sept. 1987), 133.

circumstances. She brings up her son, Marcos, as a Jew, and cannot forgive him for "ter casado com uma *gói*," having married a *goy*.[19] Even Leiser, the leader of the *Zewi Migdal*, whose crimes will eventually involve and corrupt high government officials (a frequent Scliarian motif), attempts to preserve his religion. "Outra vez viu Leiser rezando, com o chale e o livro de orações e os filactérios colocados nos braços. Movia os lábios com fevor, inclinando-se na direção do oriente, na direção da distante Jerusalém: e era uma lágrima que lhe corria pelo rostro?" ("Another time she saw Leiser praying, with a shawl and a prayer book and phylacteries wound around his arms. He moved his lips fervently, inclining his head to the East, to a distant Jerusalem and was there a tear running down his face?")[20] At work's end Esther is portrayed in a home for the aged "passa o dia sentada num velho sofa, trauteando canções em iídiche," ("passing her days seated on an old sofa, humming Yiddish melodies").[21]

II

It was Martin Buber who wrote that "Messianism is Judaism's most profoundly original idea...it was not a question of whether the future might come: it had to come: every moment guaranteed it—and so did God."[22] It is false materialism and the loss of messianic fervor that Moacyr Scliar depicts in much of his writing. Scliar's work implicitly underscores and laments the rapid assimilation into an easygoing Brazilian way of life. He reflects upon this loss of religious values in one of his best-known pieces of short fiction, "A balada do falso Messias," ("The Ballad of the False Messiah"), 1976. The story is framed with a divided vision of Shabtai Zvi, Sabbatai Zevi, the seventeenth century self-proclaimed messiah, now old and worn out, seated at a local bar in Porto Alegre. Scliar converts the sociohistorical drama of Zevi's life and ideals into a modern setting. The narrative itself begins on an immigrant ship where Zvi is anachronistically traveling to southern Brazil in 1906. Scliar creates a disjointed world where Zvi then attempts to convince new colonists to one of Brazil's Jewish agricultural communes to give up their earthly goods and return to Palestine and a life of prayer. The community rejects Shabtai Zvi out of fear that they will "provocar os anti-semitas," ("provoke

---

19. Moacyr Scliar, (*O ciclo das águas*) (Porto Alegre: Edtora Globo, 1977), 131.
20. Scliar, 29–30.
21. Scliar, 133.
22. Israel Shenker, *Coat of Many Colors* (New York: Doubleday, 1985), 19.

the Jew-haters").[23] They opt to follow the pragmatic Leib Rubin. The group abandons their agricultural commune—the hope of the Jewish Colonization Association—and heads for the city of Porto Alegre.

Zvi then joins the others in the city where Leib Rubin prospers and finds a job in one of Lieb's furniture stores. It is an allegorical tale of the renunciation of all that is mystical in favor of the worldly and the practical. Imprisoning a quasi-mythic figure—a larger than life symbol of messianic hope—in a secular life in Porto Alegre is Scliar's ironic vision of lost cultural and religious values. The tale ends with Shabtai Zvi and the narrator meeting nightly in a neighborhood tavern, silently drinking wine. Scliar, the eternal ironist, leaves both the narrator and the reader with a despairing sense of loss. "Perto da meia-noite ele fecha os olhos, estende as mãos sobre o coro e murmura palavras em hebraico (ou em aramaico, ou em ladino). O vinho se transforma em água. O dono do bar acha que é apenas um truque. Quanto a mim, tenho minhas dúvidas." ("Just before midnight he closes his eyes, lays his hands over the glass and murmurs some words in Hebrew (or in Aramaic, or in Ladino). The wine is changed into water. The bar owner thinks it is just a trick. As for himself, I'm not so sure.")[24]

Here Scliar directly incorporates two major biblical promises, two themes central to Jewish life, into the flow of this narrative: the notion of finding a homeland and the notion of final redemption by a Messiah. His work turns upon these biblical concepts to show that there exists a movement away from these basic Jewish values. Scliar's fiction expresses a tension born of a growing acceptance of acculturation and assimilation into a self-satisfied way of life in the new Eden: Brazil.

Moacyr Scliar's novels and short fiction have incorporated various, and little known, aspects of Judeo-Brazilian historiography: the settling of Baron Hirsh's agricultural communes in Quatro Irmãos; the Jewish gaúchos; the aftermath of the Soviet Union's attempt to establish a Jewish state in Birobidjan; the world of the Yiddish Mafia, the *Zewi Migdal*; an anachronistic accomodation of the life of Sabbatai Zevi, the charismatic false messiah; the long history of Brazil's Sephardim; and the Jewish white slave trade in Rio Grande do Sul. However, Scliar, who has a large and devoted international following, has written very little on the subject of the Holocaust. Perhaps in response to the Yiddish admonition, *M'ken nisht,*

---

23. Moacyr Scliar, *A balada do falso Messias* (São Paolo: Atica, 1976), 19. The work was published in English as *The Ballard of the False Messiah*, trans. Eloah F. Giacomelli (New York: Ballantine, 1988), 7.

24. Scliar, 19, 8.

one cannot, he felt the subject too sacred to be dealt with. In one of his most challenging pieces of short fiction, "Na minha suja cabeça, o Holocausto," Inside My Dirty Head—The Holocaust, he undertakes it only tangentially and from a very unique perspective. Events are recounted from the "suja cabeça," "the dirty head," of a young boy whose father's religiosity encompasses the Yiddishkeit ideal of mentchlekeit, a clamor to live by ideals for the communal good, a commitment to a strong humanistic ethic. "Meu pai toma conhecimento desta penosa situação e fica indignado: é preciso fazer algo, não se pode deixar um judeu nesta situação, principalmente um sobrevivente do massacre nazista. Chama os vizinhos para uma reunião." ("My father is filled with indignation: something must be done about it, one can't leave a Jew in this situation, especially when he is a survivor of the Nazi massacre. He calls the neighbors to a meeting.")[25]

The narrator wants to believe that Mischa, an impoverished Holocaust survivor who is found sleeping in doorways in Porto Alegre, is a fraud. He imagines that he is able to unearth the truth of Mischa's dissimulation for he can't bear his stories, especially those related to the piles of soap. The narrator then reconstructs a scenario where he exposes Mischa; his childish reasoning is a narrative device to tangibly express the sense of guilt of many Brazilians who were personally unaffected by the events in Europe. The boy observes his father's suffering and struggles to come to grips with the Holocaust as it intrudes upon his present life.

At work's end the purposefully unnamed narrator imagines having his mouth washed out by Mischa with the soap bars from Auschwitz. For the young boy the events of Auschwitz and the full realization of the human suffering finally take root. He awakens from a dream aware of the magnitude of the Holocaust and the extent of its suffering. "Acordo soluçando, acordo em meio a um grande sofrimento. E é a este sofrimento que, à falta de melhor termo, denomino: Holocausto." (I wake up sobbing, I wake up in the midst of great suffering. And it is this suffering that I, for a lack of a better word, call the Holocaust.")[26]

The story of Mischa can be viewed, symbolically, as one man's rebirth into Knesset Israel, the mystical community of the House of Israel, and literally, as his integration into Jewish Brazilian society. Scliar's vision falls within the "divine drama of creation" motif. Mischa was lost and it was through the menschlekeit of the narrator's father and the good will of the

---

25. Moacyr Scliar, O olho enigmático (Rio de Janeiro: Editora Guanabara, 1986), 20. The work was published in English as The Enigmatic Eye, trans. Eloah F. Giacomelli (New York: Ballantine, 1988), 6.
26. Scliar, 23, 9.

community that in Lurianic terms, *Tikkun*, this "Divine Spark of Light" is raised up. Thus, Mischa is released from his exile and the redemptive process is complete.

In dealing with the redemptive possibilities of life in the aftermath of the Holocaust, Moacyr Scliar, like the young boy in the story, is drawn—almost compelled—to explore its consequences. In the process he writes a moving elegy, in Portuguese, to the cultural values of the Yiddish-speaking people of Eastern Europe.

III

Eliezer Levin, in his 1972 novel *Bom Retiro*, chronicles life in the Jewish neighborhoods of São Paulo, an area once comparable to London's East End, New York's Lower East Side, or Buenos Aires' *Barrio Once*. Levin recounts the simple pleasures of childhood and the warmth of Jewish family life. "Nosso pequeno mundo resumía-se no Bom Retiro. O que estivesse fora ficava tão distante como a lua. Não tínhamos queixas a fazer, os problemas dos adultos não entendíamos e pouco nos afligiam. Contemplávamos a vida correr sem sobressaltos nem surprêsas." ("Our small world was all tied up in Bom Retiro. What was outside was as distant as the moon. We had no complaints, we didn't understand adult problems and they bothered us very little. We watched life go by without jolts or surprises.")[27]

Levin then develops a polarity in which a childhood spent on Brazil's safe shores is contrasted with news accounts of the approaching Holocaust. As the work's young narrator grows into manhood (1930–1943) the reader is made aware that millions of lives in Nazi-dominated Europe are in peril. In the fashion of Aharon Appelfeld's *Badenheim 1939*, Levin methodically creates a menacing atmosphere that comprises the work's underpinnings. This is accomplished by utilizing portions of press releases and radio broadcasts as chapter inserts, thus widening the novel's scope. "Sabado, 12 de março de 1938—Invadindo a Austria e impondo-lhe um govêrno nacional-socialista, o chanceler Hitler agravou sobremaneira a situação européia." ("Saturday. The 12th of March, 1938. Invading Austria and imposing a national-socialist government, Chancelor Hitler greatly aggravated the European political situation.")[28]

---

27. Eliezer Levin, *Bom Retiro* (São Paulo: Martins, 1972), 12.
28. Levin, 10.

This structuring device is a topos not unlike that which the Italian-Jewish writer Elsa Morante would employ in her 1975 masterwork, *La stória, History a Novel*. Levin also parallels the tranquil existence of Brazil's largest Jewish community with magazine and newspaper articles related to the rest of the world's Jewry. The reader is well aware of the two layers of historical reality that comprise the novel as excerpts from Jewish movie magazines are juxtaposed to the menacing commentaries of the tragic events in Europe. The reader's response is factored in as an essential component of this novel's structure as the boy reaches manhood, his Bar-Mitzvah is in 1943, one of the worst years for Jewish suffering in Europe.

Clarice Lispector, who has long represented Brazil as a world-class writer, is usually described as of Russian or Ukranian descent when, in fact, she was from a family of poor Jewish immigrants to the northeastern city of Recife. Her early abstractly philosophical narratives were in the nouveau roman tradition; however, late in her life, she examines the Jewish value of *Oshek*, the prohibition of oppressing workers. In her last and most passionate novel, *A hora da estrela*, (*The Hour of the Star*), 1977, she bases the book's thematic content solidly on Judaic symbology drawn from Old Testament sources. "Embora a moça anônima da história seja tão antiga que podia ser uma figura bíblica." ("The anonymous girl of this story is so ancient that she could be described as biblical.")[29] Macabéa, the work's heroine, is a virginal and unskilled office worker like the thousands of other women from the barren North who are exploited in the big cities by men. The nominal Judaic symbology is employed ironically, for Macabéa (a name that is almost non-existent in Brazil) is as inert as her biblical namesake is aggressive. At work's end she faces a syphilitic soothsayer, Madame Carlota, who sends her to a foreseen death. Madame Carlota lies to her much in the way that the Holocaust victims were deceived and led to their deaths. Macabéa is killed by a yellow Mercedes as big as an ocean liner, driven by a blond foreigner named Hans. In this minimalist and strangely magical characterization of Madame Carlota can be found correspondences and prefiguations of the Holocaust. The novel concludes ironically by juxtaposing Richard Strauss's vision of redemption, the illusionary false promises of Madame Carlota, and the hideous and painful death of Macabéa.

While Lispector's ethnic background is not readily perceivable in her writing, her elder sister Elisa unabashedly draws upon the rich heritage

---

29. Clarice Lispector, *A hora da estrela* (Rio de Janeiro: Nova Fronteira, 1984), 38. The work was published in English as *The Hour of the Star*, tran. Giovanni Pontiero (Exeter, England: Carcanet, 1986), 20.

of their youth spent in a historic Jewish neighborhood in Recife's downtown area. Her 1948 novel *No exílio*, (*In Exile*), explores recent Jewish history and customs from lives of persecution in southern Russia to resettlement in Brazil. The work reflects upon the intense *Yiddishkeit* world that surrounded both women. In the 1971 reissue of the book there is even an extensive Portuguese-Yiddish-Hebrew glossary.

IV

Francisco Dzialovsky's *O Terceiro Testamento*, (*The Third Testament*), 1987, chronicles the Jewish immigrant experience in present day Rio de Janeiro. As expected, the book underscores the inevitable loss of valued traditions. Dzialovsky's book confidently focuses upon the comic incongruities of an Eastern European family's adjustment to the heat and openness of Brazilian life.

The novel centers upon a weekly Yiddish radio program called "The Third Testament." A young Brazilian-born narrator, his sisters, and his Polish-born parents gather together for their ritual Sunday meal, the mother preparing Old World delicacies for which she is beginning to forget the recipes, and the father dressed in his best wool suit in the suffocating humidity of the tropics: "Sabia que seus filhos, criados numa vizinhança católica, não tinham o conforto de uma igreja onde o padre separava tão bem o sagrado do profano, o permitido e o não permitido. . .Portanto seu ideal era fazer de nossa residência a um só templo lar e templo." ("He knew his children, brought up in a Catholic neighborhood, didn't have the comfort of a church where a priest would separate the sacred from the profane. . .Therefore his aim was to make our residence into both a home and a temple.")[30] The Yiddish radio program becomes an important weekly event, an education that links Jewish traditions with the new culture. "Rainha Ester, fundadora do nosso festival de Purim, ancestral do nosso carnaval." ("Queen Esther, founder of the Purim festival, that great ancestor of our yearly Lenten carnival here in Rio.")[31] The book's narrator tells about the program's focus in a somewhat ironic fashion— Brazilian writing and the Brazilian *zeitgeist* in general is often scathingly satirical. The narrator recounts the radio announcer's tepid affirmation of Judeo-Christian friendship: "Afinal, após quasi dois mil anos de acalorados debates e não menos acalorados autos-de-fé, onde volatizavam

---

30. Francisco Dzialovsky, *O Terceiro Testamento* (Rio de Janeiro: Anima, 1987), 13–14.
31. Dzialovsky, 15.

as cinzas dos recalcitrantes, os teológos chegaram à conclusão que não foram os judeus que mataram Deus." ("Finally after two thousand years of heated debates and no less heated *autos-da-fé*, Catholic theologians arrived at the conclusion that it wasn't, in fact, the Jews who killed God.")[32]

The announcer also recounts biblical stories and lectures on religion, history, politics, and Jewish accomplishments. The program is a link with the past but its language, *o iídishe*, (Yiddish) is used only spottily by the narrator as each day "na conversa entre os velhos se introduzia cada vez mais palavras em português," ("among the old people more and more Portuguese words were introduced into their conversations.")[33]

Dzialovsky's secondary focus is on the weekly visit to the *Asilo*, a retirement home located in the middle of one of Rio's red light districts. Many of the book's tales and stories are recounted by two members of the *asilo*, two very distinct personalities. Through this shifting vision the novel is able to comment on the Jewish experience in both the Old and New World, from the *shtetl* to the warm beaches of the Atlantic. There are Simão's frequent disquisitions on topics like the full import of the word *lerner*, as meaning not just a studious person, but one who "lê o espaço em branco entre as letras," ("reads the white space between the letters.")[34] There are also the more worldly teachings of Rafael who leads the narrator on tours of the infamous neighborhood where they meet doña Ruth, the madam of one of the local brothels. Here Brazil and Poland coalesce as doña Ruth recites *Kaddish* for her favorite employee, a beautiful Indian girl, in a room filled with Catholic statuary. Rafael's stories contain resonances of Yiddishists like I. B. Singer and Sholom Aleichem: there are the bawdy accounts of his coming to the "New World," tales of life under the czar, and another reference to the stories of how young Jewish girls were lured into lives of prostitution.

The mother of the household adds an earthy touch to the various episodes as she wryly combines elements of Judaic folklore with a comic cynicism that is endemic to the Brazilian national character: "Como? *Dibuk* não existe?. . .Com esse calor e com essa inflação qual a alma penada que vai querer encostar em alguém?" ("What! Dybbuks don't exist?. . .With this damn heat and this inflation what tortured soul is going to want to possess someone here?")[35]

---

32. Dzialovsky, 15.
33. Dzialovsky, 12.
34. Dzialovsky, 57.
35. Dzialovsky, 89.

The novel's carnivalesque conclusion is embodied in the "Fourth Testament," a television program for the younger Jewish community. The language is now Portuguese and the show is ushered in with an old liturgical melody played with a lively samba beat. Six stately and scantily clad mulatto girls bring on the program's announcer, who looks and acts like a sleezy MC from a Copacabana review.

Francisco Dzialovsky's novel is an exploration of Jewish family life wedded to, and more often than not at odds with, the contemporary Brazilian social scene. This rendering of the "tropicalization" of the Diaspora experience is suffused with Dzialovsky's unique brand of humor. His *Third Testament* is a tender but questioning vision of an all too rapid assimilation into a new land and a new way of life. In a thoroughly assimilated community, Dzialovsky, like Scliar, questions the "Brazilianization"—the secularization—of Jewish life in present day Brazil. For this author the past intrudes upon the present and in a large measure defines it.

However, his writings also evoke forgotten traditions and attitudes that have long encompassed a timeless sense of communal Jewish life. For this reason the inclusion of Jewish tales and stories also evolve as a positive act that brings the situation to the attention of his readers. The very act of writing is his direct affirmation of the *Yiddishkeit* tradition, for it is through the recounting of Jewish legends, tales, myths, beliefs, and folklore that the values of the past will remain alive in the present. In their *pais tropical* that is the comfortable home to a large and assimilated community of Jewish-Brazilians, Dzialovsky offers a questioning work to a new generation, a primer in the values of *Yiddishkeit*.

V

The preceding study has attempted to point out the rich residue of *Yiddishkeit* that continues to flourish within the mainstream of contemporary Brazilian fiction. In dealing with the themes and complexities of their own cultural identity, the aforementioned writers have found a large and appreciative audience. They are—in a poetic sense—mythologizing and sustaining the values of a vanishing culture while redefining Jewish identity in the "New World." In an era of postmodernist experimentation, a time when writers like Roberto Drummond, Rubem Fonseca, and Ignácio Loyola de Brandão are reconstructing reality into abstract fictional modes, authors like Ghivelder, Levin, Scliar, Lispector, Rawet, and Dzialovsky are drawing upon and perpetuating what Irving Howe calls "one of the most vibrant and humane of modern cultures."[36]

---

36. Irving Howe and Eliezer Greenberg, *Voices from the Yiddish*. (Ann Arbor: University of Michigan Press, 1972), 15.

I would like to express my appreciation to Alex Berlyne, Larry Mintz, and Yvette Miller of the *Jerusalem Post*, *Midstream*, and *The Latin American Literary Review*, where ideas were worked out in the form of book reviews and short articles. Also, I thank Aaron DiAntonio of Stanford University, Moacyr Scliar of Porto Alegre, and publisher Jacó Guinsburg of São Paolo, as their conversations and correspondence have helped shape this study. Finally, I would like to express my gratitude to the National Endowment for the Humanities for allowing me to spend two research summers in Latin America.

3

Urban Life and Jewish Memory in the Tales of Moacyr Scliar and Nora Glickman

MURRAY BAUMGARTEN

IN A RECENT INTERVIEW, Ariel Dorfman comments on the effects of bilingualism on his writing: "For a time...this really worried me, that I had these two languages. When you're in exile, you constantly examine your own actions for signs of betrayal, of forgetting where you come from." But as time went by "I started just enjoying the dialogue between the two languages."[1] Central to the work of many Latin American writers, this contested dialogue of languages and cultures is encoded in the tales of Moacyr Scliar and Nora Glickman with exemplary force. They share Dorfman's concern not to forget, knowing as he does that the power of exile creates the desire to betray origins and plunge beginnings into forgetfulness. Like him, they remember by accepting and validating cultural and linguistic dialogue, enacting it in their fiction not as punishment but as opportunity and pleasure.

Their writing dramatizes the encounter, putting antagonisms as well as mutually reinforcing qualities into play, and shows their necessary reciprocity. A dance of bilingualism, their work represents this threatening, mutually enriching, yet also potentially violent meeting as a flashing heterosexual flamboyance, thereby constituting their writing in terms of the breathtaking twirls and balletic falls and slides of the tango. Like that remarkable dance form, their writing maps the desperation of the marginal, that by its skill and imagistic force overcomes the barriers keeping it from the center. It is worth noting that Glickman's fictional world is deeply rooted in Argentinian culture and history, while Scliar's Brazilian

---

1. Peggy Boyers and Juan C. Lertora, "Ideology, Exile, Language: An Interview with Ariel Dorfman," *Salmagundi*, 82–83. Spring-Summer '89, 162.

tales take their inspiration from Porto Alegre, that southeastern province bordering Argentina both in geography and spirit.

The impact of this history leads Scliar and Glickman to create a more complex and more elaborated encounter out of what for some writers is only the agon of English and Spanish or Portuguese, North American and South American experience. The realities of everyday life in Latin America are not for them a simple Manichean struggle of good against evil, and therefore not amenable to simplistic reductions. Their fiction reframes the situation, encoding it as the interpenetration and multiple crossings of many linguistic and cultural systems. Their choreographic fiction represents the cultural diversity of South America, of Jewish exile and the possibility of secular citizenship. Part of the reason for the complexity of their work is its constant urban ambience, its implicit valuation of urbane habits. To be a city-dweller, this fiction reminds us, makes possible even at the margins the recovery of the force of civilization. To live in the city, particularly for the Jew, is to be part of a long history of urbanism rooted in the ancient Middle East and beginning well before modern Western culture. The city of Scliar and Glickman is both a mythological and realistic space in which the complexities of Jewish values encounter Latin habits and European cultural overlays.

In a world where citizenship is tenuous and differences of any kind can be life-threatening, the return of repressed Jewish memories overwhelms these characters. In this universe of discourse, political responses reveal themselves as linguistic phenomena—as an awareness of the demands of two and three languages and cultural codes akin to (but even more complicated than) Dorfman's willingness to put his bilingualism into play. Like Kafka's, they are tales that are apparently allegorical yet the keys to unlock their meanings are missing. Fragments of Yiddish and Hebrew punctuate these languages, gateways to memories of ancient traditions embodying a people's strategies for survival. In Scliar's world, characters respond to their marginalization by the constant anti-Semitic undercurrents of contemporary Latin American life and undergo somatic transformations through psychic, sexual, or medical intervention. In Glickman's representation of the woman's situation, female voyeurism carries the characters into surreal fantasies that lead to the sources of bilingualism and a child's glee in the play of languages. Nevertheless, their memories are also resources for liberating possibilities, showing them what citizenship means and suggesting the outlines of a democratic engendering of sexual roles. Even as the conditions of modern alienation attack the self with such force that strategies for maintaining sanity become ever more prominent in these fictions, forgetfulness is not possible and irony serves as the most fitting response to the absurdity of this life. Their characters cannot rely on the communal supports of organized traditional Jewish life, the ritual structure of Latin Catholicism, nor the possibility of North American individualistic self-realization; neither education nor desire nor self-abandoning sexuality provides an adequate language for their reality, yet the search for an encompassing, comprehensive code is not abandoned.

The Jewish protagonists of Glickman's and Scliar's worlds function as simultaneous translators; however, theirs is not only the cultural struggle of the Hispanic or Lusitanian worlds, but of the ancient Jewish and Christian, medieval and modern, Middle-Eastern and Western confrontations. In this multi-layered encounter none of the antagonists— neither Jewish memory, big-brother bureaucracy, Catholic habits, Israeli life and the claims of Zionism, nor Latin experience—can deploy a hegemonic discourse to marshall these varied sources into a hierarchical order without unacceptable radical distortion and reduction.[2]

In the absence of such an ordering discourse, the reader discovers in Nora Glickman's powerful phrase the *puesto vacante*—the open place within which these worlds collide.[3] A magical space, it is composed of a palimpsest of cultural scenarios. This overlay of scenes creates the effect of a jumbled group of snapshots awaiting their ordering into a family album. Similarly, the interpenetration of languages produces interference that multiplies rather than reduces possibilities.[4] Rather than patriarchal hegemony, we enter the realm staked out by Philip Roth in *The Counterlife*: "The burden isn't either/or, consciously choosing from possibilities equally difficult and regrettable—it's and/and/and/and as well. Life *is* and: the accidental and the immutable, the elusive and the graspable, the bizarre and the predictable, the actual and the potential, all the multiplying realities, entangled, overlapping, colliding, conjoined—plus the multiplying illusions! This times this times this times this. . ."[5] This pluralistic view of American and Jewish possibility, an open-ended and rich limbo of potentialities, affirms the power of the imagination and

2. See Moacyr Scliar, *A condição judaica: das tabuas da lei a mesa do cozinho*, Porto Alegre: Rio Grande do Sul, 1985; and Santiago Kovadloff, *Antisemitismo en Argentina: siete opiniones diferentes*. Buenos Aires: Centro J. N. Bialik, 1985; and *Por un futuro imperfecto: ensayos*, Buenos, Aires: Botella al Mar, 1987.

3. Also see Santiago Kovadloff, *Canto abierto*, Buenos Aires: Botella al Mar, 1979,

4. Mary Ann Caws, *The Art of Interference: Stressed Readings in Verbal & Visual Texts*, Princeton, New Jersey: Princeton University Press, 1989 Introduction, Section IV Murray Baumgarten. *City Scriptures: Modern Jewish Writing*, Cambridge: Harvard University Press, 1982, chapters 2, 8.

5. *The Counterlife*, New York: Farrar Straus, 1987, 306.

celebrates the multiple possibilities of life rather than its singular certainties. It is an affirmation not of the power of the father or the mother but, in its multiplication of names and deeds, of the vigor and world-creating passionate intelligence of the sons and daughters.[6] Thereby it echoes the ancient midrash that the Torah was given to the Jews not because of the merits of the patriarchs or matriarchs but for the interpretive eagerness of the schoolchildren in the house of study, who generate the multiplicity of meanings enriching and giving life to the Law.[7] The *puesto vacante* is also the locus of feeling in this world. Overdetermined and condensed, this compressed space makes desire possible. As the internal images of desire and external environment are overlaid upon each other in these urbane fictions, they remind us of the simultaneous rise of the modern western city and the way of seeing brought on by photography, helping us to recover the informing force of the past as part of the work of the present moment.

Commenting on the power of desire in Nora Glickman's tales, Elena Martinez notes that her characters "experimenta el placer y el dolor en el mundo de la fantasia, los juegos y los sueños" (experience pleasure and pain in the world of fantasy, in games and in dreams). Their erotic qualities suffuse their setting: house and apartment define the private domestic world which her women characters inhabit while street and field are the domain of her men. What the men seem to act out in their public worlds, women create in their private space: "Las fantasías son un espacio de libertad donde se puede realizar aquello que se nos prohibe en la vida consciente; éstas—dentro del sistema freudiano—satisfacen un deseo reprimido" (Fantasies are a zone of freedom where we can do things which our conscience would forbid in our real life. According to Freudian theory, these fantasies fulfill a repressed desire.)[8] Glickman's are tales of encounter between the two realms in which the collision of public and private releases desire.

The questing women of "Uno de sus Juanes" (One of her Johns), the title story of her first collection of tales,[9] discover the objects of their desire by venturing forth into the masculine realm and casting their eyes upon the available males in a voyeuristic reversal of expected roles. "El juego," Luisa acknowledges to herself, "consistía en el uso clandestino de otra

---

6. Murray Baumgarten and Barbara Gottfried, *Understanding Philip Roth* Columbia, South Carolina: University of South Carolina Press, 1990. 226–227.

7. *Midrash Rabbah,* Song of Songs 1:4.

8. Elena M. Martinez, "La problemática de la mujer en los textos de Julia Ortiz Griffin, Mireya Robles y Nora Glickman," 19. (Paper read at Ollantay, N. Y. March 1990)

9. Nora Glickman, *Uno de sus Juanes,* Buenos Aires: Ediciones de la Flor, 1983. Nora Glickman has provided the translations of the passages from her fictions.

persona," (the game involved the clandestine use of another person), a practice that defines her personality. "Luisa estaba convencida que su vida interior era propulsada por una serie de hurtos, por una ineludible cadena de robos secretos—siempre llevándose parte de alguien, sin que nadie se enterara, y menos que nadie, ese alguien en cuestión." (Luisa was convinced that her inner life was propelled by a series of thefts, by an ineluctable chain of secret thefts—she was always stealing a part of somebody, without anyone noticing, and least of all, the person in question.) The multiple possibilities offered by this mode of visual appropriation empower her identity. "Algo la compelía a buscar lo prohibido y a guardárselo para sí, como un trofeo íntimo. Eso le daba un sentido de independencia, de jerarquía. Con los hombres, por ejemplo, con los Juanes. Simplemente se los robaba." (Something compelled her to look for what was forbidden and to keep it to herself, like a hidden trophy. That gave her a sense of independence, of hierarchy. With men, for example, with the Johns. She simply stole them for herself.) As if she were a man, Luisa takes what she wants, playing the part of the thief and picaro, in contrast with the conventional view of women's roles.

As a child of ten she encounters a sleeping gaucho. The narrator's prose articulates this mythic reversal; not only has it dominated her sexual awakening, transforming it into an iconic image and subliminal effect of all these stories, it continues to function as a determining structure of her inner life. It is the man who sleeps and the narrator/protagonist/woman who lets her imagination play upon his suspended form and being.

> Tendría unos diez años, quizás menos, y se encontraba en el campo, donde solía pasear a caballo por horas enteras. Una tarde descubrió a cierta distancia de su casa a un hombre que descansaba recostado detrás de los piquillines, bajo un árbol tupido—el único entre tantos arbustos raquíticos que poblaban el monte pampeano. Su caballo pastoreaba cerca de un poste vecino. El hombre recién habría acabado de comer porque el aire, aunque ya limpio do humo, todavía conservaba el aroma penetrante y espeso de la carne asada. Luisa se arrimó sigilosamente para espiar al intruso. Alcanzó a notar la barba negra que enmarcaba su rostro, su ropa oscura y descolorida de baquiano: un bulto en la lona que debería llevar todas sus posesiones y unas pieles de zorro que colgaban de una rama alta, para que las secara el sol. En un instante vio todo eso y aún más; vio relucir el facón del hombre al sol: centelleante como espejo. Y sintió que se le helaba la sangre. El hombre, puma alerto a presencia extraña, se volvió bruscamente hacia ella, empuñando el cuchillo, como si Luisa ya se hallara encima suyo. Luisa picó las espuelas de su caballo con toda su alma y disparó sintiendo que el metal hacía surcos en su

pecho. Pero el hombre no hizo nada por seguirla. Se quedó en cambio, sentado a la sombra de su árbol, adormilado por el rastro caluroso de su asado. (21–22)

(She was ten years old, or less, and she was in an open field, where she used to go horseback-riding for hours. One afternoon she discovered, at some distance from her house, a man who was resting, reclining behind the *piquillines* [a wild red berry tree that grows in the Pampas] under a bushy tree—the only one with any foliage to speak of among the typical spiny bushes scattered across the Pampas. She let her horse graze in the neighboring field. The man had just finished eating; the air, already clear of smoke, still kept the thick, sharp aroma of roasted beef. Luisa approached carefully, to spy on the intruder. She was able to make out the black beard that framed his face, the faded dark clothes, the bundle under the canvas sheet that must have contained all he owned, and some fox pelts hanging from a tall branch, drying in the sun. She took it all in, at a glance, and more: she saw the glitter of the man's knife against the sun, shining like a mirror. And she felt her blood freeze. The man, like an alert puma, suddenly confronted her, grabbing his knife as if she had jumped on top of him. Luisa spurred her horse with all her might and ran away, feeling the sharp edges cutting into her chest. But the man made no move to follow her. He stayed under the shade of his tree. and slid back into a quiet doze, his figure blurred by the embers of his barbecue.)

The young girl is on horseback; the man lies below her unable, despite his conventional knife-gesture, to wound her. In the sunlight he is a mirror: this chilling phenomenon defines his function for her. *Uno de sus Juanes—* the male will echo her desire and make it possible for her to achieve it. The power of the role-reversal of expected Byronic conventions reinforces that of the overturning of the macho habits of Argentinian popular culture. He is the one who is undifferentiated and absorbed into his function as male, serving the more powerful woman. We are under the sign here not of the psychology of the Lacanian mirror stage nor the mythic encounter of Narcissus and his own reflection, but of the sexual multiples and elaborated role-playing of *Alice in Wonderland* and her travels through the looking glass.

Many of these stories skirt the dangers of consummation, substituting the spying of desire for the completion of sexual exchange. That is one strategy used by the female narrators of these stories to maintain the fullness of possibility, a method that makes possible their realization in this dream-discourse. Were interchange accomplished, institutional crystallization might result, and the patriarchal force of conventional life would push Luisa into bondage. What is sought instead is language as empowering code, the articulator of alternative reality. By contrast with "Uno de sus Juanes" (One of her Johns), "El último de los colonos" (The Last of the Colonists) takes place within the more limited realm of the Jewish family. The young girl acquires the energy, historical vision, and cultural force of Boruj Leiserman, displacing the absent male heir through her power of song, in a reversal as powerful as that biblical Jewish theme of the second son overcoming the firstborn. The narrower compass of this story functions like a tightly woven verse to focus its meanings and thereby amplify their resonance, thus Hebrew and Yiddish phrases interfere with the Spanish syntax of these sentences and function as expletives pointing to a fuller reality than everyday Argentinian life. As language and as culture, Yiddish functions as home for the female narrators of these stories, the *mameloshen*—the mother tongue—wielding power just as the marriage-broker, the *shadchan* does in "En Guardia."[10] It is worth noting that the first Spanish anthology of the major twentieth century Yiddish poets was published in Argentina in 1981, evidence both of a wider interest in Yiddish culture and literature and of the passing of the earlier generation chronicled in Glickman's story. The power of the songs that the narrator sings in that story is echoed in the title of the anthology, *El resplandor de la palabra judía* (*The Glory of the Jewish Word*), suggesting the fullness of history and biblical tradition animating Yiddish poetry,[11] which is now available to these Spanish-Jewish writers.

The success of Glickman's women in negotiating this multilingual and multicultural landscape does not depend upon the exercise of hegemonic interventions that flattens them into objects to be conquered; rather, it stems from their ability to face the surreal city world without evasions and thus participate as subjects, within its fragmentary force field. In "U.S.A. Musa S.A." the narrator plays with the alphabetic codes of the New York subway system until they lose their dominating power: BMT and D trains become counters in the nursery rhymes of children as the city loses its dismaying terror by once more becoming enchanted. What to do with all this, "con tantas palabras sin sentido (with so many meaningless words)?" She decides to keep them: "Mejor las guardo en un cajón; puede ser un cajón de vidrio, así las miro de vez en cuando. Por ahí un día las saco" (I'd better store them in a box. Maybe a glass box, so that I can look at them, now and again. And one day I might even take them out.) By this process, she overcomes their effort to have power

10. Nora Glickman, *Mujeres. memorias, malogros*, Buenos Aires: Editorial Milá, 1992.

11. *El resplandor de la palabra judía: Antología de la poesía ídish del siglo xx*, selected and translated by Eliahu Toker, Buenos Aires: Editorial Pardés, 1981.

over her. This urban graffiti is transformed from the sign of her subjugation into "puras macanas. Esto es puro lienzo vacío. Veo material escribible en todas partes, hasta donde no lo puedo ver. Lo oigo, lo toco, lo huelo. Como ese fotógrafo que se hizo famoso exhibiendo fotos de excrementos: caca de palomas, caca de perros, caca de hombre. Arte en todo. Eso no. A mí no me engaña. Lienzo vacío" (Pure nonsense. This is just an empty canvas. I see writable material everywhere, even where there is none to be seen. I hear it, I touch it, I smell it. Like that photographer who became famous exhibiting photos of excrement: pigeon shit, dog shit, man shit. Everything is art. Not for me. It doesn't fool me. An empty canvas.) (86) The city that flaunts its dirt in order to keep women in their domestic place becomes instead a source of words for her. Collecting the fragments that she will later weave into the cultural fabric of this newfound culture, the narrator is an anthropologist—"las pongo a colgar" (I hung them out to dry)—she is the baglady of this city, who in her picking up and collecting activity recreates the sexual power of Pandora's box.

The self-reflexive irony of the narrator protects her from the conventional public, male vision of everyday life. As a result, there is no closing off of the story; instead of conclusion there is transition, ambiguity, and the disquieting possibility of alternative worlds. It is the method articulated most fully in "Puesto Vacante," one of Glickman's best tales. In it, Cora Fausinez, narrator and protagonist, circulates an announcement of a position: Puesto Vacante. Se Necesita Jugador" (Vacant position. Player wanted.) What Cora seeks is not to be found in the many resumes that she receives from men, though they make valiant efforts to "demostrarme el valor de lo escrito" (prove the importance of their credentials). Her first name reveals the heartfelt passion with which she pursues her quest; her last name recalls the Faustian world-making power at work in her endeavor. The story melds the bureaucratic language game of academic job-seeking with the personals of the classified ad in order to reveal their reciprocity. In the process, we discover with the narrator the game's hidden rules, which make it possible to recuperate desire rather than to expend it in re-creating patriarchal forms.

Historical forces and psychological states are translated in this open place into competing spatial forms and figures. There is no assurance that their random encounter can become a coherent dance that holds opposing forces together; there is no guarantee of the articulation of coherent meaning, just the exhilarating possibility of continuing linguistic play. In this site, gender reversal and theatrical self-realization can be accomplished because they result from the choices of the citizen. Here she is not object or victim, but subject and maker of choices.

The open space of intersubjectivity and citizenship characteristic of Glickman's female protagonists finds its echo in the civic and parodic imagination of Scliar. The role-reversals of Glickman's women who take male parts are parallelled by Scliar's men who fulfill female roles. Their plans lead Scliar's men astray, as they become confused by their own best intentions. Instead of conquering on horseback, they discover the pleasure of being ridden, of serving, of somehow muddling through. Impelled by obscure sensations and pseudo-biblical fables that they use to account for their complicated feelings, his male characters are desperate schlemiehls.[12] They do not acquiesce in their victimization as Jews but seek through quixotic actions and dizzying flights of fantasy to transform their status. As if Sholom Aleichem's characters had suddenly transmigrated to the "New World" of Porto Alegre, their Jewish identities coexist, interfere with, and thus mark the power of their Brazilian personalities.

Scliar's characters live in a city that reflects their fantasies at the same time that it parodies the grand ideals of urban life. Similarly, the urban arena of their encounter registers in these fictions as a city poised between dissolution and articulation. *The Volunteers* live in a never-quite-settled city, whose civic structure depends upon the tastiness of meat turnovers and the availability of Elvira, the prostitute. In *The Strange Nation of Rafael Mendes*,[13] actions are accounted for by reference to Jonah, the ancestor of all these desperate wanderers seeking to escape the demands of prophecy. Like contemporary readings of this prophet's story, Scliar emphasizes its comic and parodic qualities.[14] The same motive that moves Jonah to hide from his appointed task propels the centaurs of *The Centaur in the Garden*[15] not only to band together and disguise themselves, but to submit to surgical operations that will transform them into mere humans. All these efforts, however, that echo classical patterns of Jewish assimilation with their strategies of "passing," turn out to be self-parodies. They are unsuccessful methods for avoiding acknowledgment of the Jewish past, which cannot be put to rest; their memories interfere increasingly with the present. Like the characters of these tales, the environment teeters

---

12. Ruth R. Wisse, *The Schlemiehl as Modern Hero*, Chicago: University of Chicago Press, 1971, 46–47.

13. *A estranhã nação de Rafael Mendes*, Porto Alegre, Rio Grande do Sul. L&PM Editores, 1983; translated by Eloah F. Giacomelli, New York: Harmony Books, 1987 most readily available in the edition of Ballantine Books, 1989.

14. Arnold Band, "Swallowing Jonah: The Eclipse of Parody," *Prooftexts*, vol 10, number 2 (May 1990), 177–195.

15. *O centauro no jardim*, Rio de Janeiro, Editora Nova Fronteira, 1980, translated by Margaret A. Neves, New York: Available Press, Ballantine, 1984.

on the edge either of the assertive self-realization of urban success or a shaky version of the second law of thermodynamics, impelling all to the advent of complete collapse.

Plot, character, and gesture meet in the houses of Scliar's novels. They range from the seedy Lusitania Bar—the site of narration of *The Volunteers*—[16] to the enclosed fortress home of Maria Amelia, girlfriend and wife-to-be of the storyteller of the novel; the financial investment office appropriately named *Pecunia*, with its three thousand six hundred square meters of hardwood panels, crystal chandeliers, and red carpets of *Rafael Mendes*; and the surreal operating rooms and cunningly constructed houses of the centaurs in *The Centaur in the Garden*. Each of them proclaims its function by an official synecdoche, most apparent in Pecunia's company emblem, the *Arbor Aurea* depicting a gold tree against a blue background that alludes to its owner's family name, Goldbaum, while seducing customers into believing that its legendary qualities will also turn their modest investments into gold. Like this gold tree, all these logos have something tacky about them: they reveal to the reader their willed quality; they depend upon the self-persuading imagination of the beholder for their effect. Thus, the bar of the Lusitania functions as the theatrical frame of the narrator's tale, and his own prodigious appetite for his wife's meat turnovers results in an obesity that makes him describe his stomach as a constantly changing, not-yet-explored hairy island. These are not the formal insignia of formidable institutions but the hoped-for talismans of success. They enact the not-yet-realized yet constantly beckoning promise of this country, to which the narrator's immigrant parents respond upon arrival with a mixture of his mother's dismay and his father's desire.

> De madrugada, a chuva tendo cessado, saíram a pasear pelo Caminho Novo. Os útimos noctívagos saíram dos cabarés, um que outro bêbado dormia numa soleira de porta, mulheres passavam, bocejando, cansadas, a pintura borrada, os vestidos amarrotados. Isto era o que minha mãe via, e o que via lhe causava desgosto. (15)

> (At dawn the rain stopped and they went out for a walk in the Caminho Novo neighborhood. The last of the night people were leaving the cabarets, a drunk or two lay asleep in a doorway, women walked by yawning, tired, their makeup smudged, their dresses rumpled. That was what my mother saw, and what she saw displeased her.)

---

16. *Os Voluntários*, Porto Alegre, Rio Grande do Sul: L&PM Editores, 1979, translated by Eloah F. Giacomelli, New York: Available Press, Ballantine Books, 1988.

While his mother sees the rumpled night-time world, his father focuses on what this seedy street and city might become.

> Outro era o olhar que meu pai lançava sobre esse cenário. Via bêbados, sim, via prostitutas. Mas via também uma cidade que despertava para um dia de trabalho, impaciente por realizações e progresso. Meu pai via movimiento, uma febril agitação, bondes que chegavam ao centro depejavam centenas de operosos pono-alegrenses: funcionários com suas pastas, bancários, caixeirinhas que caminhavam apressadas, o olhar fixo, os braços cruzados no busto. (15)

> (It was with different eyes that my father watched this scene. Yes, he saw the drunks and the hookers. But he also saw a city waking up to face a day of work, a city eager for achievements and progress. My father saw the feverish hustle and bustle, the streetcars that kept arriving downtown, disgorging hundreds of hardworking Porto Alegre citizens: government employees carrying briefcases, bank clerks, young salesgirls hastening their steps, walking with their eyes fixed, their arms folded against their chests.)

This is world-creating optimism.

> Ambulantes exibiam suas mercadorias: lojas se abriam, os armarinhos e as casas de ferragens, as lojas de confecções, as sapatarias; cortinas de ferro subiam, vitrinas exibiam, jogados de qualquer maneira, mas sempre a preço barato, carpins e ceroulas, japonas e caminsetas; manequins de nariz descascado sorriam fixo sob os bonés e os chapéus Ramenzoni, balconistas, bocejando, arrumavam saldos em cestos, negociantes penduravam nos varões de toldos rasgados cabides e ganchos com roupas de cores berrantes que ficavam adejando à brisa da manhã como, naturalmente, bandeiras ao vento. (15–16)

> (Hawkers were setting up their wares; stores were opening their doors: dry-goods stores and hardware stores, ready-to-wear stores and shoe stores; steel doors were being rolled up; displayed in the show windows were hoes and long johns, pea jackets and T-shirts, all thrown up together in a haphazard way, but always at bargain prices: mannequins with peeling noses smiled fixedly under their caps and their *Ramenzoni* hats: yawning salesclerks were busy placing remnants in hampers; on the frames of torn awnings, merchants were hanging garish clothes, which kept flapping in the morning breeze like, naturally, flags in the wind.)

The father fails to notice the shabby quality of these tawdry heaps of objects; he is deep in the effort to recover in his imagination the past grandeur of old decaying buildings on the Rua Voluntários da Patria. It is his image of grandeur that he bears before him, like the "banners the Crusaders used to carry before them at the time of the conquest of the Holy Land."(4)

The street of the volunteers of Porto Alegre is the architectural spine of this world, reflecting not only the status of its inhabitants but also expressing the desperation of life on the edge. These people overcome natural disasters, inadequate facilities, and the frustrating urban infrastructure of their city by living in their imagination.

In this novel past difficulties become challenges overcome and opportunities seized. The looming force of the large urban centers of Brazil serve as a touchstone for successful urban life. Nevertheless, the self-parodying effort of these volunteers to attain a heroic life echoes that of the liberators of Brazil and Latin America and their efforts at adventure in devising a plan for a hare-brained, abortive voyage to Jerusalem worthy of Luís de Camões's heroes. Aspiring to the status of classical heroes conquering a continent and building a city, they manage to achieve not the act but the idea. Shlemiehls and luftmenschen, their accomplishments remain in the realm of the imagination.

Where Manuel Puig, Mario Vargas Llosa, and Guillermo Cabrera Infante have led, Moacyr Scliar and Nora Glickman follow, adding as Jews an additional ethnic marking; the result is narrative relying on interference, Spanish and Portuguese here inflected by Yiddish and Hebrew that in their reliance on city life and an urban irony, link them to classic North American Jewish writers. Like them, Scliar and Glickman build their fictional worlds in relation to the city achievements of their immigrant predecessors.

4

The Complex Roses of Jerusalem: The Theme of Israel in Argentinian Jewish Poetry

FLORINDA GOLDBERG

El viejo galeote había escrito cuando joven versos que hablaban de Israel, de la leche y la miel y la esperanza y el desierto que no había visto porque en aquel tiempo se mataba el hambre en las lecherías del Once y se acostaba con grandes polacas que aprendían a cantar el tango.

(The old galley-slave had written in his youth poems that spoke of Israel, the milk and the honey and the hope and the desert he had not seen because in those times he used to kill his hunger at the dairies of the Jewish neighbourhood and go to bed with big Polish women who learned to sing tango.)

> Pedro Orgambide, *La buena gente* (*The Good People*)

Las rosas de Jerusalém son complicadas
(The roses of Jerusalém are complicated)

> Luisa Futoransky, *La sanguina* (*The red-pencil drawing*)

THIS CHAPTER ANALYZES the theme of Israel—the state, its pre-statehood period, and its founding ideology, Zionism—in Jewish poetry written in Argentina from the second decade of the century through the 1980s.[1]

---

1. In the texts considered, "Israel" is also used as a synonym of "Jewish people" or "Judaism."

The theme of Israel comprises a very limited portion of the space devoted by Argentinian Jewish writers to issues related to Jewish identity. Moreover, the treatment of the issue is not emotionally and ideologically neutral, as it reflects the challenge posed by Zionism and the existence of the Jewish state to the Jews of the Diaspora.

I

The first period under consideration extends from 1910 to about 1950, a period of massive Jewish migration both to Israel and to Argentina. In those decades, Jewish immigrants in Argentina gradually achieved economic and cultural integration, mostly within the developing urban middle class. In 1910, the publication of Alberto Gerchunoff's *Los gauchos judíos* (*The Jewish Gauchos*) introduced Jewish themes into mainstream Argentinian Jewish literature. It also established an issue that would continue to concern Argentinian Jewish writers, namely, the successful integration of Jews into their host society, even at the cost of omitting explicit references to the tensions and conflicts that occurred during this process.

The Argentinian way of being Jewish and the Jewish way of being Argentinian were not fully accepted as poetic subjects during those years. Therefore, it is not surprising that in the works of such writers as Lázaro Liacho (1898–1969), Carlos M. Grünberg (1903–1968), and César Tiempo (1906–1980), emphasis was placed on the "content" of poems as being more important than mere "form" (this, in a period that favored experimental, form-oriented poetry).[2] The aim of these writers lay, indeed, beyond the pure esthetic realm: it was meant to explain, justify and legitimize the existence of a Jewish literary discourse, and through it, the Jewish cultural presence in Argentina in general—an apologetic attitude.

In theory, the Jewish theme was not difficult to legitimize, at least for the broad-minded, democratic, and receptive audience that the general reading public was supposed to be. Furthermore, in the 1930s and 1940s, the tragedy of European Jewry granted full rights to Jewish literary protest, indignation, and sorrow. Trouble arose from another central event in Jewish contemporary history, the development of the independent Jewish state. Writers still busy with asserting themselves as good Argentinians and good

---

2. See Lázaro Liacho, *Siónidas desde la pampa y Sonata judía de Nueva York* (*Zionist Poems from the Pampa and Jewish Sonata of New York*), Ed. Candelabro, Buenos Aires, 1969, especially pp. 12, 16; and Jorge Luis Borges's preface to Carlos M. Grünberg, *Mester de Judería* (*Art of Jewish Poetry*), Ed. Argirópolis, Buenos Aires, 1940, XII–XIII.

Jews found themselves confronted with an issue that was characterized as "dual loyalty": Is it acceptable for a citizen of one state to feel attached to another, to the point of lending to it not only moral and spiritual, but also financial support and, most importantly, to consider living there? Jewish poets, like other public figures, had to find a way out of that divisive situation, a way that could accommodate their feelings toward Israel without jeopardizing their hard-earned, but never assured, integration into Argentinian society. In their poetry these questions would be resolved through specific themes: the search for a conciliation between the two loyalties—which often produced ambiguous results; the reference to the history of the Jewish people, both ancient and modern, to legitimize their need for a state and a historical homeland; and even the use of derogatory language in their references to the concrete reality of Israel.

In Lázaro Liacho's introduction to *Siónidas desde la Pampa* (*Zion Poems from the Pampa*), he declares that "todos mis poemas están en la linea sionista" (13) (all my poems are in the Zionist line) and then "soy un patriota argentino y un defensor del judaísmo" (17) (I am an Argentine patriot and a defender of Judaism.) The same delicate balance is sought in the poems. In "Presencia de Jerusalem" ("Presence of Jerusalem") (29–30) a rhetorical first person designs an ideal, remote Jerusalem as his "Novia de Sión" ("Bride of Zion"): while in "Nostalgia del retorno imposible" ("Nostalgia of the Impossible Return") dated 1931, Zion is collectively loved but unattainable: "despierta nuestra alma colectiva, pero no la podemos alcanzar" (28–29) ("it arouses our collective soul, but we cannot reach it"). In the vocabulary of Argentinian Jewish literature established by Gerchunoff, "wandering Jew" excluded the fortunate Jew who had found a haven in Argentina; therefore, such lines as "Ya veo los jalutzim, el instante / en que feliz llega el judío errante, / pleno, a Tel Aviv, de puerto en puerta" (52) ("I see the pioneers, the moment in which the wandering Jew reaches happily, in foul soul, Tel Aviv, from port to door") can be understood as exclusively referring to other, unfortunate Jews. The rhetorical first person, though greater involvement appears in "Patria" ("Homeland"), in which Israel is presented as redeeming the Jew from the "sanguinario pogrom" ("bloody pogrom") (71): "Para que mi niño sea / tal como los niños son / el mundo debe brindarle / eterna patria en Sión" (70) ("For my child to be as children are, the world has to offer him an eternal homeland in Zion"). "Canto al nuevo Estado Judío" ("Song to the New Jewish State"), dated 1948, ends with the lines: "el hombre que estima al hombre / está de pie bajo tu cielo / cantándote, Eretz Israel" (86) ("the man that respects man stands under your skies singing to you, Land of Israel"); here the Zionist project attains legitimacy by means of a universal value. The poem that closes the book reaffirms strategically the Gerchunoffian solution to the dual identity issue: "Porteño de armas llevar, / judío a buen razonar, / ni cordero ni león, / estoy frente al porvenir, / dispuesto a ser gran peón / en el mundo a construir" (87) ("Son of Buenos Aires, fighter and a sensible Jew, neither lamb nor lion, I face the future, ready to be a great laborer in the world that has to be built")

The work of César Tiempo also stems from "el deseo raigal de expresar el anhelo del judío immigrante en pos de arraigo y naturalización. . .a la sociedad huésped. transformada en la verdadera Tierra de Promisión" ("the radical wish to express the immigrant Jew's longing for roots and integration. . .to the host society, seen as the real Promised Land").[3] Such a "radical wish" could only collide with the challenge presented by Zionism and Israel. However, Tiempo does not explore the dual loyalty conflict as Liacho and Grünberg did. His few poems dealing with Israel omit any linkage with his favorite issue, everyday Jewish life in Buenos Aires, as if the two subjects had nothing in common. A partial exception appears in his poem on the death of Chaim Nachman Bialik, the poet of the Jewish national renaissance.[4] Here Bialik becomes the symbol of the paradigmatic poet as opposed, together with some "jóvenes que supieron sacudirse como lobeznos / y sus dientes agudos despedazaron nuestra humillación" ("youngsters who knew how to revolt as young wolves, and their sharp teeth tore our humiliation to pieces") (a possible reference to Zionist pioneers), to the meanness of the Argentinian Jewish bourgeoisie and of the Jewish people as a whole. In "Canto fúnebre a un bar desaparecido", ("Mourning Song to a Disappeared Coffee Shop")[5] he ironically refers to those "sionistas infractos" ("unyielding Zionists") whose ideology is solely verbal bravado.

"Sabadomingo herido" ("Wounded SabbathSunday"), opens with "Canción de cuna"[6] dedicated to Saul Tchernichowsky, an almost literal version of the latter's "Lullaby" written in 1936. Tiempo has kept some Hebrew words: the original title "Shir eres", "jhalutz y jhalutza" [sic] ("pioneer man and pioneer woman") and "kevutzah" (settlement), to add local color. The mother sings to her newly-born son. The surroundings are sad and frightening: grenades explode, a jackle howls, the settlement is small and its corral is broken, the mother is exhausted and weeping.

---

3. Leonardo Senkman, *La identidad judía en la literatura argentina (Jewish Identity in Argentinian Literature)*, ed. Pardés, Buenos Aires, 1983, 155, 154.

4. César Tiempo, *Sabadomingo (SabbathSunday)*, Centro Editor de America Latina, Buenos Aires, 1966, 42–45. The book was first published in 1938.

5. *Libro para la pausa del Sábado* (Book for the Sabbath Pause), in César Tiempo, *Poesías completas* (Complete Poems), Stilman Ed., Buenos Aires, 1979, 78. The book appeared in 1930.

6. *Ibid.*, 168–169.

All this appears in the original, but the contexts of both poems result in different readings for each. In Tchernichowsky's patriotic writings of those years, the child represents the hope for a better future in spite of the difficult circumstances. He is, as it were, the hero who will bring about change. This optimistic undertone is absent in Tiempo.

Tiempo also devotes poems to the glory of the newborn state. "Tornaviaje" ("Return trip"), subtitled "Lamentación desconsolada" ("Disconsolate Wail"),[7] is again somewhat ambiguous. Its first five stanzas summarize the long Jewish Diaspora to present Israel as the glorious closing of an historical cycle: "Pero no hay noche sin mañana / y lo que fue de nuevo es. / Tallado en trueno y en espiga / se alza Medinat Israel" ("But there is no night without morning, and what there was is here again; carved in thunder and stalk there stands the State of Israel"); glory somewhat diminished by its territorial reductions (a notion that will appear also in Grünberg). In Sábado pleno (Full Sabbath), "Medinat Israel" ("The State of Israel") he again frames the legitimacy of the state in its historical and religious roots: "el hoy vale por el ayer. / Por el camino del retorno / volvemos a Jerusalén" (208) ("The present avails itself of the past. By the return road we come back to Jerusalem"). The exclusive use of mythological concepts and the lack of and direct perceptions of a concrete reality confers vividness to the best of Tiempo's portrayals of Argentinian Jewish life, reducing this poem to a rhetorical panegyric. There is nevertheless, one brief text in which patriotic enthusiasm combines successfully with vivid images:

PASA UN AVION
Banderas de Israel: tremolan manos,
flotan barbas talmúdicas al viento.
El cielo se enriquece de miradas
y nosotros de cielo

("A Plane Passes"—"Israeli flags: hands wave, Talmudic beards float in the wind. The sky gets rich with glances, and we with sky")[8]

It is in the poems of Carlos M. Grünberg that the ambiguities and the problems troubling Argentinian Jews regarding Israel are more fully explored. His earlier book Mester de Judería (Art of Jewish Poetry)[9] proclaims the joy of being Jewish in Argentina: "Quien exclama Argentina ha exclamado / libertad y Argentina a la vez/. . .Patria mía: tu encanto ha

---

7. Sabadomingo, 61–63. Not included in the 1979 Poesías completas.
8. Libro para la pausa, 69.
9. See note 2.

rendido / al antiguo león de Judá /. . ./ Has curado las llagas de Job" ("1916," p. 17) ("He who exclaims Argentina proclaims Argentina and freedom at once. My homeland, your charm has subdued the ancient lion of Judah. . .You have healed Job's wounds"). "Sión" ("Zion") sets a clear distinction between the Jew who needs a Jewish state and the (Argentinian) Jew who does not: "Tal vez Sión constituya la flaca panacea / de algunos de nosotros, que no de los demás" (97), ("Maybe Zion is the frail panacea for some of us, not for all"), where the relevant word is the adjective "flaca" ("thin" meaning frail, precarious). "Mestizo" ("Half-breed") will state it more clearly incorporating the historical argument: "Si, yo quiero una patria judía en Palestina, / allá en el suelo en que Isaac nació; / pero mi patria propia la quiero en Argentina" (119) ("Yes, I want a Jewish homeland in Palestine, on the land where Isaac was born. But I want my own homeland in Argentina"). The poem develops a series of parallels between ancient Jewish and Argentinian historical figures, closing with a rather long elaboratian of his "dúplice realidad" ("dual reality") as an Argentinian and a Jew.

Junto a un río de Babel (By a River of Babylon)[10] includes poems published since 1950, i.e., after the creation of the state. The singular "un río" ("a river), as opposed to the plural of the Biblical original, again stresses the fact that the poet lives in a diaspora state that is different from others. Two sections of the book, "Promisión" ("Promise") and "Siónidas" ("Songs of Zion")—significantly located after "Hitlermedio" (Hitlerinterval")—are devoted to Israel, and some of them express straightforward Zionist enthusiasm. This enthusiasm lessens in other texts that underscore the reality of the new state. The land is barren by nature; furthermore, its historical territory has been severely reduced. But most troubling is its human aspect, the kind of Jews who are populating Israel. The implication is that nothing glorious or even positive can be expected from the young state: "Tan sólo vuelven los despojos / de los galeotes de la grey; / tan sólo tornan a un harapo / de los eriales de Israel" (70) ("Only the spoils of the nation's galley-slaves go back; they return to just a rag of Israel's wasteland"), Zion is "tu única esperanza / de una vida menos ajena. / Pero también es una trampa / también es una ratonera" (85) ("your only hope of a less alienated life. but it is also a trap, a mousehole"). The Jewish state should be morally superior to others, but he can only hope that it will be "la menos / indecente del montón" (104) ("the least indecent of the lot").

---

10. Carlos M. Grünberg, *Junto a un río de Babel* (By a River of Babylon), Acervo Cultural Ed., Buenos Aires, 1965.

Grünberg candidly expresses the negative consequences of Israel's existence on his Argentinian Jewish status. In "Volver" ("Return"), he resolves the dual loyalty issue by frankly and boldly stating his three reasons for not emigrating to Israel: the first is emotional: "no puedo / desprenderme de mi patria" (130) ("I can't turn myself away from my homeland"); the second is ethical and patriotic: "no debo / sustraerme a mi terruño /. . ./ tengo que participar / en el denodado esfuerzo con que mis conciudadanos / tratan de hacerse un gran pueblo" (131) ("I must not withdraw from my land. . .I have to join my countrymen in their brave effort to become a great people") and the third has the absolute ring of sincerity: "Porque no quiero" (132) ("because I just don't want to"). Therefore, "así es mi sionismo / sionismo sin Sión" (133) ("so my Zionism is Zionism without Zion"). But two shadows dim the clarity of this solution. The first is that the Argentinian Jew's love for his country "is not always returned"—"Unilateralidad" (115) ("Unilaterality"). The other is that the existence of Israel has turned the Diaspora Jew into a "judío / de segunda" ("second-class Jew") (138), a "subjudío" (140) ("subjew"). At the end of "Siónidas", Grünberg finds a solution, at least rhetorically, in the common destiny of both Diaspora and Israeli Jews: both "comparten la misma suerte / son consortes" (142) ("share the same sorts, are consorts"), because all migration lands are equally cruel: "La tierra de leche y miel / como las de migración / tierra de lucha y de hiel" (143) ("The land of milk and honey, as any migration country, is a land of strife and bile"). Unable to find a satisfactory solution within the boundaries of history, Grünberg looks for it in a universal metaphor: "La Tierra y todos los astros / son los judíos del cielo" (147) ("The Earth and all the stars are the Jews of the skies").

II

The establishment of the State of Israel in 1948 encouraged a great deal of enthusiastic verse in Argentina and elsewhere, most of which was the raw, amateurish expression of personal and collective feelings. Two interesting poets of this period deserve closer attention.

León S. Pérez (1922) published in 1953 *Israel de setiembre* (*Israel of September*).[11] His style is heavily influenced by Pablo Neruda's great epic poem *Canto General* which had appeared in 1950. Two of the motifs found

---

11. León S. Pérez, *Israel de septiembre* (*Israel of September*), ed. Pueblo Judío, Buenos Aires, 1953.

in the older generation reappear in the book. One is Israel emerging from the history of the Jewish people, from the "patria bíblica, insepulta" (21) ("biblical, unburied homeland"), from "tu raíz ardida" (17) ("your burnt root"). The second is the unavoidable issue of dual loyalty. Pérez finds a metaphorical solution by placing the fatherland not in a land but in time: "He nacido en tu tierra sobre el tiempo / . . . un país flotante, indemne / en el espacio sin hitos de la historia" (13) ("I was born in your land on time. . . a floating country, untouched in the unbound space of history"), not within external political boundaries but in the inner soul: "He nacido de un barro de patria / interior a mi piel, / sumergido en el huevo de mi propia frontera" ("I was born from a homeland's mud inside my skin, submerged in the egg of my own boundary"). When compared with earlier poets, Pérez's texts present two striking differences. Written after spending a period in Israel, his images of Jerusalem, Safed and other places possess the vividness of direct observation. Besides, Israel is for him more than the fulfillment of the Jewish dream: it is the realization of a universal political project. The ingathering of the exiles—"Un infinito abrazo de hombre a hombre / recoge nuevos hombres en la playa" (18) ("An infinite embrace from man to man gathers new men on the reach")—is as much an end in itself as the beginning of a new society based on social justice. In this society, labor is the central value, the working class both the builder and the leader: "Una cohorte de plúmbeos aldeanos, / de corajes, de blusas marineras, / de soñadores obreros imbatibles, / te rescató de tu sitial angélico" (25) ("A cohort of plumbeous peasants, of courages, of sailor shirts, of dreaming invincible laborers, rescued you from your heavenly seat"). "Hermandad de colmenas" (91) ("Brotherhood of beehives"), is indeed the better country in which Grünberg did not believe: "Los pobres -sólo los pobres- se alegraron / . . . / ¿Por qué, si no, naciste, / Israel de septiembre, árbol y piedra en la colina, / carretera de mundos desiguales?" (47) ("The poor, only the poor, were glad. . .Why if not were you born, Israel of September, tree and rock on the hill, highway of unequal worlds?").

Fine Nerudian resonances can also be observed in the poetry of Fernando Bielopolsky (1921–1970), which deals extensively with the tragedy of the holocaust in his book *Espera* [*Waiting*], published in 1946.[12] Bielopolsky was, like Pérez, an active militant in the Zionist left; however, the state-in-the-making is the subject of only one poem in *Espera*: "Ve, camarada. . ." (53–54), ("Go, comrade. . .") a farewell to three friends leaving

---

12. Fernando Bielopolsky, *Espera*— (*Waiting*—), ed. Feria, Buenos Aires, 1946.

for Israel. The possessive pronoun "our" marks the yet unseen land as the object of collective desire: "cuando llegues a nuestra costa, a nuestra estrella sin rejas" ("when you reach our coast, our fenceless star"); with them, the Jewish people are returning to direct contact with the soil: "en la mañana sin par, en los sembrados, cuando beses temiendo la tierra de tus dedos" ("in the unequalled morning, on the sown ground, when fearfully you will kiss the soil in your fingers") (54).

Bielopolsky settled in Israel in 1947 and was among the defenders of the Kibbutz (collective settlement) Negba during the Egyptian attacks in July and August of 1948. His *Diario de Negba* (*Negba Diary*) is a dramatic testimony of those months of work, hope, fear, and struggle. He changed his surname to Loven and his poetic language to Hebrew, publishing poems, a drama, and articles on Latin American authors such as Neruda and Guillén. After his untimely death in 1970, a group of friends published an anthology of his writings.[13] Unjustly forgotten, Fernando Loven was a pioneer among Latin American poets in Israel, and a promoter of Latin American literature in that country.

Still, Israel never became the central subject of his poetry. His work was mostly lyric, and when he dealt with collective issues, his focus was universal. Isolated images taken from his Israeli experience, "estoy exprimiendo piedras y pomelos / y los copio, y los traduzco en cantos" (56) ("I am squezing stones and grapefruits and I copy them, and translate them into songs") are integrated into poems devoted to his feelings of anguish, "amiga oscura amiga de mi nombre" ("friend dark friend of my name"), which the new life in Israel had not eliminated: "creí que no me seguirían tus mudos ojos huecos / hasta esta tierra antigua de locura divina / donde la piedra se abre presintiendo el tiempo, / donde la hoja se recorta y perfuma transcendiendo / y donde es mi logro y mi comunión / la del alma y del viento" (30) ("I believe your mute hollow eyes would not follow me to this ancient land of divine madness, where the stone opens with the presentiment of time, where the leaf gives forth its transcendent fragrance, and where the communion of soul and wind is my achievement and my communion").

Loven wrote only two epic poems, concerning the death of his comrades during the Negba combats. In both we find the notion of continuity beyond and in spite of personal pain. This continuity is achieved

---

13. Fernando Loven, *Obra literaria* (*Literary Writings*). Tel Aviv, julio de 1975. Includes both Spanish and Hebrew texts. A selection of the *Negba Diary* is included in Florinda Goldberg and Iosef Rozen, eds., *Los latinoamericanos de Israel—Antología de una aliá* (*Latin American in Israel: Anthology of an Aliya*), ed. Contextos, Buenos Aires, 1988.

through the survivors, and also through the dead body's rejoining the soil and breeding new life: "los que sabemos que no serás tierra porque serás raíz; los que no te sabremos llorar porque en Israel no se llora; / los que apretamos los dientes contra el fusil para matar la muerte, / para que sean palomas lo que ahora hiere el aire, / para que sean naranjas lo que revienta en los campos" ("We who know that you will not become soil because you shall become root; we who do not cry for you, because in Israel nobody cries; we who clench our teeth to the gun to kill death, so that what hurts now the air be doves, so that what bursts in the fields be oranges") ("Oración leída ante su tumba cuando pudimos hacerlo" ("Prayer Read at His Tomb When We Could Do It") (86).

III

The writers born in the thirties and the forties absorbed the optimistic belief of the 1960s in the power of spiritual creations to forge a better world; at the same time they lived through Argentina's political and economic crises that culminated in the so-called "dirty war" in the seventies and the beginning of the eighties. On the Jewish scene, the enthusiasm toward Israel in its pioneer years had given way to preoccupation with the concrete problems of the country's development and international stand. A kind of "realpolitik" dismissed the classical imperative of Zionism, settling in Israel, as the only viable alternative. It also became increasingly popular to get first hand knowledge of the country through tourism or study periods.

The existential situation of the Argentinian Jew now presented new problems that went beyond the well-known issue of dual loyalty. If Liacho could contend in his times that only verse could confer the necessary "transcendency" to his historical testimony,[14] the new insight demanded a deeper and more detailed analysis. Not surprisingly, the treatment of such issues was mainly put forth in prose—novels, short stories, and essays. This process, obviously, continues to the present day.

Ricardo Feierstein (1942) has devoted most of his writings to that crossroad existential experience. His narrative trilogy, *Sinfonía inocente* (*Innocent Symphony*)—written in Buenos Aires after having lived for some years at a kibbutz—closes with a long poem, "Nosotros, la generación del desierto" ("We the Generation of the Desert").[15] The poem summarizes

---

14. See note 2.

the struggles and frustrations of a generation that believed in the imminence of a better world as an outcome of ideology and art: "el mundo ideal al alcance de la mano / las casas sin fronteras, el destino que nos hermanaba, / la poesía como flecha de plomo hacia el futuro" (208) ("the ideal world at arm's length, the houses without boundaries, the destiny that made us all brothers, poetry as a leaden arrow towards the future"). "Aquellos de nosotros que nacimos judíos ("Those of us who were born Jews") are even more frustrated: born after the destruction of the traditional Jewish life, they were also born too late to be among the pioneers of the Jewish homeland. Feierstein assumes his existential situation as unsolvable: "No somos la historia ni el futuro" ("We are neither history nor future") (205), "Estamos en el medio / generación del desierto /. . ./ y pagamos un precio desmedido / enhebrando una metralla de preguntas culposas / por nuestro temor de haber perdido algo" (207) ("We stand in between, the generation of the desert, and we pay an excessive price while firing a barrage of guilty questions, for we are frightened to have lost something").

The issue is therefore no longer the apologetic denial of dual loyalty; this generation, though it "admits its ambidextrous and fruitful roots" ("reconoce raíces ambidextras y fecundas,") (215) has lost the chance of proving its point and finding its place, being rejected from both sides: "y de allá nos dicen / galúticos, dispersos, vergonzantes / y de acá usureros, vendepatrias, desiguales" (207) ("and from there they call us diasporic, disperse, shameful, and from here usurers, traitors, unequal"). In the context of this new configuration of the Argentinian Jew—"generación del desierto / destinada a vislumbrar la Tierra Prometida / con una elíptica lupa de inmigrante" (207) ("generation of the desert, bound to glimpse at the Promised Land through an eliptic immigrant's magnifying glass"). The expression "Promised Land" plays with two meanings: the real State of Israel, and the symbolic connotation of utopia—both assumed to be unattainable. The previous generation's search for a definite answer to the dual loyalty issue has given way, for Feierstein, to the hopeless presentation of an open-ended existential problem.

A similar ambiguity can be read in the poems of Eliahu Toker (1934). As in Feierstein, there are no apologies for the dual roots. But for Toker, this is less of a generational problem than it is a personal, spiritual one that stems from an impossible choice. In fact, for Toker the issue is not dual loyalty, but dual exile. "Nací en el extranjero / y vivo expatriado entre

---

15. Ricardo Feierstein, *Escala uno en cincuenta* (*Scale one in fifty*), Ed. Pardés, Buenos Aires, 1984, 205–217.

amigos" ("I was born abroad, and live exiled among friends"), he writes
in *Piedra de par en par* (109):[16]

Fui concebido en el vientre de una ciudad querida,
quedé embebido en el jugo de su idioma
y en la sombra viva de sus calles,
y ya soy para siempre el que Buenos Aires hizo.
Pero traigo de pie en mí
la luz de otro pueblo
con cuya historia levantada y fuerte
estoy comprometido desde siempre

("I was conceived in the womb of a beloved city, remained soaked in the
juices of its language and in the live shades of its streets, and I am forever
what Buenos Aires made. But within me stands the light of another
people, and I am since eternity involved in its strong, standing history").

Eliahu Toker has chosen to remain in Argentina. His poetic persona
accepts the ambivalence of his choice: though Buenos Aires is "esta ciudad
/ donde tienen lugar mis sueños y pesadillas" ("this city where my dreams
and nightmares take place"), he confesses his awareness of the fact that
"vivir en Buenos Aires / debe de ser algo distinto de esto que hago" ("to
live in Buenos Aires must be something different from what I do"),[17] and
that "en el país de los judíos están las raices de mis manos" ("my hands'
roots lie in the land of the Jews").[18] His ideal solution to exile can only
exist in fantasy: "Quisiera alzar una casa en otro continente, / de pie sobre
un andamio levantado aquí mismo, / para borrar de mis palmas la línea
del exilio" ("I would like to put up a house in another continent, standing
on a scaffold right here, to wipe out from my hands the line of exile").[19]
Ultimately, the choice and the inevitable loss are accepted as positive:
"Optar entero es mi conciente acto de amor, / de un amor que vence a
otro amor" ("To choose entirely is my conscious act of love, of a love which
overcomes another love").[20]

Free not of tensions but of any apologetic compulsion, Toker can
assume a sympathetic observer's approach to Israel in the four poems in

---

16. Eliahu Toker, *Piedra de par en par* (*Wide Open Stone*), Rocamora Ed., Buenos Aires, 1972.
17. "Buenos Aires", *Papá, mamá y otras ciudades* (*Daddy, Mummy and Other Cities*), ed.
Contextos, Buenos Aires, 1988, 33.
18. "A Germán Rozenmacher" ["To German Rozenmacher"], *Piedra*, 90.
19. "Entretanto" ("Meanwhile") (dedicated to César Tiempo), *Lejaim*, (To Life), ed. de la
Flor, Buenos Aires, 1974, 39.
20. "Nací en el extranjero" ("I was born abroad") *Piedra*, 109.

Piedra...devoted to "Seis días en junio" ("Six Days in June"), where impressionistic images—"Entre un aire amarillo / acribillado por el lento vuelo de las esquirlas" ("In a yellow air pierced by the slow flight of splinters")—combine with expressionistic descriptions: "un desierto reptante, / hastiado de arena / y atragantado de manos atrapadas" ("a crawling desert sated with sand and choking with trapped hands").[21] In the poems on Masada, Jerusalem, and Israel in *Homenaje a Abraxas*, immediate perceptions integrate with symbolic significance taken from historical motifs, not as a legitimation of the new state, but rather as an additional dimension that coexists with factual reality and multiplies its significations. The insistence in words and construction implying continuity—"memoria," "recuerdo," "pasado," "futuro," "siguen de pie," "son todavía," "vuelve a,"—privilege historical memory as the ultimate giver of sense: "Tierra cortejada por arqueólogos / que extraen de los socavones y del recuerdo / las pruebas de un prolongado amor / hecho vasijas y espigas, pergaminos y pomelos" ("Land courted by archaeologists who extract from caves and memory the proofs of a long lasting love that became vessels and wheat, parchments and grapefruits").[22]

For contemporary Argentinian poets, history remains an unavoidable and necessary mediator that conditions their perception and poetic account of today's Israel. In *Ciudad en fuga y otros infiernos* (*City in Flight and Other Hells*) by Manuela Fingueret (1945),[23] again the paradigm of memory and continuity connects contemporary reality to history and myth: "Un hálito de piedra / que recuerda el primer día" ("A stormy breath that recalls the first day") ("Desierto I" ["Desert I"], 32), "recibo el fuego sagrado / de mis antiguas palabras" ("I receive the sacred fire of my ancient words") ("Safed" ["Zefat"], 35), "las cien puertas / por las que regresamos" ("the hundred doors through which we come back"), "la memoria como el maná" ("memory as mana") ("Jerusalem," 37). These motifs cluster in the poem "Jerusalem dorada" ("Golden Jerusalem"), where direct contact with the contemporary Israeli reality is simultaneously possible and impossible: "Cuánta distancia / Oh Jerusalem / entre tu antiguo olor / y el canto que anuncia / la caída del sol. (39) ("How great the distance, oh Jerusalem, between your ancient smell and the song that announces sundown").

---

21. "Seis días en junio: Sinai" ("Six Days in June: Sinai"), *Piedra*..., 93.

22. "Homenaje a Israel" ("Homage to Israel") en *Homenaje a Abraxas* (Homage to Abraxas), ed. Nueva Presencia, Buenos Aires, 1980, 35.

23. Manuela Fingueret, *Ciudad en fuga y otros infiernos (1976–1983 (City in Flight and Other Hells [1976–1983]*), ed. Botella al Mar, Buenos Aires, 1984.

IV

If, in a sense, Feierstein's and Toker's texts paradoxically close the dual loyalty motif showing that it cannot be resolved, Daniel Gutman (1954) creates a different kind of closure in his book *Erosión* (*Erosion*),[24] by presenting the subject as nonexistent. The title of the book postulates an ideal entity that integrates "Eros" and "Sion," symbols of two cultures, the Greek-classical and the Jewish-teleological, that represent two forces within the spirit of universal man—one aiming at the absolute-static and the other dynamic and goal-oriented. "Eros-Sion" is the "eterna mutación" ("eternal mutation") in which "la identidad alcanza sus pregunatas" (44) ("identity attains its questions"). To achieve this project, Zion is progressively stripped of its concrete historical and geographical contents, becoming an abstract symbol of creative impulse. Zion is "el nombre de una Tierra que no es de esta tierra" ("the name of a land that is not of this earth"), "cualquiera sea su nombre" (39) ("whatever its name").

Gutman's effort to void the concept of any national meaning seems to be a new version of the medieval Jewish notion of a "heavenly Jerusalem"—that "sitial angélico" from which Israel had been ideologically rescued in the vision of León Pérez. Such a proposal reveals the effort to avoid that conflict which in other poets resulted in apology, defense of Zionism, or acceptance of an existential fatality.[25]

V

A brief, intense poem by Luisa Futoransky (1939) synthesizes many of the motifs that have been presented in connection with the theme of Israel in Argentine poetry: history and challenging present, universal values and personal involvement. In "Jerusalem, una copa de vértigo" ("Jerusalem, a Cup of Vertigo"),[26] the roses that embellish the streets and public gardens of modern Jerusalem all year round are found to be "complicated," a complication that has to do with humanity's permanent quest for absolute truth, to finally become a matter of personal feelings. It is the "vertigo" of a unique encounter of the eternal and the self:

---

24. Daniel Gutman, *Erosión* (*Erosion*) Ultimo Reino, Buenos Aires, 1989.

25. See a more developed analysis of this aspect of the book in Florinda Goldberg, "Daniel Gutman: *Erosión*", *Noaj*, n. 5, Jerusalem, July 1990, 109–110.

26. Luisa Futoransky, *La sanguina* (*The Red-Pencil Drawing*), Taifa, Barcelona, 1987, 13. See also "El lenguaje arquetípico de mi judeidad" ("The Archetypical Language of my Jewishness"). in *Noaj*, No. 3-4, Jerusalem, May 1989, 160–168.

Las rosas de Jerusalém son complicadas
Los peregrinos desesperan
El camino de las rosas de la verdad
es absoluto

Y me duele/s tanto.

("The roses of Jerusalem are complicated / Pilgrims despair / The road
of the roses of truth / is absolute / And it hurts me, you hurt me, so much")

5

Jacobo Fijman: Jewish Poet?

NAOMI LINDSTROM

THE AVANT-GARDE POET JACOBO FIJMAN (born Bessarabia, 1898: immigrated to Argentina 1902; died 1970, of Jewish family background, converted to Catholicism in 1929. While the phrase "Jewish writer" may always be inherently problematic in some longer view, Fijman generates a more immediate uncertainty: should he be included when Jewish Argentine writers are considered?

One aspect of this question, whether a convert to Christianity should still be considered a Jew, lies outside the realm of literary studies. Without entering into technicalities, though, one may say that Fijman's conversion appears less than binding because it occurred during a time when the poet, who had always been eccentric, was growing bizarre in his everyday speech and behavior and having difficulty caring for himself; he would never again remain self-sufficient for long. Fijman's extreme fragility colors the general perception of his identity. Leonardo Senkman conveys this idea by entitling his essay on Fijman "Bautismo y locura" (Baptism and Madness). Senkman further observes that, unlike many Jewish converts to Christianity, Fijman was not seeking social acceptance (295). Much more could be said about the exceptionality of Fijman's Christianity, elaborated well beyond clerical guidelines. The following discussion, though, concerns itself with the literary aspect of the issue, assessing the evidence for and against perceiving Fijman as a poet who expressed himself Jewishly.

Molino rojo is the only one of Fijman's three collections of poetry that antedates his conversion, though the poet's fascination with Christianity was evident by the mid-1920s. While *Hecho de estampas* (Made of Images, 1930) and *Estrella de la mañana* (Morning Star, 1931) have a number of Christian allusions, *Molino* displays few (in fact, the frequency of religious allusions is lower than elsewhere in Fijman's work). *Molino* has been viewed (particularly by Fernandez) as the most likely repository for Jewish thought in Fijman's works. For this reason, the present study takes its textual examples from the 1926 work.

A useful starting point for examining Fijman's identity, although its status as evidence is equivocal, is his Delphic self-account, the 1970 *El pensamiento de Jacobo Filjman; o, el viaje a la otra realidad*. This one-of-a-kind work, part collaborative essay and part interview, was compiled by Vicente Zito Lema from conversations with the poet, then advanced in years and long institutionalized. It shows that Fijman continued to include Jewish thought in his personal system of ideas. He objects to Zito Lema's saying "su conversión de judío a católico" (your conversion from a Jew to a Catholic), insisting that "lo de judío no se pierde" (78) (it doesn't mean the loss of Jewishness). When Zito Lema inquires into the sources of Fijman's recurring image, "la noche de los corderos" (the night of the lambs), the poet evokes the flourishing of Judaic ritual before the destruction of the Second Temple: "Cuando eran sacrificados [los corderos) en el Templo Judío..." (When [lambs] were sacrificed in the Jewish Temple...). Fijman then utters both sides of this dialogue: "¿Quién te enseñó la física? Los egipcios. ¿Quién te enseñó la magia? Los caldeos. ¿Pero quién te enseñó el misterio de la unidad la magia? El pueblo de Israel" (67). Who taught you physics? The Egyptians. Who taught you magic? The Chaldeans. But who taught you the mystery of divine unity? The people of Israel (67). Fijman retains Jewish ways of discussing religious issues. For example, though he adopts the Christian practice of calling the Hebrew Bible "el Antiguo Testamento" (The Old Testament; 53), he employs in the same utterance, as a global term for canonical scriptures, "la Ley" (the Law); (53), he at times avoids direct naming of God in favor of circumlocutions, e.g., "El Que Sabía" (The One Who Knew) (53), in his account of the revelation on Mt. Sinai. Many other Jewish tendencies of thought appear in *Pensamiento*, including the association of piety with textual study and interpretation, reasoning, and ethical conduct, with a corresponding elimination of the Christian ideal of unquestioning faith. Fijman appears to filter nostalgia for pre-Diaspora Jerusalem into his allusions to the *City of God*, of which he has made an idiosyncratic, personal adaptation.

Most significant for this study are those passages in which Fijman adopts a mode reminiscent of Jewish prophetic writing, as when he inveighs against Buenos Aires as "una ciudad de maldiciones. Por la depravación. Y fundamentalmente por la carencia absoluta de moralidad. Hoy es una ciudad de pecado. Una ciudad hipócrita..."(26) (...a city of accursedness. For its depravation. And fundamentally for its absolute lack or morality. Today it's a city of sin. A hypocritical city....).

It should be noted that *Pensamiento* also features many assertions that are religious, but hardly Christian or Jewish. Fijman reveals a *sui generis* set of beliefs in which he occupies a central—messianic or divine-role. "Yo soy Dios. Jacobo Fijman es Dios" (47) (I am God. Jacobo Fijman is God), he states, and clearly does not mean a spark of divinity latent in all humankind. Of the ideal city, he says "Y su lengua no será el latin o el castellano sino la lengua de Jacobo Fijman. Dios y yo enseñaremos la verdad" (50) (And its language will not be Latin or Spanish but the language of Jacobo Fijman. God and I will teach the truth). There are such assertions as "yo estuve en la Luna antes que nadie. Dios quiso que el primero que realmente la viera fuera Fijman" (51) (I was on the moon before anybody. God wanted Fijman to be the first really to see it). Fijman explicates a personal magic, convinced that he holds revealed knowledge that goes beyond all existing religions.

While *Pensamiento* possesses an oracular beauty, it can neither count as part of Fijman's imaginative writing nor as analytical commentary on his work. A critical assessment of his literary Jewishness must come from an examination of his poetry. One approach, the identification of allusions, has been pursued by Ruth Fernandez in her 1985 *Jacobo Fijman, el poeta celestial y su obra* (Jacobo Fijman: The Celestial Poet and His Work). Fernandez, going through *Molino rojo*, compiles a list of recurring lexical items that she sees as evidence of an expressive debt: "Los libros del Pentateuco están llenos de frases similares: el uso reiterado de 'erizar,' 'candelabros,' 'espanto,' 'pavores,' 'palomas,' 'corderos,' 'estrella,' confirman la cristalización de un idioma legado desde antiguo y, a la par, la exhumación del mismo a través de nuevas expresiones" (The books of the Pentateuch are full of similar phrases: the reiterated use of 'rise,' 'candelabra,' 'fright,' 'fears,' 'doves,' 'lambs,' 'star,' confirms the crystallization of a language bequeathed from ancient times and, at the same time, the exhumation of this language by means of new expressions) (Fernandez 22). The immediate difficulty here is that these items also have meaning in Christian culture, as in the time-honored figures of the Holy Ghost as a dove and Jesus as a lamb. They can also function symbolically outside religious tradition, as in this statement of despair from "Subdrama" (50–52): "Han caído mis esperanzas como palomas muertas" (My hopes have fallen like dead doves).

Beyond the multiple associations of many religious symbols, there are other difficulties in an inquiry that starts with individual, overt allusions to religious culture. Consider the line "Me hago la señal de la cruz a pesar de ser judío" (I cross myself even though I'm Jewish). Occurring in the opening poem of *Molino*. "Canto de cisne" (Swan Song, 5–6), this utterance appears to be of electrifying interest to anyone seeking clues to Fijman's identity. But the poem, seen as a whole, has scant bearing on the issue; it is dedicated to suggesting the pain and chaos of disordered thought, in an uninterrupted progression from its opening line, "Demencia" (dementia). For example, the lines that follow "Me hago la señal de la cruz" are: "¿A quién llamar? ¿A quién llamar desde el camino tan alto y tan desierto?" (To whom can I cry out? To whom can I cry out from such a high and lonely road?) Since "the highest, loneliest road" has already been established as a metaphor for madness, crossing oneself becomes a desperate appeal and a sign of the anxiety of dementia.

Throughout *Molino*, the expression of suffering and disorientation has priority over the suggestion of religious messages. Fijman's choice of lexical items or allusions at times reflects his preoccupation with religion, but such options are better accounted for, in these particular poems, as working to convey the pain of a malfunctioning mind. Consider the opening stanza of "Máscaras" (Masks, 30–31). Its figurative language incorporates the Christian image of a bleeding heart and the term *crucificado*, as well as allusions that could easily be part of religious culture, such as those to purity, a star, and soothing fragrance. The items chosen may be drawn from the cultural inventories that develop around religions. Beyond doubt, Fijman had such repertories in his mind, as a reader of many types of religious texts and an admirer of the mystical and scholarly aspects of Catholicism. Yet this stanza, as the poem in its entirety, has at its center mental torment:

> Sangró mi corazón como una estrella
> crucificada.
> Dolor:
> del sándalo purísimo del sueño
> trabajaron la balsa de mi vida.
>
> (My heart bled like a crucified
> star.
> Pain:
> From the purest sandalwood of dream
> they wrought the raft of my life.)

At this point, two preliminary findings may be summed up: (1) *Molino* is not only the least Christian book by Fijman, but also stands out among his collections by the subordination of all religious elements to the generation of secular meanings; (2) the individual items that *Molino* has drawn from religious discourse are not reliable guides to this area of concern.

Clearly, the inquiry into Fijman's religious identity as manifested in *Molino* must begin with larger samples of his discourse: entire poems or groups of poems. One such possibility is suggested by Fernandez's very insightful observation that the lamentations in *Molino* resemble passages in the Book of Job (20). She goes on to cite a wider similarity between *Molino* and "los libros sapenciales del Antiguo Testamento" (20) (the wisdom books of the Old Testament). Here it grows unclear which portion of the Bible Fernandez has in mind: she has just been discussing Job, and by "wisdom books" seems to refer to the more philosophical writings, but actually her subsequent descriptions apply more accurately to the prophets. In addition, her well-launched argument loses force as she proceeds to contrast *Molino* with Fijman's later, more Christian, collections: then there is an unfortunate reliance on the stereotypical polarity between the Christian value of mercy that she sees in the post-conversion books, and the threat of divine wrath that she perceives in both the Hebrew Bible and *Molino*. e.g., "los pecadores (necios) recibirán de Dios ruina y desgracia. Fijman, que conoce la Biblia, sabe de la naturaleza justiciera y terrible de estos cantos sagrados" (20) (...sinners [evildoers] will receive from God ruin and misfortune. Fijman, who knows the Bible, knows of the justice-dealing and terrible nature or those sacred songs...).

Perhaps it would bring the discussion more clearly into focus to delimit better the parallel Fernandez has discerned. Let us try considering *Molino* as a modern extension, not of the Hebrew Scriptures globally, but of Jewish prophetic writing, in which urgent moral messages are conveyed through such stylistic conventions as curse, harangue, invective, and lamentation. Fernandez appears to have in mind the repertory of prophetic speech when she describes the biblical elements in *Molina* as "gritos" (cries) and "gemidos y anatemas" (moans and anathemas). *Molino* can be seen as continuous within this tradition; it would be an argument for seeing Fijman as Jewish in his poetic expression (remembering, though, that the biblical books of the prophets are often cited in Christian liturgies and theology).

Where should the search for prophetic modes in *Molino* begin? The collection contains three general types on writing, although not every poem exemplifies only one type. One variety uses as a backdrop more rural and depopulated locales, whose inhabitants are imbued with such attributes as simple dignity, earthy appeal, and an understanding of the universe. "El hombre del mar" (The Man of the Sea) (88–89) exemplifies this type of poem; the speaker is a dissatisfied urbanite who eagerly apprentices himself to the weathered and seasoned hero, possessor of "todos estos secretos" (all these secrets) and "una cósmica simpatía" (a cosmic sympathy—less literally, either a cosmic warmth or attunement to the cosmos). "Paraguaya" (Paraguayan Woman (64–65) offers a more sensual variant of this pro-rural writing; it celebrates a peasant lover whose body reiterates the features or the earth. Again, the speaker expects healing and purification through contact with individuals simpler than himself. A second category of poems presents a poetic speaker in isolation from other human beings, exulting over the ecstatic state in which he finds himself. This jubilant mode is most purely represented in "Alegría" (Joy) (45–46). "Antigüedad" (Antiquity) (53–55), and "Las blancas torres" (The White Towers) (80–81). These poems are few and their expression of joy is modified by warnings that the speaker has reached a dangerously extreme condition.

However, the most cited and anthologized poems in *Molino* are not those realized in Fijman's bucolic or ecstatic modes, but those featuring a distraught and angry *I* who surveys scenes of grotesque, sordid deterioration. The chaotic flux of images in these poems is no doubt the factor that has earned *Molino* its enthusiastic following among readers who prize surrealistic expression (noted by Herrera, 244). Now the setting is more heavily populated and may be marked as a city. It is sometimes intimated to be a depraved version of what should rightfully be a holy place and has failed in its mission to the speaker's indignation. This third type of writing is the best source of passages that echo the characteristically enraged voices of prophets asserting that wherever they look they see moral deterioration and lawlessness.

While each of these poems of horror and outrage has its individual traits, a reader looking at them in the aggregate abstracts a composite portrait or a landscape of depravation. In some instances, the scene includes a disorderly crowd abandoning itself to ritual merrymaking. "Feria" (Fair) (39–40) is dominated by the angered depiction of an open-air festival. The poetic *I*, speaking from the midst of a confusing whirl of sensory stimuli, inveighs against the "Feria maligna de rostros tostados" (Malignant fair of sunburnt faces) and exclamatively decries "Las máscaras estúpidas/ de los atormentados" (The stupid masks/ of those in torment). Mass carousing disgusts the poetic speaker in other poems. In "Subdrama" (50–52), following a profession of despair, he reports sights and sounds suggesting public revels: "Murga carnavalesca./ ¡Las risas rojas!" (Carnival band. Red peals of laughter!)

In these cases, the *I* can reasonably be likened to a prophet pronouncing a harangue against degraded, often actively idolatrous or blasphemous, collective celebrations. This speaker shares the prophets' typical rage at ritual devoid of spirituality or heartfelt involvement. It is true that the poems of *Molino* cannot be made to correspond with the particular stylistic conventions, as invective and harangue, that may be distinguished as prophetic writing (research into these conventional patterns is summarized by Muilenberg) (24–29). But modern writers are entitled to make a free adaptation of ancient modes of expression. The similarity is in the stance taken by the *I*: he is filled with revulsion at the human scene around him and eager to convey the wrongness and the imminent downfall of all that meets his eye. The poems of *Molino* do not threaten the errant multitudes with retribution, but do speak of a perilously eroded unstable world: the *I* expresses apprehension and anxiety at what is to come. In sum, Fijman's poetic speakers often resemble the prophets in their rhetorical posture and outlook on society, but stop short of enunciating actual predictions (of course, the prophecies recorded in biblical books are frequently so vague that they scarcely go beyond a general warning of impending calamities). The correspondence between portions of *Molino* and the prophetic writings is far from exact, but it is strong enough to be readily recognizable once a reader looks for it.

For all the resemblances between certain passages in *Molino* and the pronouncements of prophets, still, as previously noted in other respects, Fijman seldom remains for long within the bounds of those religious precepts common to an entire group. His tendency is to express an idiosyncratic constellation of beliefs. As in his remarks in *Pensamiento*, he is eager to convey the experience, not merely of expecting an apotheosis or the coming of the messianic era, but of being part of the whole of what is awaited. The poetic *I* in *Molino* can be not only a prophet, but the prophet of himself. For example, the revelation of a one-man religion, with the *I* at the center of the system as its generator, explicator, and principal actor, is the outcome of the poetic soliloquy "Vísperas de angustia" [Eve of Anguish) (41–42). The *I* repeatedly intimates that there is an extraordinary dimension to his perception of, and way of being in, the world; he hears celestial music and has sensory experiences that do not correspond to his surroundings. The closing line offers a way of accounting for these troubling phenomena: "Yo soy el prometido, el anunciado" (I am the promised one, the one foretold).

While "Vísperas de angustia" stands out in *Molino* for its overt assertion of a messianic identity many other poems are similar in that the expression of religious ideas and preoccupations is dominated by the extraordinary sensations of the poetic *I*, and by his awareness of his special situation. "Ciudad santa" (Holy City) (16–17) is in Fijman's diffusely prophetic mode;

the *I* describes with horror a place where matters have gone amiss. The site titularly referred to as a holy city quickly reveals itself to be an accursed place. The elements to which all others are subordinated are the sensory information the speaker registers while traversing this abomination and his feelings of revulsion and fear.

Throughout the texts in which he inveighs against the decadence surrounding him, Fijman's poetic *I* frequently makes assertions that draw attention away from the deterioration he views and places him and his exceptionality in the foreground. For example, the speaker in the above-discussed "Feria," while abominating the carousers among whom he finds himself, makes remarks that suggest that the carnival may be at least to some degree a sensory manifestation of his inner turmoil. By alluding to the "agrios soplos de mi locura" (bitter gusts of my madness), he raises the possibility that the celebrants may be mere hallucinations or projections of his disordered mind. In "Mortaja" (Shroud, 28–29), the *I* resembles an embittered, denunciatory prophet to some extent; isolated and alienated from fellow beings, "miro las multitudes" (I look upon the multitudes). Nonetheless, he offers no observations concerning the masses who are the object of his gaze. Instead, he directs the reader's attention to his own extraordinary mode of being. As is occasionally the case in *Molino*, the speaker casts himself as a new incarnation of a celebrated and remarkable being drawn from religious tradition. In this case, he becomes, of all the many secondary figures from the gospel narratives, perhaps the one who underwent the most astonishing supernatural experience: "Estoy siempre desnudo y blanco: / Lázaro vestido de novio" (I am always naked and white: / Lazarus dressed as a bridegroom).

The question posed at the outset of this discussion has not been fully answered through the examination of *Molino rojo*, and it is doubtful whether any analysis could isolate an unambiguously Jewish strain in Fijman's poetry. The most obvious difficulty is the overlap between the symbolic repertories of religious traditions, especially those of Judaism and Christianity. Fijman, at the time he wrote *Molino*, was a Jew being drawn toward Christianity; he was also a wide-ranging student, and to some degree a creator of religion, mysticism, and magic. It is a reasonable supposition that in struggling for coherence in religious outlook, Fijman favored elements compatible with more than one system, particularly those that could link his Jewish background with the Christianity toward which he was moving and his miscellaneous or *sui generis* beliefs.

This situation clouds with ambiguity the identification that might have been provided by Fijman's adaptation of Jewish prophetic tradition. The great prophets, those whose pronouncements hold a place in the canon of scripture, form part of the history of Jewish religious thought and discourse. Fijman continues this tradition into the twentieth century, but it can be said that he takes up the prophetic mode in a purely Jewish way. The problem is not primarily Fijman's exposure to the Christian reading of the prophets, but rather his reworking of prophetic modes to suit his own expressive needs. In Fijman's poetry, prophetic speech becomes united with surrealistic language, the description of bizarre sensory experiences, and the affirmation of one's own elect status. It seems probable that Fijman's choice of prophetic models was not altogether religions or moral. Prophets enjoy a time-honored license to emit messages in unusual ways, whether symbolic acts (as Isaiah's naked walk through the streets and Jeremiah's wearing of a yoke) or language (as in the imagery of Ezekiel, the prophet whom Fijman most resembles in his descriptive language). Fijman was ineluctably peculiar in his self-expression (according to Zito Lema and Toyos his penchant for bizarre dress goes back to childhood). From the prophets he took a tradition in which manifestations of eccentricity are an expressive asset. Fijman's poetry echoes the strangeness of prophetic discourse as much as its message.

Given this general picture, there is logic to such measures as Senkman's decision (295) to recognize Fijman as a poet of Jewish inspiration but not to seek precise confirmation in the poetry. Fijman was individualistic and idiosyncratic in the construction of his poetry and his religious vision. *Molino rojo* highlights this originality. The collection centers on and draws primary attention to the voice of a self subject to exceptional perceptions and aware of its own exceptionality.

REFERENCES

Fernandez, Ruth. *Fijman, el poeta celestial y su obra*. Buenos Aires: Editorial Tekne, 1985.
Fijman, Jacobo. *Estrella de la mañana*. Buenos Aires: Editorial Número, 1931.
———. *Hecho de estampas*. Buenos Aires: Gleizer, 1930.
———. *Molino rojo*. Buenos Aires: Editorial "El Inca," 1926.
———. *El pensamiento de Jacobo Fijman; o, el viaje hacia la otra realidad*. Ed. Vicente Zito Lema. Buenos Aires: Rodolfo Alonso, 1970.
Herrea, Francisco. "Jacobo Fijman." *Enciclopedia de la literatura argentina*. Pedro Orgambide and Roberto Yahni, eds. Buenos Aires: Sudamericana, 1970. 244.

Muilenberg, James. *The Way of Israel: Biblical Faith and Ethics*. New York: Harper and Row, 1961.

Senkman, Leonardo. "Bautismo y locura." *La identidad judía en la literatura argentina*. Buenos Aires: Pardés, 1983. 195.

Zito Lema, Vicente, and Héctor Toyos. "Elementos para una biografía." *Talismán* [Buenos Aires] No. 1 (1969): 3-4.

6

Matrimony and Religious Conflict: Bernardo Gravier's *El hijo del rabino*

DAVID WILLIAM FOSTER

REB CALMAN: Las cosas son así, porque
                     Dios lo dispuso. (6)
DAVID: Hablemos de otra cosa. (33)[1]

(REB CALMAN: That's the way things are because that's the
                       way God arranged them.
DAVID: Let's talk about something else.)

IT MAY WELL BE LEGITIMATE to consider César Tiempo's *Pan criollo* (Native Bread; 1937) the classic Argentine drama dealing with racial and religious conflicts brought to the fore by the love between a young woman and a man of different religions and customs. Tiempo cheerfully touted the possibility that *lo criollo* (what is "native" or prototypically Argentine) would prevail, even if it was at the expense of the implied element of contrast (the *pan judío*, literally, Jewish bread—that is, any Jewish baked goods, but typically the bagel in Argentina). Surely, in addition to Tiempo's excellent sense of stagecraft, it is this hearteningly nationalistic note, so important in the Argentina of the 1930s, that gave *Pan criollo* such an enthusiastic reception at the time of its original performances and allowed it to occupy such an important place in the history of Argentine drama.[2]

---

1. Bernardo Gravier, *El hijo del rabino*, in *Argentores, revista teatral* 125 (1936): 1–35.
2. For a discussion of *Pan criollo*, see David William Foster, *The Argentine Teatro Independiente, 1930–1955* (York, S.C.: Spanish Literature Publishing Company, 1986): 110–116. These comments on *Pan criollo* also appeared in Spanish as "César Tiempo y el teatro argentino-judío," in Rose S. Minc, ed., *El cono sur: dinámica y dimensiones de su literatura* (Upper Montclair, N.J.: Montclair State College; 1985): 43–48.

Bernardo Gravier's *El hijo del rabino* (The Rabbi's Son; 1932) did not enjoy similar fortune, although it is also a paradigmatic work in dealing with the confrontation between the Christian and Jewish communities in Argentina at a time hardly propitious for interfaith understanding. In contrast with Tiempo's play a few years later, *El hijo del rabino* is dramatically clumsy (as we shall see, it essentially sets the characters up as antagonists in a religious debate) and eschews the facile happy ending typified by *Pan criollo*. Zayas de Lima observes that the play "levantó interesantes polémicas" (sparked interesting polemics) without providing any characterization of what these might have been.[3]

However, the harshness with which Gravier characterizes the historical misunderstanding between Christians and Jews (personified in the play by the protagonist's father, the rabbi, and by the bishop, the uncle of the protagonist's fiancée and later wife), and the manner in which the rabbi scores the best points in the debate with the bishop can only have alienated touchy spectators and a conservative Catholic press. Moreover, the decision by the protagonist and his wife to remain nonreligious and to raise their son as neither a Catholic nor a Jew, but to allow him to choose his own religion, cannot have been to the liking of either traditional Catholics or traditional Jews in the Argentina of the 1930s.

David is a young doctor who gives every indication of being quite well assimilated into the professional upper middle class of the adoptive country of his Polish Jewish parents (it is significant to note that a name like David belongs to both a list of typical Jewish names and a list of acceptable Hispanic-Catholic ones). David had made the acquaintance of Luisa at medical school. She is the daughter of a devoutly Catholic household and the niece of a bishop of the church. After five years of secret meetings, David and Luisa decide to announce to their parents their intention to wed; David takes the initiative to ask Luisa's father for her hand in marriage.

It is important for the dramatic postulates of the play that David and Luisa handle themselves, in the face of the inevitable high emotions and conflicts that their decision will provoke, with exemplary decorum and respect toward their elders. As one would expect, David is disowned by his father, who sees nothing but perdition and disgrace in the decision of his son to marry a *goie*, seeing all Christians as persecutors of the Jews. In the same spirit, Luisa's father, supported by his brother the bishop, denounces her intentions to wed a son of, according to accepted Catholic

---

3. Perla Zayas de Lima, *Diccionario de autores teatrales argentinos, 1950–1980* (Buenos Aires: Editorial R. Alonso, 1981): 86.

doctrine of the time, the assassins of Christ. He states that he would rather see his daughter dead than married to a Jew, and on this note the irreconcilable differences between the two traditions, the two major components of Argentine society, are starkly defined.

The first act of the play portrays the confrontation between David and his family, prefaced by a series of vignettes that serve to specify the traditional Jewish character of the family and the Old World values by which it lives. The second act of the play centers on the confrontation between Luisa and her family and concludes with the interview between her father and David, who arrives to make the customary petition to the father of the intended bride. The crucial exchange between the two men expresses the impasse beyond which, because of history, social conventions, and religious beliefs, it is impossible to move:

DAVID: Yo lo he perdido todo, todo. Mi padre me expulsó de su casa por esta misma razón. Yo afronté todo contra todos, contra mis propios padres y hermanos, todo por ella [Luisa]. Ahora estoy ante usted, (*Trémulo.*) como un culpable...(*Pausa.*)

DIEGO: (*Contrito*) Es verdad todo lo que dice, pero no puedo..Somos católicos, usted es judío...(22)

DAVID: I've lost everything, everything. My father threw me out of the house for this very same reason. I stood up to everybody over everything, including my own parents and my own brothers and sisters, all for her [Luisa]. And now I'm standing before you (*his voice shaking*) just like a criminal. ...(*Pause.*)

DIEGO: (*Contritely*). Everything you say is fine, but I just can't. ...We're Catholic and you're a Jew....)

The first two acts of Gravier's three-act *comedia* are, as can be surmised from the foregoing characterization, quite schematic in nature. In more technically rhetorical terms, they are bimembers of a single proposition, the symmetrical nature of the lack of understanding and acceptance between Catholics and Jews in Argentina, patriotic slogans to the contrary. (Significantly, in the initial segment of the first act, the rabbi defends the position that the Jews have found a hospitable setting in Argentina, although later he will pray for the chance to emigrate to Eretz Israel in the face of what he sees as his son's betrayal.) The symmetry of the dramatic interplay between the two acts involves, in general terms, the need of David and Luisa to confront their families with their matrimonial intentions and to plea that the deep personal love between them must take precedence over the equally deep but impersonal antagonism between Christians and Jews. The predictable repudiation by the fathers and their supporting characters generates the specific dialogues, which are a fabric of social and religious commonplaces.

In more specific terms, the parallelism between the two acts assumes the form of an echoing of speeches. Thus, each father berates his child in roughly equal terms, underscoring the betrayal of the family, the loss of filial respect, and the violation of sacred trusts and codes. In each case, the argument culminates in the sense of an awesome transgression, with the result that there is a semantic equivalence that binds the two acts together as the two sides of the same coin of misunderstanding and blind hatred of the Other, the Different One. David's father denounces his intentions in the following terms:

> RABINO: Entregar tu corazón a aquéllos, que aún sus abuelos—lee la historia argentina—tenían las manos teñidos con sangre de hermanos nuestros, enviados a la hoguera por el auto da fé; cuando recién en la independencia mandaron a quemar los elementos de tortura....¿Y a los hijos de aquéllos pretendes entregar tu corazón? ¿eh? ¿eh?... ¡Y con tu vil ejemplo—el hijo del Rabino—entregar sentimentalmente lo que no nos pudieron arrancar en miles de años de tortura y martirologio! [...]¡Rasgad los vestidos, poned ceniza en vuestras frentes, encended velas, cubríos de luto, que Israel ha perdido un hijo! ¡Hemos perdido un hijo!... ¡Un hermano!... (11, 13)
>
> RABBI: The very idea of giving yourself to them whose very grandparents—all you have to do is read Argentine history— stained their hands with the blood of our brothers and sisters who were sent to the stake in *autos da fé*. It was only during the time of independence that they ordered the instruments of torture burned.... And you have the gall to hand your heart over to their children? Huh? Huh? And by your vile example—you, the Rabbi's son—you would out of love turn over what they could not extract from us in thousands of years of torture and martyrdom! [...] Rend your clothes, mark your foreheads with ashes, light candles, cover yourself with shrouds, for Israel has lost a son! We have lost a son!...A brother!...)

Luisa's father, seconded by his brother the Obispo, articulates roughly the same sentiments from the point of view of his social and religious convictions:

> DIEGO: (*Mirándola.*) El podría ser un hombre muy digno, pero es hijo de la raza maldita, que ambula por el mundo bajo el peso de sus crímenes. (16)

OBISPO: Hija, ¿sabes lo que significa tu actitud para nuestra Santa Religión? ¿Ignoras que los judíos crucificaron a Jesús, y que sus almas han sido entregadas a manos de Satanás, lo mismo que las de los que entran en contacto con ellos? ¡Y no sólo casarse, Dios libre, sino estar cerca de un judío, es ya un pecado mortal, un pecado mortal! (18)

DIEGO: (*Looking at her.*) He could be a very dignified man, but he is the son of a cursed race, one that wanders the world beneath the weight of its crimes.

BISHOP: My daughter, do you realize what your attitude means for our Holy Religion? Are you ignorant of how the Jews crucified Jesus, of how they yielded their souls to Satan, which is also what happens to the soul of anyone who comes into contact with them? And not just to marry a Jew, God forbid, but to live alongside a Jew is a mortal sin, a mortal sin!)

There is a hiatus in time between the curtain of the second act and the events of the third. We deduce from the setting and the dialogue of the characters that David and Luisa have married against their parents' wills; that, although David sees his sister Sara and Luisa her mother, they have had no contact with their fathers; that they have had a son; and that, last but not least, they have established mutual respect for their differing cultural frames of reference (Luisa praises her husband for his support of Jewish causes and urges him not to forsake his taste for *sopas coloradas* [red soups, i.e., borscht] and other elements of Jewish folk culture).

The dramatic action of the third act is tea time around their table. Initially we see them in the company of David's Jewish friends, and the conversation deals with Zionism, which is discussed in both positive and negative terms. Sara is expected, but in her stead, David's parents arrive unexpectedly to see their new grandson. Amid gestures of reconciliation between father and son, the Rabino hopes to claim his grandson for Judaism (Ana is David's mother):

RABINO: (*Mirándolo.*) Un verdadero angelito, pobrecito. ¿Y qué dice el médico? (*A David.*)

ANA: Pobre palomito, no se puede todavía circuncidar. Santificado estaría bien...(*Luisa y David cambian miradas.*)

DAVID: (*Sonriendo.*) Sí...El médico...(*Señalándose.*)...declaró que apenas esté bien, mi padre y no otro lo santificará.

RABINO: (*Satisfecho.*) ¡Cuidado, mucho cuidado, David!... Cuando se halle bien...(29)

RABBI: (*Looking at him.*) A veritable angel, poor thing. And what does the doctor say? (*Addressing David.*)

AMA: Poor little dove, it's too soon to circumcise him. He would be well blessed....(*Luisa and David exchange glances.*)

DAVID: (*Smiling.*) Yes. . . .The doctor. . . .(*Pointing to himself.*) declared that
as soon as he's well, my father and none other will bless him.
RABBI: (*Satisfied.*) Be very careful, David, very careful! When he's feeling
better. . . .

This happy family scene is interrupted by the arrival of Luisa's mother,
Inés, accompanied by her brother-in-law, the bishop. The latter makes it
clear that, despite his diplomatic deference toward the rabbi, he has come
to claim the child for Catholicism:

OBISPO: Es preciso que esa criatura sea cristianada.
LUISA: Monseñor. . .
INES: Hazlo cristianar. . .
LUISA: Por la misma razón podrían exigir ellos que lo hiciéramos
judaizar.
INES: Hijita, si la mamá del nene es cristiana, justo es que el nene sea
cristiano. (*Detrás vuelven David con el Rabino y la Madre, que
murmuran oraciones.*)
OBISPO: Debo advertirte que aquí no se trata de sexos. Es algo más
importante y fundamental: es común que el niño nazca en la
religión católica en atención al ambiente que es católico, al país
que es católico, al porvenir que es católico y la mayoría católica;
la mayoría. . .(31)
BISHOP: This child must be baptized a Christian.
LUISA: Monsignor. . . .
INES: You be the one to baptize him. . . .
LUISA: They could demand by the same token that we have him
circumcised as a Jew.
INES: My child, if the mother is a Christian, it only makes sense that
the boy be a Christian too. (*David approaches from behind with the
Rabbi and his mother, who are murmuring prayers.*)
BISHOP: I should like to remind you that we are not dealing here with
a question of sex. There is something more important and
fundamental involved: it is customary that the son be born into
the Catholic religion out of respect for his environment, which
is Catholic, his country, which is Catholic, his future, which is
Catholic, and the Catholic majority; the majority I say. . . .)

The bishop is interrupted by the rabbi, who can contain himself no
longer. There ensues a long debate between the two men of religion, in
which the bishop insists on the moral and historical supremacy of
Christianity,[4] while the rabbi underscores the long history of Jewish

---

4. Between October 10 and 14, 1934, Buenos Aires was the site of an Eucharistic Congress
that brought Catholic churchmen from all over the world. As an officially sponsored event,
the Congress was seen as an aggressive and tendentious affirmation of Argentina's historical
identity with the Church.

persecutions by the Church that belies the benevolent image of Jesus and points out what, from the Jewish point of view, appear to be the gross irrationalities of Christian theology (e.g., How can Christians accuse Jews of executing Christ, one of their own, while preaching that Jesus's sacrifice was preordained in order to save mankind?). Although the outlines of the argument must have been scandalous to conservative Catholic audiences in the early 1930s—indeed, it would still be rather bothersome to the nonecumenical Argentina of the mid-1980s—it provides the play with the opportunity, via the heated debate of the two religious authorties, to demonstrate the profound differences between two perspectives sustained by immeasurable historical hatred and incomprehension. David pleads first for a change of subject, for the conversation to focus on what brings them together (i.e., presumably the newborn child) rather than what alienates them from one another. But his plea is in vain, leading him to the follow despairing interrogatives:

> DAVID: (*En un arranque.*) ¿Por qué no terminan?. . . ¿Por qué traer a esta casa que no conoce más palabras que el amor, el sordo lenguaje del odio?. . . (34)
> DAVID: (*In a fit of anger.*) Will you please all shut up?. . .Why bring into this house, which knows only words of love, the unhearing language of hatred?. . .)

In contrast to the happy reconciliation of different religious and traditional points of view in Tiempo's *Pan criollo*, the dénouement of *El hijo del rabino* demonstrates the futility of David's pleas: the subject cannot be changed, and an idyllic love cannot escape the generalized outpourings of religious hatred and social misunderstanding. The rabbi makes better points than the bishop in their debate. (It would have been a nice theatrical touch to have the baby crying in fright in the background as the innocent's response to this cacophonous exchange.) But the parents' decision, enlightened in their own eyes, not to select any religion for their child and to allow him to make his own choices in this regard signals that the rhetoric of the play recognizes the equally damaging influence of both points of view. The play ends on the "happy" note of David's and Luisa's firm conviction as new parents (thereby justifying Gravier calling his work a *comedia*), but their decision is at the expense of the apparently definitive rupture with their families and the internally unified and coherent interpretation each represents.

Two textual strategies of *El hijo del rabino* are worth noting in the overall presentation of religious and social conflict: the overwhelming reliance on clichés, social formulas, and religiocultural tropes; and the degree to which the characters speak elliptically. As has been noted, the opening segment of the first act is a series of vignettes regarding Jewish customs and beliefs (interestingly, Tiempo opens *Pan criollo* with a series of similar sketches). The rabbi is a central figure in these vignettes, as he answers questions concerning observances and dispenses traditional wisdom and interprets Talmudic law. The sequence of cultural allusions is not abandoned when the main action of the play begins. Rather, the rabbi relies precisely on these concepts to refute his son's arguments and to persuade him that he is about to embark on a course of disastrous consequences. To the extent that the second act of the play is a counterpoint to the first act, Luisa's family addresses her in similar terms, with the bishop becoming a veritable spring of Catholic and anti-Semitic commonplaces. Commonplaces assume antiphonic proportions in the confrontation between the two families in the third act. The Bishop's cry of frustration, "¡Jesús Santo! O no me ha entendido, o no me quiere entender o tergiversa mi pensamiento" (In the name of Christ! Either you have not heard me or you do not wish to hear me, but rather to twist my thoughts: 33), is simply a tacit admission that an exchange of information, a dialogue of mutual persuasion, has not taken place. The fact that the communication between the characters of the play and the basis of the conflict are based on the exchange of clichés is a confirmation of the justification of the new-born's parents' abandonment of religious traditions.

The fact that the characters speak primarily in verbal formulas that promote conventional or folk wisdom as though it were absolute truth allows them to speak elliptically, since it is often possible to enunciate a commonplace or a sequence of structured commonplaces in a partial manner: one's interlocutor is able to complete the phrase or sequence on the basis of shared knowledge. It is against this verbal backdrop of conventional wisdom that David's and Luisa's interpretation of their personal and social imperative vis-á-vis their newborn son becomes compelling as an appeal to the audience to accept a new shared wisdom of religious ecumenicalism: "DAVID: Aquí respetamos todas las creencias" (Here we respect all beliefs; 35).[5]

5. This essay is part of a global investigation on Argentine Jewish dramatists funded by the Memorial Foundation for Jewish Culture (New York), the principal segment of which appeared as "Argentine Jewish Dramatists: Aspects of a National Consciousness, "Folio 17 (1987): 74–103. See also "*Krinsky* de Jorge Goldenberg y la identidad étnica argentina," *Noaj* 5 (1990): 51–54.

7

Jewish Identity, Pluralism, and Survival: Feierstein's *Mestizo* as Minority Discourse

EDNA AIZENBERG

How DO YOU CONSTRUCT a Latin-American Jewish identity? With what materials do you cohere a personality anchored in its surroundings yet faithful to its ancestral voices? Ricardo Feierstein's novel, *Mestizo* (1988), is an inquiry into these questions, an inquiry that employs the conventions of detective fiction to explore in depth what it means to be Jewish in contemporary, post-dictatorial Argentina.[1]

To summarize the plot would be fruitless and impoverishing; here are just a few leads: David Schnaiderman, an unemployed sociologist and the only witness to the murder of a woman on a Buenos Aires street, is struck with amnesia as a result of the emotional shock. The novel tells the story of his struggle to regain his memory, to find the links with the past and the present, and to solve the mystery. But what mystery? The name of the unknown murderer? The obliterated personal past? The murky Jewish identity, fragmented and in search of integration? In *Mestizo* these versions of the mystery—and others—are joined to produce a densely woven text. By bringing into play diverse sociocultural spaces (Europe, the Middle East, Argentina), diverse characters (grandfather Moishe Burej, Arab and Jewish childhood friends), and a variety of grammatical voices (I, you, he, we) the text gradually traces a family tree rooted in the hybridities of yesterday, but branching out to the pluralities of tomorrow.

The tree points to the basis of the novel: that *pluralism* and *survival* are the twin axes of a Latin-American Jewish identity. Within the context

---

1. The term *mestizo* is commonly used to refer to a person of European and Native-American descent. In Argentina the military dictatorship of the seventies was officially and euphemistically known as "el Proceso de Reorganización Nacional," the Process of National Reorganization.

of a renewed democracy (the book ends with a massive demonstration for human rights) survival and pluralism can create an identity by forging a link between Jew and Argentinian, both survivors of oppression, both *mestizos*—the hybrid products of wandering and immigration. To put it another way, what holds the promise of true integration is a dual process: a "minorization" of the majority and a "majorization" of the minority through their shared experience of endurance and heterogeneity.

If we go back to the canonical proposal for the conformation of an Argentine-Jewish identity, the one put forth by Alberto Gerchunoff in the early part of the century, we can measure the distance traveled between the hopeful georgics of the patriarch and the revisions of the ephebe. Gerchunoff's collection of stories, *Los gauchos judíos* (The Jewish Cowboys) (1910), the first literary work written in Spanish by a Jew in Argentina, was based on his early years in the Jewish agricultural colonies of the pampa. The book propounded a program of integration based on three principles: territorialism, language-as-nationality, and liberalism.[2] The "Jewish gauchos"—the name Gerchunoff gave to the immigrant Jews who were in reality farmers, not cowboys—symbolized the desire to belong to *one* specific place and *one* specific history. The gaucho was the embodiment of the Argentine land, and to be a gaucho implied being rooted on that land and no other. By positioning Jews alongside gauchos, Gerchunoff sought to erase the complexities and discords of Jewish multiterritorialism and to embrace the apparent simplicity and quietism of uniterritoriality. As one of his contemporaries put it: The Jews received their Argentine naturalization papers thanks to *Los gauchos judíos*.

Linguistically this naturalization could be achieved through the harmonizing of Jewish greenhorns' speech with medieval and Cervantine Spanish—"pureblooded" Spanish, in other words. The Sephardic key was especially important in this regard, for Gerchunoff portrayed the Ashkenazic-Russian newcomers, whose real language was the prestigeless Yiddish, as inheritors of the legacy of Sepharad, particularly the sweet tongue of Spain. His book displayed a studied linguistic archaism, a going back to the old Castilian sources of the language, in a style calculated to give his writing—and the immigrants—a high-bred Hispanic linguistic lineage.

The third element in Gerchunoff's proposal for identity, liberalism, was reflected in the author's adherence to the official philosophy of the

---

2. Liberalism in Argentina included a written constitution; limitation on trade restrictions; and formal equality before the law. The ideology was European-oriented and against the "despotism" of the masses.

Argentina of 1910. According to the image projected by its governors in its first centenary of independence, Argentina was a prosperous, progressive melting pot; people of the most varied backgrounds were happily shedding their "exotic precepts" to become amalgamated into an Argentine ethnic type living contentedly under the centenary rubric of "Peace and Fraternity." The image of this Country-in-Technicolor (Szichman) did not have room for the malaise—strikes, assassinations, anti-Semitic incidents—of a nation undergoing rapid social change. Neither, by and large, did Gerchunoff's book, published in honor of the centenary and committed to the authorized version of the Argentine "Land of Promise."

In an earlier study I analyzed what I called the "parricide on the pampa," the challenge to Gerchunoff by recent writers. I discussed how these parricides question and dismantle Gerchunoff's proposal point by point, replacing *enracinement* with exile, language-as-nationality with language-as-estrangement, and liberalism with the critique of liberalism. Their works postulate an errant and rebellious writing as the mark of Jewish-Argentine identity. This writing is rift with internal and external dislocations—failure of the agricultural experiment, migrations from the country to the city, anti-Semitic outbreaks, revolutions, exile. Its language is a babelic Spanish shot with Yiddish, Hebrew, eccentric and immigrant speech patterns—a language that upsets all pretense to linguistic "purity," disturbs the limpid surface of an exclusionist, monolingual code and rejects maneuvers of harmonization.

Politically, the parricidal writing calls into question the evolution of liberal Argentina in the direction of an elitist-repressive nationalism and advocates the definition of the national in terms of the multiple. Examples of the new writing can be found in novels such as Mario Szichman's *Los judíos de mar dulce* (The Jews of the Fresh-Water Sea) and *A las 20:25 la señora entró en la inmortalidad* (At 8:25, Evita Became Immortal), Gerardo Mario Goloboff's *Caballos por el fondo de los ojos* (Horses in the Depths of the Eyes) and *Criador de palomas* (Pidgeon Breeder), Pedro Orgambide's *Adventuras de Edmund Ziller en tierras del Nuevo Mundo* (Adventures of Edmund Ziller in the New World) and *Historias imaginarías de Argentina* (Imaginary Histories of Argentina), Edgardo Cozarinsky's *Vudú urbano* (Urban Voodoo), Antonio Elio Brailovsky's *Identidad* (Identity); and in critical studies such as those by David Viñas, Saúl Sosnowski, and Leonardo Senkman.

Feierstein's novel also forms part of this counterdiscourse. In place of a single territoriality, *Mestizo* favors a sense of belonging that is fashioned out of various spaces: Europe, represented by the Polish village from which the Schnaiderman family emigrates; Israel, the site of the kibbutz where the protagonist spends some years; and Latin America, whose emblematic space is the Buenos Aires neighborhood of David's childhood. In *Mestizo* multiterritorialism is not a shameful condition in need of elimination. It is the very substance of Jewish (and Argentine) existence, a condition willingly assumed as a necessary part of one's identity, and as the indispensible building block of a kaleidoscopic national "we" that can serve as a counter to the essentialist and authoritarian "I's." Just how needed this counter is can be gauged from recent Argentine history, when the armed forces took it upon themselves to defend the narrowly-defined "fundamental Christian moral values" of the nation, falling particularly hard on Jews, who did not constitute part of that unchanging space termed the "national essence." (In a penetrating essay, Santiago Kovadloff, a contemporary of Feierstein's, discusses the role of the armed forces and the church in the configuration of a theologically and spacially restricted *esencia nacional*.)

Language is likewise seen as a zone of hybridity in *Mestizo*. A poetic meditation entitled "Nuestra Babel" (Our Babel) by Gerardo Mario Goloboff, another of the parricides, has asserted that Yiddish was the absent yet present substratum in the language of many Latin-American Jewish authors. Even when it scarcely appears in the Spanish text it is there, notes Goloboff, modulating the choice of words, the rhythm of the writing (74). The same could be said of *Mestizo*, although here Yiddish is not merely a substratum but a visible code. The Yiddish vocabulary, expressions, proverbs, and names incorporated into the book recreate a certain texture of Jewish life; they conjure up a storehouse of cultural experience that, despite its apparent caducity, continues to nourish contemporary Jewish identity. *Mestizo* does not hide these roots nor excise them in the name of an artificial hispanism; on the contrary; the loss of Yiddish on the part of David, the son and grandson of Yiddish speakers, is an important aspect of the amnesia that he is struggling to overcome.

David says, referring to Moishe Burej: "El, sentado. . .y el idish de acento eslavo repleto de consonantes. . .Nunca lo entendí y ahora lo extraño. . .Estoy seguro que, de haber comprendido en ese entonces, todo me sería mucho más sencillo ahora" (31) (He, seated there, his Yiddish, with its Slavic accent, full of consonants. . .I never understood him and now I miss him. I'm sure that had I understood then, everything would be much easier for me now.) What a painful and acute commentary on the price paid by those who eagerly jumped into the melting pot; above all those who in the name of "belonging" erased from their memory a millenary linguistic-cultural heritage. For Schnaiderman (and Feierstein) multiplicity of language—the ancestral Yiddish; the Polish, Hungarian, and Czech that the grandfather also spoke; the father's Russian and German; his own Hebrew—is a source of pride, another significant element in a pluralized identity that undermines essentialisms.

And above all there is the political revisionism. The greatest challenge for Latin-American prose fiction, Feierstein argues, is producing a literature that is at once political and expressive, that achieves a fusion between societal concerns and the requirements of the imagination. *Mestizo* is the latest of his works to attempt such a fusion (private communication). If the smooth and quietist rhetoric sanctioned by the establishment in 1910 was the textual counterpart of its vision of Argentina, the fractured and questioning counterdiscourse of Feierstein and other parricides reflects another state of the nation—fissured, in search of alternatives to established political postures.

In his novel, Feierstein traces a genealogical line of descent starting from the progressive political circles in the European *shtetl*, and proceeding through Labor Zionism, the union movement in Argentina at the turn of the century; left-wing activism during the sixties, both in Latin America and in the Israeli kibbutz; opposition to the dictatorship of the seventies; and the human rights movement of the early eighties. But this oppositional line forms part of what Feierstein calls a "dialectic equilibrium" between a "centered" majority and a "decentered" and rebellious minority. He writes: "Estos últimos aportan el fermento necesario para producir el cambio y, sin ellos, el avance no sería posible. Pero es peligroso entregarles luego, la *totalidad* del poder, ya que sus saltos imaginativos, en cada disciplina, no podrían ser digeridos a tiempo por el resto de la sociedad. Se convierten, de manera paradojal, en desintegradores de todo el marco social. Así posibilitan la llegada de la reacción conservadora, que viene a restaurar el 'orden.' En suma, se trata de un delicado balance" (279) (These latter provide the ferment necessary to effect change, and without them progress would be impossible. But it would then be dangerous to place power *entirely* in their hands, since their imaginative leaps in every field could not be digested quickly enough by the rest of society. They would paradoxically become the unravelers of the entire social fabric. In this way they would facilitate a reaction from the right, which would come to restore "order." In short, it's a delicate balance.)

Feierstein clearly remains sympathetic to the nonconformist minority, and is antagonistic to any peaceable assimilationism in the mode of the *gaucho judío*; at the same time, he does not advocate the violent and totalitarian solutions of various political messianisms. In this sense *Mestizo* represents a later stage in the counterdiscourse to Gerchunoff. While it shares the wandering, linguistic "impurity" and political disconformity of other parricides, it likewise contemplates the possibility of belonging to that "extraño país, mi Argentina" (strange country, my Argentina)—a belonging more in tune with current exigencies and the painful experiences of Argentine and Jewish history (206). This belonging is built on linguistic and political openings: the formation of an Argentine idiom that recognizes not only Latinisms but also words with many consonants and vowels together—Yiddish words, for instance—and an Argentine political practice that vindicates moderation, the mature give and take of those who have survived more than one dictatorial "process." (127). In place of the desperate rootlessness of earlier works, of the linguistic estrangement that led to silence or to the grotesque, and of the political absolutisms that demanded extremes (Zionist emigration to Israel or nothing, guerilla warfare or nothing, right-wing dictatorship or nothing), Feierstein posits a hope for the future. Such a future would allow a Jew to say "my Argentina" by forging an identity based on the balance of minority and majority, a delicate balance most important in the sociopolitical and cultural areas.

If the challenge to Gerchunoff and his replay of Argentina's master discourse provides a useful model for understanding *Mestizo* and kindred works, it is also illustrative to examine them within a broader contemporary dismantling of *grand récits*. In particular, the question of "minority discourse" is of growing interest, a reflection of the need for paradigms more appropriate for the study of third world, postcolonial, ex-centric, and minority literatures. "Minority discourse" is oppositional writing— the type the parricides produce—and its characteristics are largely those I have described: linguistic-spacial deterritorialization, political disconformity, and a vindication of collectivity over singularity (JanMohamed and Lloyd).

The issue of abrogating authorized versions of major languages is primordial, because it is through these versions that hierarchical structures of power and conceptions of "truth" or "order" become established. Minority discourse often subverts "normative" language by releasing the "creative potential of *intersecting* languages"—various dialects, varying languages and levels of speech—much in the way Feierstein intersects and replaces Spanish to produce a new, non-hegemonic Argentine idiom (Ashcroft 7, 44).

The matter of place, more accurately of displacement, is central as well. A dialectic of multiple spaces caused by the shared experience of migration, transportation, exile, or colonization, is a common feature of post colonial and minority writing. (8–9). Many works are marked by a desire to expose the difficulties of belonging unproblematically to a single place and a single history, for identity almost always implies recognition of multiple origins. To elaborate identity thus means to interrogate restrictive accepted definitions, and, as in *Mestizo*, to expand the possibilities of "place."

Political challenge to established power is implicit within the linguistic-spacial repositioning of minority discourse. By contesting predominant readings of language and location, the conformers of national identity writers undermine nonpluralism and champion a polivocality in the political order (the kaleidoscopic "we" as opposed to the authoritarian "I"). "The desire and the quest for a genuinely plural reality are at the heart of minority discourse," Josaphat Kubayanda writes in a study of Black literature in the Americas. "The African presence in the New World... not only undermines mainstream monolithism but makes possible, theoretically at least, a unique multifacetedness which admits to collective or multiple existence in America" (12). The project of collective or multiple existence in America is precisely Feierstein's, and the liberating and constructive potential that Kubayanda finds in Black minority discourse is precisely that of Jewish minority discourse in *Mestizo*.[3]

Mestizo, then, ends on a note of hope: the hope of rearticulated opportunities for identity and belonging by applying of minority discourse to the Argentine circumstance—which brings us back to Gerchunoff. In the midst of the optimism of *Los gauchos judíos*, Gerchunoff had told the "Tale of the Stolen Horse" ("Historia de un caballo robado"), about a Jew falsely accused of stealing his Christian neighbor's nag. At the end of the story the author reflects that perhaps without quite understanding its ultimate consequences, the accused man had experienced the beginning of a new period, in which the "eternal judgement" (juicio eterno) about the Jews would be transplanted to Argentine soil. But he adds immediately: "Yo quiero creer, sin embargo, que no siempre ha de ser así, y los hijos de mis hijos podrán oír, en el segundo centenario de la República, el elogio de próceres hebreos, hecho después del católico *Tedeúm* bajo las bóvedas santas de la catedral" (I would like to believe, however, that it doesn't always have to be that way and that on the second centenary of the Republic my children's children will be able to hear Praises of the Hebrew founding fathers sung after the Catholic *Te Deum* beneath the holy vaults of the cathedral) (80–81).

Just two decades away from that second centenary, despite the fulfillment in large measure of what Gerchunoff scarcely wanted to foresee, Feierstein wants to believe that it doesn't always have to be that way. He no longer advocates the legitimation of Jewish identity and of the Jewish contribution to Argentina beneath the vaults of the cathedral—that is, through assimilation to an authorized, nationalist Hispano-Catholic code—but he continues to propose that there is hope for the future. Despite everything that has happened, one wishes to share his faith.

REFERENCES

Aizenberg, Edna. "Parricide on the Pampa: Deconstructing Gerchunoff and His Jewish Gauchos." *Folio* (1987): 24–39.

Ashcroft, Bill, Gareth Griffiths, and Helen Tiffin. *The Empire Writes Back: Theory and Practice in Post-Colonial Literatures*. London and New York: Routledge, 1989.

Deleuze, Gilles, and Félix Guattari. "What Is a Minor Literature?" *Kafka: Toward a Minor Literature*. Trans. Dana Polan. Pref. Réda Benamaia. Minneapolis: University of Minnesota Press, 1986. 16–27.

Feierstein, Ricardo. *Mestizo*. Buenos Aires: Mila, 1988.

Gerchunoff, Alberto. *Los gauchos judíos*. 1910; Buenos Aires: EUDEBA, 1964.

———. *The Jewish Gauchos of the Pampa*. Trans. Prudencio de Pereda. New York: Abelard Schuman, 1955.

Goloboff, Gerardo Mario. "Nuestra Babel." *Noah* (Jerusalem) 1.1 (1987): 72–74.

JanMohamed, Abdul R., and David Lloyd. "Introduction: Minority Discourse—What is to Be Done?" *Cultural Critique* 7 (1987): 5–17.

Kovadloff, Santiago. "Un lugar en el tiempo: La Argentina como vivencia de los judíos" (A Place in Time: Argentina as a Jewish Experience). *Por un futuro imperfecto* (For an Imperfect Future). Buenos Aires: Botella al Mar, 1987.

Kubayanda, Josaphat B. "Minority Discourse and the African Collective: Some Examples from Latin American and Caribbean Literature." *Cultural Critique* 6 (1987): 113–30.

---

3. The discussion of *Mestizo* is part of a longer study on Latin-American Jewish writing as minority discourse. A major source for JanMohamed and Lloyd is Deleuze's and Guattari's essay on Kafka, but their collection of articles contains nothing on later Jewish writers.

8

Metaphors of Disorder and Displacement in *Mil años, un día,* by Ricardo Halac

NORA GLICKMAN

A FEW MONTHS BEFORE Christopher Columbus's voyage in 1492, Queen Isabel of Castille (1451–1504) enacted the Edict of Expulsion, which compelled Jews to leave the country or to convert to Catholicism, under threat of death. Those who did not comply with the Edict were handed over to the Inquisition for trial. While an estimated 200,000 Jews began an exodus to other European countries (Portugal and Holland in particular) and to North Africa, others became "New Christians" and remained in Spain. Under continuing pressure from the Inquisition, many of those New Christians who had only pretended to convert (known as crypto-Jews) seized opportunities to come to the "New World," where it was easier to find safety in obscurity.[1]

The reign of terror that the Jews endured during the Spanish Inquisition is the subject of a number of contemporary plays written both in Spain and in the Americas. The first one was Golcalves de Magalhaes' *Antonio José ou o poeta e a Inquisição.* (Antonio José, or the Poet and the Inquisition).[2] Written in 1838, the play is a celebration of Brazil's independence from Portugal. It centers on the life of the martyred poet Antonio José, himself a victim of the Inquisition. More recently, several other plays have dealt with the subject of the Jews and the Inquisition

---

1. By 1492, the number of Jews remaining in Spain had been greatly reduced, since their persecution and exodus had begun more than a century before. The Inquisitional tribunals were responsible for determining the validity of the mass conversions of Jews, and whether those remaining were sincere New Christians, Marranos (forced converts), or crypto-Jews (Jews clandestinely continuing to maintain Jewish practices while outwardly adopting Christianity).

2. Gonçalves de Magalhaes, *Antonio José ou o poeta é a Inquisição,* 1838.

as symbols of the oppression by totalitarian regimes. In Brazil, Alfredo Días Gomes's *O Santo Inquêrito* (1966, The Holy Office) centers on the sacrifice of Branca Días, a young woman accused of being a crypto-Jew, who was burned at the stake. In Portugal, Bernardo Santareno wrote *O Judeu*;[3] in Mexico, Sabina Berman's play *Herejías* (1983, Heresies) is based on the tragic fate of the Carvajal family, who fell victim to the Spanish Inquisition in Mexico in the early part of the sixteenth century;[4] Susana Torres Molina's play *Chris Crosses* (1988) is a romanticized recreation of Christopher Colombus's, life and of his controversial relationship with Queen Isabel of Castille.[5] Finally, Ricardo Halac's play *Mil años, un día* (1986, One Thousand Years, One Day) which will be analyzed here, focuses on the impact of the expulsion of the Jews from Spain, and on their attempts to find explanations for their predicament.[6]

Mil años, un día, deals with the earthshaking events that took place in 1492: the end of the Christian reconquest of the Moorish kingdoms in Spain, Colombus's first voyage, and the final expulsion of the Jews from Spain. The new myths, symbols, paradigms, and political structures that were generated from these events continue to be reevaluated today, even five hundred years after Colombus's voyage and the Edict of Expulsion.

Throughout Halac's play we find repeated references to historically documented characters, such as Abravanel and Santángelo, two prominent Jews who were responsible for financing Colombus's voyage from Puerto de Palos in Portugal. Although there is mention of "the three ships" departing from Palos, there is no other direct reference to Christopher Colombus in Halac's play.[7] Several allusions are made to the events leading to the reconquest, which meant the end of religious tolerance and economic prosperity for Jews and Moors alike. Halac makes reference, in

---

3. Bernardo Santareno's *O Judeu* (Narrativa dramática em tres actos (Lisbóa: Edições Atica, 1966) 1st ed.

4. Sabina Berman, *Herejías* (Heresies) translated into English by Timothy Klinger (1989, Klinger). Berman's published plays are anthologized in *Teatro de Sabina Berman* (Mexico: Editores Mexicanos Unidos, 1985).

5. Sandra Torres Molina *Chris Crosses*, staged in New York, at the Puerto Rican Travelling Theatre, in 1989.

6. Ricardo Halac, *Mil años, un día* translated by Nora Glickman and Gloria Waldman, *One Thousand Years, One Day*. All quotes are taken from this unpublished version (Halac, 1985).

7. The play alludes to the coincidental historical fact that the same night when the time limit for Jews in Spain elapsed, Christopher Colombus left Puerto de Palos on his first voyage. In fact, Colombus's travel diary records that on the night of his departure a ship filled with Jews was bound for North Africa. It is also well established, that some (if not most) of Colombus's crew were Jews and *conversos* (converts). Other plays by Ricardo Halac include: *Soledad para cuatro* (1961); *Fin de diciembre* (1965); *Estela de madrugada* (1965); *Tempempié I y II* (1968); *Segundo tiempo* (1976); *Ruido de rotas cadenas* (1983); and *El dúo Sosa Echague* (1984).

particular, to the capitulation of Boabdil—the last Islamic Sultan—and to the fall of the last Moorish stronghold in the south of Spain.

Nevertheless, Halac does not merely reproduce reality; he selects from it what he regards as components essential to his drama and creates innovative images that serve to intensify the pathos endured by his characters. By attaching an increased importance to metaphorical elements, to expressionistic pranks and games, and to a distorted use of traditional religious objects, the author creates an atmosphere of disorientation.

Mil años, un día reenacts the intense feelings of a people faced with instability and change. By creating sustained images of uncertainty and displacement, Halac reinforces the link between the predicament of the Jews in 1492 and their ancient history. The *Kabbalah* (from the Hebrew, "that which is received"), is the most prevalent manifestation of their search for relief from their despair. Out of their search for a solution comes a faith in the *Kabbalah* and in supernatural interpretations of reality. In Halac's play, Isaac Levy, the spiritual leader of the Jewish community, mourns over the inability of the Jews to control their own destiny. Levy and his followers resort to the mystical formulae contained in the *Kabbalah* because they believe these provide them with essential keys to understanding human behavior and divine mysteries. They also put their faith in the *Kabbalah* because they hope that the popular superstitions, traditions, and mythological motifs contained in it will provide them with a way of transcending the misfortunes of the physical world.

Because the Jews attribute cosmic significance to their prayers as well as to their actions, they strive for a harmonious balance between the "upper" and the "lower" worlds to prevent disorder and chaos. The *Zohar* (from the Hebrew, "splendor"), which is the most important literary component of the *Kabbalah*, explores the correspondence between the "upper" and the "lower" worlds. Its central doctrine is that a harmonious union with God can be achieved through leading a religious life that includes good deeds and mystical meditations. This balance, however, can be disturbed by man's sins and improper thoughts.

The year 1492, in which this play is set, marks a time of imbalance in both the "upper" and "lower" orders. This can be seen in the mood of skepticism and disbelief that pervades the characters' actions and adds to the sinister meaning of their words: Jehuda, a secular Jew, feels ambivalent about the methods used by all the Spanish Jews who ". . .tiran ahora letras al aire. No piden sólo quedarse. ¡Ahora quieren que esto se transforme en la tierra prometida!" (p. 29); (". . .throw letters in the air. They not only demand to stay. Now they want this to become their promised land!"). And Devoto, a converted Jew, complains of the idiosyncratic nature of Jewish mysticism and its use of black magic and rituals to supplement religious prayers. Devoto concludes, in a statement reminiscent of Hamlet's opinion of Polonius' madness, that "Cada cabalista tiene su método" (p. 21); ("Each *Kabbalist* has his own method").

Along with the *Kabbalists*, Isaac sees a parallel between the present exile of the Jews from Spain and the original exile, described in the book of Genesis. In trying to understand the nature of events, Isaac turns to biblical sources when he relates the Queen's Edict to Adam's Expulsion from the Garden of Eden. Isaac tends to blame the Jews themselves for their expulsion from Spain, and despairs of finding a reason that will justify why and where the Jews have failed to deserve such severe punishments as expulsion and death.

The pervasive presence of ritual objects in the play is meant to strengthen the identification of the Jews with their religion: the *shofar* (ram horn), the candelabra, the *talit* (ritual shawl), and the secret numbers and letters related to the *Kabbalah*. When Isaac keeps his arms raised high— like Moses did in the desert to help the Jews against their enemies, and like Joshua did in Jericho to prevent the walls from crumbling—he hopes to invoke a miracle that will cancel the Edict. Similarly, before the Jews are forced to leave Spain, they follow their tradition of visiting the tombs of their relatives. Covered in their ritual shawls, they perform a ritual dance sing *jarchas* at the cemetery to commiserate with their loved ones.

In *Mil años, un día* the mournful tone of the *shofar*, which is only sounded during the sacred Jewish holidays, is an important Jewish symbol that provokes an immediate response, as it draws attention to events of high religious significance. Here the *shofar* "reproduce los lamentos del corazón" (p. 16); ("reproduces the lamentations of the heart"). It is a symbol of Jewish tears, and "anuncia la llegada del Mesías" (p. l6); ("it announces the coming of the Messiah").

Another prominent metaphor in the play is that of the bride wishing to join her beloved, Israel. Here the *Kabbalah* teacher, an androgynous character named Luz (from the Spanish "light" or "splendor"), pleads to God in the name of (its) people. Before leaving Spain, Luz—whose real name is Ibn Pérez—is seen sleep-walking, dressed as a bride with a garland of flowers on (its) head and saying: "¡Dios! Tu pueblo ya fue tu novia mucho tiempo...llegó la hora de casarte con ella!" (p. 37); "God! your people [Israel] have been your bride too long already; the time has come for you to marry her"). Luz's plight as the abandoned bride of Israel is echoed by the more literal plight of Isaac's daughter Raquel, also abandoned before her wedding by her fiancé—a Jew who fled Spain following the Edict.

Queen Isabel herself is fascinated at first by the *Kabbalah*, although it soon becomes evident that her "openness" to the *Kabbalah* is only a ploy to persuade Isaac Levy, her physician and lover, to identify with her own Catholicism. The Queen's confused and ambiguous love toward her physician manifests itself in her chronic physical ailments of skin boils and rashes, which her priest interprets as "un castigo por coquetear con el demonio" (p. 11); "a punishment for flirting with the devil"). Isabel perceives the Jewish doctrine as a spurious set of superstitions, no more effective than the rabbit's foot that she gives Isaac for good luck.

The Christian symbols recognizable in *Mil años, un día* serve to arouse the Christian crowds into acts of patriotism and religious zeal. The Queen appeals to the emotions of her people because her country has become "un caballo desbocado" (p. 11), ("a runaway horse"). The author uses symbols and emblems such as the flag and the banner; the sword and the cross are used interchangeably to reinforce each other. The cross, the most powerful symbol in Christian religion, is constantly related to the sword, symbolic of military strength, Queen Isabel puts her faith both in God and in the sword as a means to reconquer Spain from the heathens. She reflects: "No hubiéramos reconquistado España si hubiéramos confiado sólo en Dios. El confía en nuestras espadas también" (p. 9). ("Had we trusted only in God we would not have reconquered Spain. He [God] trusts in our swords too".) Furthermore, the Queen believes that God has empowered her with a sacred sword that brings her fame throughout the world: "¡Por algo me llaman Isabel la Católica!" (p. 11); ("They have good reason for calling me Isabel la Católica!"). Finally, Isabel inverts her sword and thereby turns it into a cross when she asserts her authority, by forcing Isaac Levy to convert to Catholicism.

The bells, which traditionally toll when someone is coming or leaving town, are a signal of celebration for the victorious Christians who remain in Spain. But the tolling of the bells is defined quite differently for the Jews, who mourn at the sound and regard it as an ominous announcement of their imminent departure.

The suitcases, more than any other metaphor in *Mil años, un día* represent the futility and impermanence of the times. In a style recalling that of Beckett's *Waiting for Godot*, the characters frantically carry their luggage across the stage, thus emphasizing their state of flux and incertitude. Sara, Isaac's wife as well as the Queen's rival, is always prepared to move, but hopes that that moment will never come. Although her common sense teaches her what to take and what to leave behind, she is worn out by constantly "packing and unpacking" her suitcases (p. 29). Her son, Yehuda, a young, spirited man, is also seen repeatedly crossing the stage carrying suitcases. Yet, when the time to leave Spain finally comes, he resists vehemently and is consequently tortured by the Inquisitors.[8]

The plight of the Jews best illustrates their precarious condition: their destiny is likely to change from one moment to the next. As Devoto remarks, "La vida de muchos depende de un pequeño detalle" (p. 21); ("The life of many hangs on a small detail").

The relentlessness of fate and the irreversible movement of time is symbolized by the wheel. The wheel that turns is literally "La rueda de tormento" (the wheel of torture), or the rack, an instrument used by the inquisitors to torture infidels and force them to confess. Ironically, the wheel of torture also represents progress, for the rack is introduced to the "New World" by a proud Christian official named Rodrigo as a symbol of modernity.

The wheel is also used figuratively to indicate the passage of time. After ten centuries of relative calm in Spain—as the title of the play suggests, Mil años, un día—after one thousand years of peace and prosperity, the fate of the Jews has been altered in one day when they are arbitrarily forced to uproot themselves and leave their homeland. With the Edict of Expulsion, their political and economic prestige is eradicated.

Interestingly, Halac's play repeats the same leitmotif expressed by the messenger in T.S. Eliot's play Murder in the Cathedral: ". . .that the wheel may turn and be forever still."[9] Eliot's play has an illusion of progression because the action takes shape in a pattern that is repeated, making any change seem imaginary. In La cabala y la cruz the Jews despair because the world does not respond to the injustice against them. Carrying the metaphor of the wheel a step further, Isaac insists: "Tenemos que encontrar la falla. El mecanismo del mundo está atrancado en algún lugar. La rueda del tiempo gira, pero sigue en el mismo sitio. . ." (p. 7); ("We must find the flaw! The mechanism of the world is jammed somewhere. The wheel turns, but it stays in the same place"). Isaac's comment is significant, as it represents the exasperation of those who feel impotent to control their own lives. The events that lead to the Inquisition show that no matter what they do, the Jews are unable to affect a change. The prospect of exile creates an atmosphere of unpredictability and instability.

---

8. In her play Efectos personales (Personal Effects), trans. by Nora Glickman and Gloria Waldman, Diana Raznovich develops the metaphor of suitcases to signify the condition of paranoia that affects individuals living at the mercy of rigid rules and inhuman regulations.

9. T. S. Eliot, Murder in the Cathedral (London: Faber and Faber, Ltd. 1955), 9.

Eventually Isaac Levy comes to acknowledge the senselessness of his will for advancement and self-determination. He aspired to a power that turned out to be illusory. "Ese poder estúpido e invisible que conquistamos los judíos, y que cuando llega el momento, nos barren de un soplo" (p. 38). ("That stupid and invisible power that we Jews conquer, which when the moment comes...is swept away from us in one breath").

Halac creates a technical device whereby his characters find a means to escape their oppressive reality through expressionistic games. As the play unfolds, Isaac and Isabel are able to act out some of their most audacious fantasies through make-believe, thus averting or pretending to escape real punishment by the Inquisition. When the Queen symbolically "anoints" Isaac as a king, he exercises his power by issuing three commands. First he orders that those inquisitors who believe in the efficacy of torture throw themselves into the flames of the stake to prove its purifying powers as "scientifically" valid. Next, Isaac orders that the "wheel of time" be stopped from turning, to make the Queen forget having signed the Edict. Isaac's first two wishes—punishing the guilty and relieving the innocent—are therapeutic in nature. His third and final command, "Abdico en nombre de mi mujer" (p. 44); ("I abdicate in favor of my wife") is ambiguous because he appears to be referring to his real wife, Sara, while at the same time he is attempting to win back the Queen's favor. For Sara, the Queen's two-day postponement of the Edict is the ultimate "miracle." For it is she who, along with her daughter Raquel, carries Isaac to the ship that will lead them safely out of Spain.[10]

In the course of the play Isaac grows from being a complacent man, proud of his position in court, into an awareness of the vanity and futility of his endeavors, as he cannot extricate himself from his heritage. This he comes to accept—first by insisting that his immediate family settle with him at the Queen's court, and then by explaining to the Queen that more names are missing which include the larger Jewish community: "¡Faltan! Porque ahora mi familia son todos" (p. 22); ("More are missing! Because now my family is everybody"). Subsequently, Isaac comes to terms with his own faith by accepting that the *Kabbalah* can be deceptive and treacherous: "Sacrifiqué a mi viejo y ningún ángel llegó a tiempo para detenerme" (p. 35); ("I sacrificed my old man and no angel came in time

---

10. Historically, those Jews who went to the Spanish colonies in the New World could do so only if they converted prior to their departure. If their conversion was not sincere, they would be punished by the local Tribunals of the Inquisition. In this play, paradoxically, the Queen intercedes in favor of Isaac so he can go to New Spain, and continue practicing his own faith.

to stop me!"). Finally he resists his own conversion to Catholicism on the grounds that he can only live as a Jew. When forced by the Queen to convert, he retorts:

"¿En qué? ¿en un sapo? ¿una culebra? ¿El Santo Inquisidor? ¿un caballero? (Se suelta. Nadie sabe qué hacer.) Veo el manual de zoología fantástica que se abre ante mí y no encuentro ningún papel que pueda interpretar. ¡Menos a la fuerza! ¡Soy Isaac! (p. 48).

[To convert] (to what? To a frog? A snake? The Holy Inquisitor? A knight? (He frees himself. No one knows what to do.) I see the manual of fantastic zoology open before me, and I can't find any role for me, least of all by force! I am Isaac!)

As the situation worsens for the Jews, their symbols of faith and trust begin to fail them, and Christians abuse religious symbols in order to torment them. Isaac's former friends, who represent Christian authority and the church, play dangerous, diabolical games at his expense. Just at the moment when Isaac is in ecstasy, believing that there has been a miracle and that the Jews will finally be saved, Isaac's Christian companions cover his eyes with a "talit" (a Jewish ritual shawl), thus desecrating a religious symbol, and spin him around to play the game of blind man's buff. At this point Isaac, blinded, is entirely at their mercy, and no divine intervention can save him.

Later on his "friends" play another trick and disguise themselves as statues, each representing a different aspect of terror: an inquisitor, a henchman, a devil, a conqueror, a cardinal, and death itself. They surround Isaac to announce that the deadline to leave Spain—midnight— has arrived. Partially in jest, when one of them unsheathes his sword to kill Isaac for disobeying the Edict, the Queen announces that she has issued a proscription deferring the expulsion of the Jews for another two days. The Queens's sudden change of mind regarding the deadline of the Edict, like the capricious behavior of the Spaniards toward the Jews, creates feelings of anguish and confusion in the Spaniards' victims.

Another apparently harmless make-believe game that the peasants play upon Ezra—Isaac's old father—turns out to be of the utmost seriousness. The peasants' choice of amusement at Ezra's expense is just as cruel as the psychological torture Isaac himself had to endure when playing blind man's buff. Faithful to the end, Ezra stands by his religious convictions: He is ritually baptized and renamed Benedictus, as an initiation into the Catholic faith. His name is also a code, since Benedictus means "blessed" in Latin, but means "son of" (ben) in Hebrew; that is, Ezra is the legitimate "son of the Edict," or the first heir of the exile.

The common peasants who beat up Ezra are not only indifferent to the injustice toward the Jews, but are most concerned about their own plight. They hate the Jews and the rich indiscriminately. They complain that the rich will exploit the money left behind by the Jews in order to pay their own taxes, and plead: "Mejor nos lo dejan a nosotros, que no tenemos nada!" (p. 30) ("Better leave it to us, who have nothing!"). The peasants feel just as cheated as the Jews, for rather than improving their condition, the expulsion will perpetuate it, and their condition will remain as miserable as before.

In a fundamental way, Halac's metaphors dramatically express the failure of the individual to change the course of events and the inefficacy of the answers provided by mysticism.

The strength of *Mil años, un día* lies in Halac's ability to establish a natural connection between the Jewish exodus from Spain in particular, and the condition of exile that has become recurrent in Jewish chronology—a predicament also shared by the mass displacement of innocent victims throughout human history. In a personal interview, the author referred to a memory that remained fixed in his mind since he was ten years old: Upon first reading of the horrors of the Holocaust, his father told him that the fate of the Jews is to always be prepared to leave at the first signs of impending danger.[11] The lack of logic in this idea—that Jews would have to leave when they had done nothing wrong—puzzled and disturbed Halac, of Argentine birth but only one generation removed from Syrian immigrants.

Mil años, un día was written only over a decade after the years of the "Proceso" in Argentina (1968-1972). As in other periods of uncertainty and persecution, the Jews endured those years and remained in Argentina because they trusted that reason would prevail over barbarism, and that better times would come in the future. Halac's play is a study of contemporary situations of repression and of man's precarious condition under totalitarian regimes.

---

11.   Nora Glickman, "Entrevista con Ricardo Halac," *Latin American Theatre Review*, pp. 1990.

Noah in the Pampas: Syncretism in Goloboff's *Criador de palomas*

LOIS BARR

Ya ves cómo al final nos mezclamos todos.
(So you see how in the end, we are all mixed together.)[1]

Criador de palomas (Dove Breeder)

I admire the gauchos as much as I admire the ancient
Hebrews. The gauchos, too, are patriarchal and noble.

Albert Gerchunoff, *The Jewish Gauchos*

GERARDO MARIO GOLOBOFF was born in Carlos Casares on the
Argentine plain in 1939 and in his adolescence witnessed the great social
upheavel and anti-Semitism of the forties and sixties.[2] He writes of the
tensions in his village, which became so great that his family did not even
feel free to speak at home in front of the maid. ("La pasión según San
Martin", 190). In exile since 1973, he now teaches Latin American literature
and literary theory at the University of Paris at Nanterre. Goloboff's love
for the Argentine plains gives a strong gaucho flavor to his fiction. He,
like so many Argentine intellectuals and writers, wrestles with gaucho
themes and the meaning of life in the pampas. At the same time, he claims
to be "Jewish to the marrow."[3] Although his work does not deal primarily
with Jewish themes, he confirms his religious identity by the language,
imagery, and illusions to biblical stories in his fiction. As Leonardo

---

1. This translation and all subsequent translations are mine.
2. An earlier version of this paper was given at the 1990 Kentucky Foreign Language
Conference. I greatly appreciate the comments of Dan Reedy, Joe Schraibman, Phyllis
Silverstein, and Kenton Stone which led me to understand the text more fully.
3. Conversation at Latin American Jewish Studies Association Conference February 23,
1987.

Senkman explains in his discussion of Goloboff, language becomes the fatherland of the Jew (335).

Goloboff is aware that the human condition is one of exile, since Adam and Eve were expelled from Eden, and suggests that sense of the wandering Jew in the plot and the imagery of his novel *Criador de palomas* (1984), becomes a vehicle of return.[4] In this work the struggle between good and evil, innocence and venality, life and death is told with images that suggest the story of the flood in Genesis. The Ten Commandments gave the Jews a mooring during their forty years of wandering in the wilderness. The Torah and other scrolls and texts carried by the Jews into successive exiles have retained their past. Similarly, Goloboff's narrator returns via words to a special and primordial place. In *Criador de palomas* two disintegrating patriarchal worlds—that of the gaucho and that of the Jewish patriarchs—are synthesized. There would not be, as Gerchunoff's *Los gauchos judíos* suggested, a bright new future for Argentina and for the Jews, but rather an unstable society destined to suffer the sacrifice of the innocent.

Criador de palomas is told in the first person by an unnamed orphaned Jewish youth living in the pampas. The time frame is deliberately very vague, but the boy's early youth and adolescence probably coincide with the Peronist and anti-Peronist clashes of the fifties and sixties. The boy's parents die when he is an infant, and he is separated from his brothers and raised by his uncle, the aloof and strong Tío Negro, who lives and works according to a dual code. Like the gaucho, the uncle is basically a loner: never married, he is a self-sufficient man, a skilled horseman, and most adept in the wilderness. Just like Moises, (arguably the only Jewish gaucho in *Los gauchos judíos*) he dies on horseback under mysterious circumstances. While Tío Negro teaches his young charge about horses and about the pampas topography, he also shows him what remnants of Jewish patriarchal tradition remain in the boy's life and in the village. Under his uncle's tutelage, the boy moves in this novel from a marginal and ineffectual role as an orphan to a role of authority, as the teller of his own tale. When the boy (now probably a young man) moves back to Algarrobos after an unexplained and extended absence, he restores and protects his home. His return to Algarrobos in some ways echoes the gaucho tradition of the return. But unlike Martín Fierro, the narrator has not lost wife and family. Like Noah, who was more than anything else a breeder and a restorer of the creatures of the earth after the cataclysmic

---

4. See: Mario Goloboff, "Paroles d'Exil," *Magazine Littéraire* 221 (August 1985): 44–45 and "Restos de Bitácora," (The Remains of Bitacora) *Teoría del discurso poético*. Travaux de l'Université de Toulouse-le Mirail (Série A 37) (1986): 87–89.

flood, the boy is a dove breeder who cares for his little house and land as though he could replenish the earth.

The setting of *Criador* is the pampas' town of Algarrobos, a blend of fact and fiction, of the author's own memories of Carlos and Casares and stories of other villages told by his elders.[5] Goloboff's depiction of Algarrobos is at once a primordial Garden of Eden and a strange inferno in which evil and mysterious events happen in a random manner, and against which there is no protection. This story alludes to the story of the Garden of Eden and of the flood—complete with the return of the dove to announce that the period of destruction and death has ended. Algarrobos is the Edenic garden, the *locus amenus*, the lost innocence of youth, and the womb—all together. Its name is that of a tree upon whose seeds birds feed. Algarrobos is a tree of life, a place which sustains. The orchards of the wealthy foreigner, the count, are so luxuriant and the neighbor Jorda's pool is so refreshing that the cruel events which occur are almost unexpected. The rainbow, which Tío Negro explains to the boy as being a sign of the covenant, is an omen of good, but the mention of various natural disasters—floods, cyclones, and droughts—as well as the boy's dream of a black rainbow, foreshadow the ominous death of his beloved doves and the boy's eventual exile.

Just as its images hark back to Old Testament events and places, this novel also reflects gaucho literature. Algarrobos, with its twelve asphalted streets at the center and surrounding forty blocks, is the first word of the book and becomes, as it were, the demarcation of space in a novel in which boundries and open spaces are symbolic. Interestingly, the narrator of *Don Segundo Sombra* also sets out the exact geography of the pampas town in the first page of that novel, and both Algarrobos and the village in Güiraldes' novel are made up of some forty blocks. Each important vignette in *Criador* is separated from the others, not by chapter headings or numbers, but by large blank spaces—spaces that suggest the great distance from one town to another or from one tree to another. As is so often the case in *Don Segundo Sombra*, this space is also indicative of the distance between one individual and another and a mutual respect that keeps a barrier of fraternal silence between these inhabitants of the pampas who have an almost religious zeal, "un gusto casi religioso," (81) (for distance and privacy).

Despite the distances, there is still some sense of community in this town, the roots of which go back to old-time ranchers, cowhands, and

---

5. Olver Gilberto de León, "Un mítico viaje hacia la infancia," *La Prensa* 8 (December 1985): Suplemento dominical, 3.

Jewish colonizers. The preparation and consumption of *mate*, the salutes on horseback, and the guitar music at a wedding are remaining gaucho customs that create a sense of solidarity between many of Algarrobos' residents, both Jews and gentiles.[6] But the most syncretic act in the novel—the one which most subtly and yet significantly melds the gaucho and Jewish worlds—is the consumption of meat at the *parrilladas* (barbecues). Perhaps out of obedience to the rules of *kashruth* (kosher), perhaps merely copying the pampas tradition, Tío Negro always roasts and salts the meat he consumes.[7] At one point while the uncle roasts the meat, the boy breaks off a little piece of bread and drops it into the flames. In this simple incident—the importance of which is underscored by the ample space that separates this vignette from others—homage is paid to the Jewish custom of breaking off a small portion (the size of an olive) of the dough for the Sabbath bread and burning it. This custom—one of the few remaining which in any way resembles earlier sacrificial rituals—commemorates the destruction of the temple and within the novel may foreshadow the violence which will ensue in Algarrobos.[8]

The slaughter of meat is also symbolic of the divisions in the community, not only of Algarrobos, but also of Argentina. The unexplained sporadic killings of the boy's beloved and gentle doves go hand in hand with other mysterious signs of violence, disintegration, and destruction in Algarrobos. Midway through the novel, the uncle takes his young nephew to visit the municipal slaughterhouse where his old friend Doble Feo (Two Times Ugly) works. (Doble Feo, Tío Negro explains, is a *shochet*, certified to slaugher animals according to Jewish ritual.) Inside, the boy becomes dizzy and nauseated from the cold, the sight of blood running throughout channels in the floor, and the smell. But most disturbing of all, is when Doble Feo hacks open a cow and her unborn calf comes into view. Here the slaughter of the innocent could not be more apparent, nor the text more in line with Argentine literary tradition. Echeverria used the *matadero* to decry Rosas's butchery and Goloboff's Argentina is a slaughterhouse where the innocent, like the gentle doves, are repeatedly sacrificed.[9]

---

6. The boy's first sip of *mate* is treated as a rite of passage.

7. The Jewish custom of salting sacrifices as prescribed in Lev. 2:13–14 was also carried over to the table, considered to be as sacred as the alter. See also Trepp, 58.

8. Ezek. 44.30 "ye shall also give unto the priest the first of your dough, to cause a blessing to rest on thy house." For an explanation of the custom of burning a bit of *challah* see: Trepp, 72 and Richard Siegel, et. al, ed., *The First Jewish Catalogue* (Philadelphia: The Jewish Publication Society of America, 1973) 37–38.

9. When interviewed, Goloboff has agreed that the doves may be seen as Argentina's disappeared. See, for example, his interview with Oscar Taffetani, "El poder de la ficción," (The Power of Fiction) *La Razón* (13 October 1985): Cultura 10–11. María Adela Renard suggests the influence of Echeverria in her review of *Criador* in *La Prensa* (3 February 1985): Sec. 1, 11.

Tío Negro shows the boy a rainbow with his first words in the novel, but from the novel's opening the death and destruction which are to grip Algarrobos are prefigured by the allusion to storms and floods and the neighborhood hit by the cyclone. The boy's nightmare the night he gets his first dove also suggests a brutality that seems preordained. In his dream a dove rides on the back of his little horse along a stream. Silvery fish jumping from the water startle the horse, who rears up and gallops off. The frightened dove cannot get off the horse's back. A black rainbow and lightening form a backdrop for the frenzied galloping of the horse. After that dream the violence is sporadic. From time to time the boy awakens early to feed his doves, only to find one dead in a pool of blood.

> Corrí hacia el nido de Verana. Lo encontré vació. Busqué a tientas bajo la parra casi oscurecida. En el huerto, junto al tronco del duraznero, yacía mi paloma con un tajo profundo en el cuello. La sangre brotaba todavía caliente. Le habían cortado las patitas; las grandes alas estaban retorcidas, muchas plumas habían sido arrancadas brutalmente. (43)

> (I ran to Summer's nest. It was empty. I groped around in semi-darkness under the grapevines. In the garden at the base of the peach tree lay my dove with a deep gouge in her neck. The blood which spurted out was still hot. They had cut off her feet; her big wings were twisted, many feathers had been brutally pulled).

His doves are killed at various points in the narration. There are snatches of political discussions and allusions to big problems ahead. The Soria furniture store burns down and finally the narrator leaves Algarrobos furtively in the early morning hours. At that point the situation of the town is likened to that of a natural disaster, and the storm mentioned in the first line of the novel is mentioned once again: "Como en medio de un ciclón quedó Algarrobos: una lluvia finita lo vaciaba, el cielo estaba gris cuando me fui." (Algarrobos seemed engulfed in a cyclone: a light rain emptied it, the sky was gray when I left, 139). Just as the flood almost destroyed the earth, the boy's entire world has practically disappeared.

Understanding why evil exists is beyond the comprehension of man. The narrator never knows who has killed his doves or why they were killed. The count tells the young boy on his sickbed that there's a lot of evil in the world. The narrator never knows why the Soria furniture store burned down or even how his parents died. Tío Negro's death is also cloaked in mystery.

Yet another mystery in a novel full of enigmas, is the young boy's lack of a name, so contrary to a biblical tradition that emphasizes male lineage and names. The narrator's beginnings as an orphan, however, are not unknown in the paradigm of the hero, and certainly here the model is the young and nameless narrator of *Don Segundo Sombra* who so admired Don Segundo just as the boy in *Criador* admired Tío Negro, whose name so closely echoes that of the legendary gaucho.[10] He has lost both parents. His past is a mystery just as the one the *gaucho* (orphan) in *Don Segundo Sombra* describes ". . .en torno mío también existía un misterio que nadie quiso revelarme" (186, ch. 22); (all around me there was a mystery that no one would reveal to me). If the narrator of *Criador* knows the circumstances of his parents' deaths, he does not share them with the reader. He is raised by a bachelor uncle, el Tío Negro, suckled by a wet nurse through an open window, and attended during a period of serious illness by a gracious but mysterious immigrant known as the count. In the course of the novel when the boy is a young teen, the uncle dies. He is forced to leave his beloved village mysteriously, ostensibly because the political situation has worsened. When he returns, the count has gone and the generous man's estate has been turned into a country club. Much of what he loved in Algarrobos has changed.

He is also an orphan from Jewish heritage. It is quite obvious that many of the characters in the novel are Jewish; however, there is little Jewish ritual. His uncle takes him to see the Jewish cemetary. The boy cannot read the inscriptions (nor, he suspects, can his uncle) on the tombs whose disarray suggests that Algarrobos's Jews have abandoned their religious tradition. The notable exception is an old man who dismounts his horse before sundown on the Sabbath eve. As we have seen, the *pibe* (kid) found the slaughterhouse repulsive. Only bits of Yiddish are recorded in the story and the boy does not understand most of what he hears. What remains of the culture are simply those snatches of Yiddish and a curious blending of Argentine rural life and Jewish custom. The Bar Mitzvah has become a secular thirteenth birthday party. Even the narrator's gift to his brother—a book of Quiroga's short stories—becomes a syncretic act. As was seen with the preparation of meat, the customs of the Old World often guided the Jewish immigrants in choosing which customs of the new world they would embrace.

---

10. In *Don Segundo Sombra*, Chapter 22, the narrator answers the question as to what his name is: "Quisiera saberlo, señor." (I would like to know, sir.) He later adds that sometimes people call him "gaucho" or orphan. In the second novel of the trilogy, (*La luna que cae*) (*The Falling Moon*), the boy's name becomes El Pibe, the kid. At one point in *Criador* the uncle calls out to the boy "¡Pibe!" but it is not clear whether it is used as a nickname of simply to get his attention. Even in *El soñador de Smith* (*The Dream Man from Smith*), the narrator is still *El Pibe*.

The uncle explains a great deal to the boy, in fact, most of the nurturing and teaching in the novel is done by males for males. The uncle holds his nephew's hand and gives him a clean and comfortable, if economically disadvantaged, home. Male friends sip *mate* and share their circle of friendship with the *pibe*. They sit in a circle and rarely talk; they just pass the aromatic mate and warm fraternal looks. Tío Negro and his male neighbors share a sense of communion, which permeates his every act. The narrator's two older brothers lavish affection on their younger sibling whenever possible. The obese Francisco, a mysterious fortune teller from the nearby town of Smith, serves as the uncle's confidant. Even the pleasure of eating freshly baked bread is afforded him by the old baker Malamud.

In many ways, the narrator of *Criador* partakes of male bonding in the gaucho tradition. In *Don Segundo Sombra* the *pulperías* (gaucho outposts which were part grocery store and part tavern) are a male domain in which no woman can undermine the freedom and daring of the men. All of gaucho literature stresses a sense of loyalty of one gaucho to another, but wastes little time on women.[11] Just as the young man in *Don Segundo Sombra* worships the mysterious and larger-than-life gaucho, Segundo Sombra, the boy in *Criador* venerates his Tío Negro. Segundo Sombra rides off as the sun sets at the end of the novel and Tío Negro dies on horseback. The boy decides to keep Negro's neckerchief, a gaucho symbol, as his reminder of the uncle and as a way of being stoic in his sadness.

Similarly, in gaucho literature there is not room for family. Gerchunoff's Don Remigio knifed his son in the back rather than allow him to retreat in a fight, and most gauchos had to sacrifice family to live a life of continual struggle.[12] In *Radiografía de la pampas (X-ray of the Pampas)* Ezequiel Martínez Estrada contemplates this lack of continuity, the childless condition of the gaucho as well as the Argentine society's lack of moral cohesiveness, dating back to the conquest period: "The sons as the perpetuation of the lineage, the house as a permanent plot, the family, the household chores which varied with the seasons, were not possible" (12–13). The open spaces always seemed to need conquering, so the conquerors went further, never stopping to cultivate. The patriarchal home is also missing in the gaucho tradition. The narrator of *Don Segundo Sombra* devalues the home and those furniture-like women who inhabit it:

---

11. Women in *Criador* belong to a mysterious, sweet smelling and starched world. The distance of that world is emphasized by the suckling of the orphaned narrator through an open window.

12. Martín Fierro's reunion with his sons seems more the exception than the rule.

La casa grande y vacía, poblada de muebles serios como mis tías, no me veía más que de paso. Seguían sus vastos aposentos siendo del otro hombre, cuya memoria no podía acostumbrarme a encarar como la de un padre. Y, además, me parecía que también ella se iba a morir, significando su presencia sólo un recuerdo frío. De haberme atrevido, la hubiera hecho echar abajo, como se deguella, por compasión, a un animal que sufre. (235)

(The big empty home, populated by furniture as serious as my aunts, never saw me except in passing. Its vast rooms continued to be those of another man whose memory I couldn't adjust to facing as that of my father. And, moreover, it seemed that the house would also die leaving only the cold memory of its presence. Had I dared, I would have had it torn down, as one chokes a suffering animal out of compassion)

Unlike the Jewish forefathers, Abraham, Isaac, and Jacob, who set down roots and proceeded to multiply, the gaucho tends to disappear.

If there is no sense of family and continuity, there is a respect in *Criador* for the home that is within biblical tradition. The males create the space for the dwellings and celebrate the sanctity of that space. A ritual of entry into Tío Negro's house is the wiping of one's shoes (although the entry of the house is a dirt floor) and a very solemn opening of the front door: "Abría la puerta con la misma solemnidad con que la cerraba al irse porque decía que el umbral es una separación entre dos mundos" (12–13); (I opened the door with the same solemnity with which I closed it upon leaving because he said that the doorway is the separation between two worlds.) Without actually referring to a deity, Tío Negro's ritual of entry calls for a sanctification of the home reminiscent in some ways to the commandment in Deuteronomy (6.9 and 11.20) to remember God each time one enters the home. It divides, as Mircea Eliade would say, the sacred from the profane. Tío Negro teaches his nephew how to build the dovecotes; that is, to promote life and protect it. As an adult, the narrator returns to Albarrobos and resumes his life in Tío Negro's home, which, although is inhabited by a squatter, has fallen into disrepair. The act of refurbishing the home after the disasters of the past reenacts the cleaning of the desecrated temple or the rebuilding after the flood. The holiness of that act is underlined by the return of a dove—which in Genesis 8.10 informed Noah that the flood had ended—at the very end of the novel:

Hacia las siete me bañaba, y después iba a enderezar las plantas o a regar arvejas. Uno de esos atardeceres, ya casi cerca del crepúsculo, cuando estaba agachado, en cuclillas, arreglando un montoncito de tierra para que no se desviara el agua, percibí un extraño movimiento junto a mí.

Un paso leve, menudo e impreciso. Miré casi sin ver hacia un bultito blanco, vacilante. Tendí, temblando, el brazo, y la paloma se acercó a mi mano. Pasé la otra por las alas, acomodándolas. Sentí bajo mi tacto el suyo que latía. Toda ella fue un cuerpo delicioso en medio de mi lecho. Cierra los ojos y descansa. (155–156)

(At about seven I usually bathed and then I went to tend the plants or water the peas. One of those afternoons, almost at sunset, when I was squatting down to pat a little mound of dirt into place so that the water wouldn't flow away, I felt a strange movement next to me. A light step, imprecise and tiny, I looked almost without seeing toward a diminutive and hesitant white bundle. Trembling I extended my arm and the dove approached my hand. I passed my other hand over her wings accomodating them. Under my touch I felt her pulse. She was entirely delicious as her body filled the bed of my hand. Close your eyes and rest.[13]

The narrator's return to Algarrobos marks his recovery of sanctuary. Through the doves, he can communicate with his brothers and Ivana. Through words the writer can return to his youth and restore it in the same way the narrator restores Tío Negro's house. Goloboff often speaks of attempts to reach a pristine and untouchable sanctuary, much like the glass bottle in which the poet travels through time in "Restos de Bitácora." So the painstaking training of the doves to go and come back is not unlike the painstaking process of working and reworking a text until it reaches the reader. The boy's doves, which always return home with a message, are the novel's words, which Goloboff treats with the same care and tenderness as the boy treats the doves.[14]

The doves are central to this tale of adolescence in a violent and yet nurturing world because the dove is a symbol of purity and innocence. The first dove in the novel appears to the boy right after he and his uncle see a rainbow, which the uncle explains as God's sign of a covenant with the world after the flood (Genesis 9.13). Just as Noah was a creator and a builder, the boy is preoccupied throughout the novel with building, cleaning, and attending to his doves. Even the title alludes to a double

---

13. The Spanish is, of course, ambiguous and could describe the bird with a jump to the present tense, in which case the translation would be: "It closes its eyes and rests." Or it could be, as I have rendered it, a tender command to the bird. To my mind it is the moment of fusion of the will of the animal and of the man, who rest as one. These same words open the second novel of Goloboff's trilogy, *La luna que cae,* in which a godlike narrator addresses the *Pibe* throughout in the second person singular.

14. In the interview with Taffetani, Goloboff states that *Criador* was written with special care: "Yo sentía que acariciaba las palabras con la yema de los dedos. . ." (11). (I felt that I caressed the words with the tips of my fingers. . .)

role of breeder and creator. The word *criador* (breeder) is close in sound to *creador* (creator), and as Corominas' *Diccionario crítico etimológico castellano e hispánico* shows, both words come from the Latin verb *creare*. So the young boy comes of age learning to fulfill the pastoral role of caring for a flock: a gentle gaucho, his flock are not cattle but doves. His vocation as a writer is a restorative and unifying principle. His earliest letters, sent by carrier pigeon, unite him with his brothers and Ivana, and his efforts at narrating his story unite him with his past. He assumes the mantle of patriarchal aloofness and sanctity by returning to the desecrated home and village and rededicating both. Virtually alone in life, his desire to connect himself with a home and with all that Tío Negro has taught him is reenacted at the end of the novel with the return of the dove. Yet though the dove rests comfortably in the palm of his hand, reconnecting the past and the present, man and nature, the protector and the protected, the missing element is the rainbow, which would symbolize an end to the violence in Argentina and a reconnection of man and the deity. The end of *Criador de palomas* brings the return of the dove, just as the dove breeder returns to Algarrobos; but it is a tentative return and there is not rainbow to assure a covenant of peace. Indeed, the last novel of the trilogy, *El soñador de Smith*, ends with a flood. Enmity, isolation, and destruction have not ended for Argentina.

REFERENCES

Gerchunoff, Alberto. *Los gauchos judíos*. 1910. Buenos Aires: Centro Editor de América Latina, 1968.
Goloboff, Gerardo Mario. *Criador de palomas*. 1984. Barcelona: Muchnik, 1989.
———. *El soñador de Smith*. Barcelona: Muchnik, 1990.
———. *La luna que cae*. Barcelona: Muchnik, 1989.
———. "La pasión según San Martín." *Caravelle* 33 (1979): 187–192.
Güiraldes, Ricardo. *Don Segundo Sombra*. Prologue Leopoldo Lugones. Madrid: Alianza, 1982.
Martinez Estrada, Ezequiel. *Radiografía de la Pampa*. 6th ed. Buenos Aires: Losada, 1942.
Rivera, Jorge B., ed. *Poesía gauchesca*. Caracas: Biblioteca Ayacucho, 1977.
Senkman, Leonardo. *La identidad judía en la literatura argentina* Buenos Aires: Pardes, 1983.
Simpson, John and Jana Bennett. *The Disappeared and the Mothers of the Plaza*. New York: St. Martin's Press, 1985.
Trepp, Leo. *The Complete Book of Jewish Observance*. New York: Behrman House, 1980.

Marcos Aguinis: Shifting Lines of Difference Between the Other and the Self

JUDITH MORGANROTH SCHNEIDER

MARCOS AGUINIS (1935–), Argentine writer and psychoanalyst, has been engaged since the 1960s in both literary and social endeavors. In addition to the practice of clinical psychiatry, his career has included the production of biographies, novels, short stories, essays, and journalistic articles, as well as work in public affairs, as the Minister of Culture from 1986–1987, and subsequently, as head of the governmental organization responsible for the redemocratization of national culture after the military repression (1976–1983). Aguinis's literary writing–not dissociated from his social and psychoanalytic concerns—is marked by criticism of the structures of Argentine society and by the recent tendency on the part of Argentine Jewish writers "to acknowledge the Jewish sources of their intellectual style or sense of social ethics" and "to focus on Jewish aspects of issues" (Lindstrom 1989, 163).

Aguinis's first published work (1963) was a biography of Maimónides. In justifying his identification with the Sephardic philosopher, the Argentine writer pointed out that they are both physicians and writers writing in languages of the diaspora (Francescato 1987, 61). As Francescato hypothesizes, underlying Aguinis's interest in Maimónides, "was the (. . .) need to put into perspective the Jewish contribution to the splendor of Spain as an indirect way of putting into perspective the Jewish presence in the Argentine soil" (61). Aguinis's choice of a Jewish theme for his first work to appear on the Argentine literary scene is indicative of a shift in position of Argentine Jewish intellectuals. It was in the post-Peronist era of the sixties that there emerged an Argentine Jewish literature, as Lindstrom has documented (23–31), which abandoned both the "centennial version of events"—Gerchunoff's praise of Argentina as the Promised Land of the Jews—and the assimilationist ideology endorsed in such works as Tiempo's *Pan Criollo*. Aguinis participated in the process through which Argentine Jewish writers began "to overcome the old anxiety that a discussant whose outlook is identified as Jewish will be perceived as insufficiently Argentine to speak of national affairs" (Lindstrom, 2). Within his own literary trajectory, Aguinis's early identification with a Hispanic Jewish figure may be seen as an affirmative statement of origins, an acknowledgement of an aspect of his identity rooted in Jewish history and tradition, that will be supplemented by a multiplicity of social identities projected in his later texts.

The mechanics of the constitution of Otherness is a theme central to Aguinis's writing and especially evident in the three works to be discussed in this chapter—*Refugiados* (1969), *La cruz invertida* (1970), and *Carta esperanzada a un general* (1983). The social construction of alterity is a question crucial to the analysis of Jewish diasporic writing. Jewish writers, in one way or another, are compelled to respond to the assimilationist ideology instituted by the Enlightenment and the French Revolution and re-echoed in modern times in Jean-Paul Sartre's (1954) definition: "Le Juif est un homme que les autres hommes tiennent pour Juif: voilà la vérité simple d'où il faut partir" (p. 84). ("The Jew is a man whom other men take to be Jewish: there is the simple truth from which our argument must begin.")[1] To escape from the position of absolute negative alterity to which, as Sartre remarks, numerous societies have confined the Jew, many Jews and Jewish thinkers choose the solution that Sartre imagines will occur only in the classless society, that is, identification with the concept of the universal man (184). Other contemporary Jewish writers have challenged Sartre's denial of a positivistic set of characteristics differentiating Jews from non-Jews.

Albert Memmi, a Tunisian born and French educated social philosopher—whose thought influenced Aguinis and other Argentine Jewish social critics of the sixties (Lindstrom, 34–35)—took exception in his *Portrait d'un Juif* (1962) to Sartre's negative definition of Jewishness by recognizing his own Jewishness as an empirical set of social facts: "La judéité est d'abord un ensemble de faits, de conduites, d'institutions que je rencontre en moi, mais surtout hors de moi, tout le long de ma vie" (p. 264). (Jewishness is, first of all, a collection of facts, behaviors, institutions that I find within myself, but especially outside myself, during the entire course of my life.) Memmi, nevertheless, was sensitive to the

---

1. All translations in this chapter are mine.

social and political risks of an ideology implying Jewish difference. In his *Libération du Juif* (1966), he makes it clear that it has been Rightist regimes which have traditionally cultivated the myth of national identity and tended to exclude Jews as a people or a race (198). Memmi considers the logical ideological position of the Jew to be on the Left, yet he underscores the dilemma of Leftist Jews, whose affirmation of Jewish identity (manifested, for instance, in some form of Zionism) seems to contradict what Memmi sees as the Marxist imperative to abolish differences (*Libération*, 201).

Aguinis's first novel, (*Refugiados* (1969), reedited under the title *Refugiados: crónica de un palestino* (1976), was first published in the midst of "massive questioning" in Argentine as well as in Western European and North American progressive political circles "of the propriety of liberal and leftist support for the Jewish homeland in Palestine" (Lindstrom, 33). Considering the polemical mood of the moment, it was an explicitly political act for an Argentine intellectual to place the question of Zionism at the core of a first novel. The novel represents the issue of alterity in a deconstructive mode; it breaks down the lines of difference defining the self and the Other within the context of the Palestinian-Israeli conflict. It speaks through the Sartrian dialectic and against it, by focusing on the instability of the social construction of difference and by denying any immutable, absolute quality to stereotypic alterity. It gives both Jewish and Islamic cultures a positivistic representation constituted, as suggested in Memmi's analysis, by a "collection of facts, behaviors, and institutions" attributed to the novel's characters, while representing these social facts and the subjectivities embodying them as open to change.

Refugiados proceeds through a series of displacements. The first displacement transfers a young Palestinian physician to Germany, where he holds a fellowship. Here he meets two displaced Israelis: Isaac Ben Aaron, a diplomat formerly involved with saving Jews from the Shoah and with founding the modern state of Israel, and his adopted daughter, Myriam, a scholarship student in the German university. The Palestinian physician saves the life of Ben Aaron, by performing his first case of brain surgery, and falls in love with his daughter. The refugee becomes friends with other displaced persons, a group of "Latin American" students of whom several are neither "Latin" nor "American"; his closest companion in the group is a Chilean Jewish doctor. The pluralism of the "Latin American" group is mirrored in the diversity among the Arab students portrayed in the novel; they are alternately united against Zionism and opposed to the Palestinian protagonist because of his insistence on preserving his friendships with a Latin American Jew and an Israeli.

The displacement of the three principal Jewish protagonists to Germany displaces the Arab-Israeli conflict with the Nazi/Jewish opposition, which itself becomes decentered by the predominant position in the novel of a German sociologist who worked in the resistance rescuing Jews, and a German lawyer, dedicated since the war to improving the plight of refugees throughout the world. After the defeat of the Nazis, this lawyer himself became a refugee, losing his wife and children in the flight from Breslau to Munich occasioned by the Allied partition of Germany. He becomes the friend of the Palestinian doctor, and later, his legal defender, when the Palestinian is accused of murdering Myriam, actually assassinated by a former Nazi who was responsible for sending her biological father, a German Jewish physician, to the extermination camps. A long narrative, embedded in the novel as the history of Myriam's escape from Nazi Germany, reenacts the Zionist struggle against the British in Palestine. By means of this historical kaleidoscope of shifting political oppositions and the shifting referents of the term "refugees," *Refugiados* suggests the possibility of a (utopian?) moment in history in which Jews and Arabs will no longer constitute for one another the inimical Other. As Myriam tells her Palestinian lover, quoting al-Farid, a poet of *his* culture: "Si no hay unión posible contigo, prométela al menos a mi esperanza" (177). ("If there is no possibility of union with you, promise it, at least, to my hope.")

The romantic relationship between Myriam and the Palestinian refugee is a metaphor, as Senkman (1983) remarks, for humanitarian, fraternal relations between Jews and Arabs. Myriam makes explicit the similarities between the two peoples of exile reflected in the novel's structure: "Ningún pueblo comprendería mejor a los árabes que el judío. Estoy convencida. Los judíos hemos padecido infinitas torturas. Casi siempre estuvimos solos" (206). ("No other people can understand the Arabs better than the Jews understand them. I am convinced of it. We Jews have suffered infinite tortures. We have almost always stood alone.") Senkman objects to the "twin identity" created for the two protagonists and the peoples they represent on the grounds that it "de-historicizes" the Palestinian-Israeli conflict (397). He accuses Aguinis of ignoring the dramatic dialectic of the Double and the Other in which the Palestinian, not the Nazi, represents alterity for the Israeli, and the Israeli, not the Syrian or Egyptian, occupies the place of the Palestinian's Other (398). Senkman views the novel's identification of the suffering of Jewish exiles with the suffering of Palestinian refugees, and its displacement of responsibility for the Palestinian defeat and evacuation in 1948 from the Zionists to the feudal fascist leadership of the Arab Mufti, as an attempt to assuage the guilt of Jewish Argentine intellectuals for the tragic massacres of the War of (Israeli) Liberation and the Six Day War and for Israeli occupation of Arab territories.

In one sense, my reading supports Senkman's argument, for *Refugiados*, subtitled in the 1976 edition: *crónica de un palestino* is constructed around a deception. It purports to speak for a Palestinian refugee, in accordance with the assumption prevalent among poststructuralist theoreticians "that intellectuals must attempt to disclose and know the discourse of society's Other" (Spivak, 1988, 272). In effect, from the opening of the novel, the subjectivity of the subaltern Palestinian is infiltrated by humanistic Western discourse. His position as a Palestinian refugee—displaced person, enemy of Israel and Zionism—is systematically appropriated. Through his reaction to saving the life of Ben Aaron (the Zionist): "No le veo ninguna trascendencia extramédica al asunto....Un hombre está herido y un médico lo cura. El médico no debe hacer diferencias con sus pacientes, eso es todo" (19). ("I see no extra-medical significance in the matter....A man is hurt and a doctor cures him. A doctor must not discriminate among his patients. That's all.") Through his friendship with Jorge Silverman (the universalist Jew): "Creo justo diferenciar a los judíos de Israel de los que no viven en Israel....Jorge me ha demostrado que un judío puede sentir afecto por un árabe y no sé si algún día llegará incluso a comprender la justicia de nuestra causa" (25). ("I think it is right to distinguish between the Jews of Israel and those who do not live in Israel....Jorge has shown me that a Jew can feel sympathy for an Arab and I wonder if one day he might not even understand the justice of our cause.") Through his susceptibility to the arguments of Freytag (the Western humanist), for whom the status of "refugee" becomes an accident of history common to innumerable citizens of our century: "Los refugiados palestinos nos hemos convertido en un pueblo espectral (como eran los judíos)....Año tras año prometen el retorno y nuestros corazones se alegran. Pero año tras año nos golpea otra frustración. Y entre alegría y frustración fue creciendo una conciencia nacional. Como ocurrió con los judíos. ¡Qué paradoja!" (60–61). ("We Palestinian refugees have become a spectral people [as were the Jews]....Year after year we are promised the return and our hearts become happy. But year after year another frustration strikes us. And between happiness and frustration a national consciousness has come into being. As it did for the Jews. What a paradox!") And, finally, through his infatuation with Myriam (the liberal Israeli): "De ella sólo conocía su nacimiento y su presente....¿Cómo Israel? Surgió de repente, con vigor, y se instaló en el centro de mi vida...¿Cómo Israel? Me fascinaba...y atemorizaba incluso" (207). ("Of her I knew only her birth and her presence....Like Israel? She appeared suddenly, with vigor, and occupied the center of my life. Like Israel? She fascinated me...and even made me afraid.")

By the end of the novel, the Palestinian's identity as a refugee has been shattered: "No sé lo que quiero...Somos y dejamos de ser casi siempre por obra de fuerzas que no nos pertenecen" (220). (" I do not know what I want...We are and we stop being what we are almost always because of forces beyond our control.") Although to some extent *Refugiados* is, as Francescato states, "an attempt to show the Palestinian's emotions, his loyalty, his suffering: to imagine the testimony of his bitter fate" (60), it is to a greater degree an apologetics seeking to convince the Palestinian (and the reader) of Zionism's definition as a movement of national liberation, of Israel's right to exist, of the willingness of liberal Israelis to establish the solution proposed by Myriam: "Un estado palestino con mayoría árabe junto al estado israelí con mayoría judía....Repartiéndonos el país" (207). ("A Palestinian state with an Arab majority beside an Israeli state with a Jewish majority....Partitioning the country between us.") The novel infiltrates the subjectivity of the subaltern, to whom the deceptively transparent author, as Francescato observes without noting the deceit, "*transfers his own desire* for peace, his repulsion for the absurdity of the sterile, frustrating, and unending war" (60, italics mine).

In spite of this appropriation of the Palestinian's discourse, the novel may be defended against Senkman's charge of misreading the dialectic of the Double and the Other in which Palestinians and Israelis are inexorably opposed. Historically, it may be argued, oppositions do become displaced. Aguinis's representation of the shifting lines of difference in the dialectic of the Palestinian and the Israeli, as well as in the German/Jewish polarity, corresponds to the application of psychoanalytic theory to social and political relations. According to this view, processes that define the self overlap with processes by which we project ourselves into images of the Other. Gilman (1985) describes the "protean" nature of these images and their historical and cultural variability in a description of the formation of stereotypes: "The models we employ to shape the stereotype are themselves protean....Every social group has a set vocabulary of images for this externalized Other. These images are the product of history and of a culture that perpetuates them....The ones that are invested with relatively greater force vary over time" (20). Gilman's presentation of psychoanalytic theory linking the processes of individuation with the social construction of the Other insists upon the shifting nature of lines of difference: "Difference is that which threatens order and control: it is the polar opposite to our group. This mental representation of difference is but the projection of the tension between control and its loss present within each individual in every group. That tension produces an anxiety that is given shape as the Other. The Other is protean because of its source, the conflicts within the individual as articulated in the vocabulary of the group" (21). Aguinis's writing, after *Refugiados*, only occasionally develops specifically Jewish themes, but the question of the shifting constitution of alterity—always relevant to the social construction of Jewish identity—continues to be a preoccupation in his major works.

La cruz invertida—the first Latin American novel to receive the Premio Planeta from one of Spain's prominent publishers—situates its story on the terrain of Latin America, although in an indeterminate country. It deals with the contemporary crisis of legitimation in the Catholic Church in Latin America. Whereas, traditionally, as Franco (1988) argues, the "paternalistic discourse of the Church" was used by capitalism in Latin America to discipline the work force of the hacienda and the mine (505), in recent years, the subversion of this discourse by the forces of social change within the institution, has been reinforced by "ferocious attacks on. . . .the Church by the very forces (the military) that rhetorically invoke" this institution (513). *La cruz invertida* delineates this process of change, in which the identification of the military and the Church—figured in the opening of Aguinis's novel in a dream image of an inverted cross resembling a sword enmeshed in a boot that is sinking into a swamp of gold—begins to come undone. The Catholic Church, which (like the Palestinian refuge) might have been projected as the Argentine Jewish writer's absolute Other, becomes instead a subjectivity in crisis divided by traditional and liberation theology discourses.

Carlos Samuel Torres, the Jesuit protagonist—created after the death of the Colombian revolutionary priest, Camilo Torres, and before the assassination of the Salvadorean archbishop, Oscar Romero—dialogues in the traditional discourse of the Church in an epistolary exchange with his uncle, Father Fermín Saldaño. For Carlos Samuel, the meaning of the Incarnation of Christ (his parish church is named Encarnación) is that God desired the physical as well as the spiritual salvation of humanity. The Church's divine mission places it on the side of social progress, of the liberation of the poor from the domination and exploitation by a handful of privileged rich. To his parishioners who cannot pay the rent or buy medicine or buy milk for their children, Father Torres cannot "asegurarles que con hambre, lágrimas y mansedumbre ganarán el cielo" (72) ("assure them that with hunger, tears, and gentleness they will get to heaven"). This would mean speaking the traditional ecclesiastical discourse that he rejects:

> Quisieron ir a la huelga. Yo los apoyé. Quisieron recurrir a la violencia. Yo los apoyé. Están desesperados e indignados. Monseñor Tardini me recriminó. Debería calmarlos, narcotizarlos. Para eso está la Iglesia, para estimular la mansedumbre, la paciencia...de los oprimidos. (72)

> (They wanted to go on strike. I supported them. They wanted to resort to violence. I supported them. I was supposed to calm them, drug them. This is what the Church is for, to encourage gentleness, patience...in the oppressed.)

Torres encourages insurgency, thus contradicting his uncle's admonition to uphold the Hispanic Church's tradition by maintaining order and a hierarchy of values:

> El comunismo penetró como un virus, circulando por todo el árbol arterial de nuestra sociedad. De su contacto no se libera el cerebro ni el corazón. ¡Ha penetrado en nuestra Santa Iglesia! Algunos sacerdotes sucumben a su infección provocando una consternación lógica entre los fieles....El aire pestilente sopla en las salas y corredores, atraviesa de parte a parte la Casa del Señor. (58)

> (Communism penetrated like a virus, circulating through the entire arterial trunk of our society. From this contact neither the mind nor the heart remains free. It has penetrated our Holy Church! Some priests succumb to its infection provoking a logical dismay among the faithful....The pestilential air blows through rooms and corridors, passes through and through the House of the Lord.)

Carlos Samuel's uncle evokes metaphorically the fissures in the monolithic subjectivity of the Catholic Church depicted in *La cruz invertida*.

Just as the discourse of the Church in Latin America becomes diversified in the novel, so do stereotypic oppositions become deflected. The militant communist lawyer Arturo Bello is the traditional projection of the Other for a priest like Fermín Saldaño, for whom he represents an infectious "virus," and, reciprocally, Bello's opposition to the Church is reflected in his own skeptical opinion of Carlos Samuel:

> Por más que quiera ser progresista, es un engranaje de la más vieja fuerza reaccionaría de la historia....Este cristianismo 'socialista' nació como

anticomunismo. No lo engendró la injusticia ni el dolor humano. Está aquí, en primer lugar, para hacernos la competencia. (10)

(As much as he wants to be progressive, he is a cog in the oldest reactionary force of history. . . .This 'socialist' Christianity was born from anti-Communism. Neither injustice nor human suffering engendered it. He is here, first of all, to compete with us.)

Nevertheless, when Torres visits Bello in jail to offer his assistance, after a night in which Colonel Pérez ordered the arrest of hundreds of "delinquents," including prostitutes and progressives, the discourses of the priest and the communist coincide in the analysis of the totalitarian strategy: "—¡Pérez es diabolicamente inteligente!—murmuró cabizbajo. —¡Ya lo creo!—coincidió Bello" (84). (" '—Pérez is diabolically intelligent!' he murmured with his head lowered. '—You said it!' agreed Bello.") While the novel bridges lines of difference between the Latin American Church and Marxist ideology, it also depicts Marxist discourse with cracks in its own subjectivity. Bello's daughter, Olga, a disciple of Carlos Samuel, opposes the "grass roots" ideological position of Latin American revolutionaries of the generation of the sixties who subscribe to the official, bureaucratic Communist Party discourse:

El escucha y respeta, papá. Es algo que en el Partido han olvidado hace mucho. Cree firmemente en su religión, pero no se cierra a nada ni se escandaliza por nada, si se lo expresan con honestidad. En cambio, ustedes tienen en funcionamiento un mecanismo en la cabeza, que sólo deja pasar por el oído lo que coincide con las últimas versiones de la Enciclopedia Soviética. (141).

(He listens with respect, Dad. That's something the Party forgot a long time ago. He believes firmly in his religion, but he isn't closed to anything and nothing shocks him, if it is expressed honestly. On the other hand, you and your comrades have a mechanism working in your heads that only lets you hear what coincides with the latest versions of the Soviet Encyclopedia.)

The anarchical tendencies of Olga's companion, Nestor, who has been disillusioned by his petty bourgeois Spanish parents' desertion of their Civil War republicanism, form still another line of difference in the split Leftist subjectivity. At the end of La cruz invertida, although the Church of the Encarnación is ravaged by the army and Carlos Samuel Torres is excommunicated, the dream sequence that closes the work places its events in a mythical, Judeo-Christian context implying perpetual repetition.

Aguinis's analysis of the constitution of the Other by social groups is explicitly theoretical and psychoanalytic in his essay, *Carta esperanzada a un general*. On one level, it constructs (from the outside) a polemical critique of the military establishment. Lindstrom has written of this essay that it is "one of the landmarks of this period" of renewed public discussion of Argentine political culture following the repression (164–65). At another level, it attempts—as in the case of the Palestinian refugee and the Catholic Church—to subvert traditional military discourse by revealing its internal cracks. Behind each militaristic gesture or appearance of authority, Aguinis's psychoanalytic discourse reveals an insecurity. Behind the uniforms and rituals there is "la angustia," (46) ("anxiety"), "la sensación de malestar, desprotección, peligro" (47) ("the feeling of uneasiness, unprotectedness, danger") that comes from the fear of disobeying superiors; behind the bravado of the call to reestablish order in society lies the obsessive fear of change perceived as a sign of chaos; behind the machistic code of honor is an adolescent doubt of virility.

The social structure of the military institution is undermined by its own ideology of uncritical submission to authority, which ultimately instills in its members the dependent mentality of a child:

> La organización militar es verticalista. No es de otra forma que un niño percibe el mundo: encima están los padres y abajo un hermanito o el pobre perro. El verticalismo permanente, sacralizado, no favorece la terminación de la dependencia. La dependencia frunce la nariz ante los riesgos de la libertad. Y sin libertad nadie es responsable. (157).

> (The military establishment is verticalist. It is in this way that a child perceives the world: above are the parents and below is the little brother or sister or the poor dog. Permanent, sanctified verticalism does not favor the end of dependence. Dependence frowns on the risks of freedom. And without freedom, no one is responsible.)

The guilty feelings of insufficiency and wickedess provoked by the authoritarian structure of the military institution can be relieved only by projecting the image of badness onto another social group:

> Para un militarista siempre existe un enemigo que lo amenaza, siempre hay un judío, un comunista, un negro, un masón, un capitalista, un marciano, en fin, que reúne los estigmas odiados (que son los suyos) a los que necesita destruir cuanto antes y completamente. Es obvio que nunca llega a la "solución final": tendría que suicidarse. (57).

> (For a militarist there always exists an enemy menacing him, there is always a Jew, a Communist, a black, a Mason, a capitalist, a martian,

who, finally, unites all hated affronts (his own) which must be immediately and totally destroyed. Obviously, he never achieves the "final solution": he would have to destroy himself.)

The *Carta esperanzada a un general* is subtitled *Puente sobre el abismo*. The subtitle corresponds to the rhetorical structure of the essay, a "letter," a gesture that if not constituting a dialogue at least suggests the possibility of a communicative exchange across distance. Here, again, there is an element of deceit, since it is Aguinis's own desire to undermine lines of difference that is repeatedly projected (not without irony) onto the general's imagined receptivity to criticism: "¿Usted sigue leyendo, General? ¡Felicitaciones! Es necesario tener fortaleza moral y confianza en sí mismo" (15). ("You are still reading, general? Congratulations! One must have moral strength and self-confidence.") By projecting (or fantasizing) a measure of comprehension on the part of his interlocutor and by evoking the history of military officers at odds with the authoritarian mentality, Aguinis seeks to broaden the fissures in the monolithic subjectivity of the military institution. Not only is the institution not what it seems—a powerful embodiment of omnipotence—but it is constituted by individual subjectivities not rigidly dissimilar and closed to other subjectivities of the society.

In an interview, Aguinis recounted the fact that publishing houses in the United States and Venezuela turned down the manuscript of *Refugiados* because they considered the novel to be anti-Semitic (Francescato, 61). On the other hand, while Aguinis served as Minister of Culture, an Argentine magazine of the extreme right featured an article labelling him as an "intellectual, democrat, Alfonsinist, psychoanalyst, Jew, Zionist" and accusing him of trying to establish "a totalitarian project" in which the morality of the masses would dominate, the primacy of the unconscious would be established, humanity would be disontologized, and God the Father would be eliminated (A. H. 1986, 6–7). The author's ideological position being pluralistic, it is not surprising that diverse ethnocentric social groups—with a rigid definition of Otherness extending to all individuals outside their narcissistic mirror image—view him as the embodiment of alterity. Ideological conflict provides the productive matrix of Aguinis's major works—*Refugiados: crónica de un palestino, La cruz invertida, Carta esperanzada a un general*—but these texts do not ultimately resolve the contradictions they represent. The ideological position of Aguinis's texts is progressive and humanistic. Placing their sympathies on the side of the oppressed, his writings point toward a moral solution to oppression through adherence to a principle that Western culture has defined as a universal human value: the view of the Other, beyond differences, as similar to one's Self.

REFERENCES

A. H. 1986. "Aguinis: Mala Letra." *Cabildo*. 102: 6–7.
Aguinis, Marcos. [1969] 1976. *Refugiados: crónica de un palestino*. Buenos Aires: Planeta.
———. [1970] 1977. *La cruz invertida*. Buenos Aires: Planeta.
———. 1983. *Carta esperanzada a un general: Puente sobre el abismo*. Buenos Aires: Planeta.
Francescato, Martha Paley. 1987. "Marcos Aguinis: A Controversial Argentine Jewish Writer." *Latin American Jewish Writers*. Folio, special issue, 17:57–63.
Franco, Jean. 1988. "Beyond Ethnocentrism: Gender, Power, and the Third-World Intelligentsia." In *Marxism and the Interpretation of Culture*, eds. Cary Nelson and Lawrence Grossberg, 271–313. Urbana: University of Illinois Press.
Gilman, Sander L. 1985. *Difference and Pathology: Stereotypes of Sexuality, Race, and Madness*. Ithaca: Cornell University Press.
Lindstrom, Naomi. 1989. *Jewish Issues in Argentine Literature: From Gerchunoff to Szichman*. Columbia: University of Missouri Press.
Memmi, Albert. 1962. *Portrait d'un Juif*. Paris: Gallimard.
———. 1966. *La libération du Juif*. Paris: Gallimard.
Sartre, Jean-Paul. 1954. *Réflexions sur la question juive*. Paris: Gallimard.
Senkman, Leonardo. 1983. *La identidad judía en la literatura argentina*. Buenos Aires: Pardes.
Spivak, Gayatri Chakravorty. 1988. "Can the Subaltern Speak?" In *Marxism and the Interpretation of Culture*, 503–515. See Franco 1988.

II

Lispector's Rethinking of Biblical and Mystical Discourse

FLORA SCHIMINOVICH

CLARICE LISPECTOR DIED OF CANCER in December of 1977 without knowing that she would become the focus of French feminist critics: "When I first encountered the texts of Clarice Lispector," says Hélene Cixous, "I remembered Celan's image of the bottle and the sea, the poem's journey to the reader. Reading Lispector, I saw the map of the world crossed by a voice, A message,"[1] Considered one of the most gifted and innovative Brazilian writers of the twentieth century, Lispector has been claimed by many groups and movements. Her works offer a wide variety of subjects and narrative strategies,[2] which are very different in nature and scope, reflecting the author's diverse intellectual and creative trajectory.

Clarice Lispector was born in Techtchelnik, Ukraine, in 1925. Her parents immigrated to Brazil when she was two months old. After living in Recife for almost twelve years, the family moved to Rio de Janeiro. In this city, Lispector became a lawyer and also worked as a journalist and a translator. In 1944, the same year that she graduated from law school, she published her first novel: *Perto do coração selvagem* (Close to the Savage Heart). This novel already anticipated the dazzling poetic imagination she would display in *The Stream of Life* (1973).

Lispector's reputation as a writer was first based on the philosophical aspects of her work; critics traced affinities between her and Heidegger, Kierkegaard and Sartre. With the publication of *The Apple in the Dark* (1961),

---

1. Hélène Cixous, "Conversation with Susan Sellers," 146.
2. Robert DiAntonio studies one of Lispector's novels, *A hora da estrela*, from both its ingenious construction as a reader-centered text and its sense of self as a pessimistic vision of contemporary philosophical, religious, and sociopolitical paradoxes. (DiAntonio, 164). DiAntonio's criticism should be read as a further development of the many issues and aesthetic responses implied in Lispector's works.

Lispector's fiction achieved general recognition. The novel was written in a style similar to Virginia Woolf's lyricism. Lispector was by nature an innovator, always willing to explore new modes of expression.

With the publication of her first novel, *The Passion According to G.H.* (1964), Lispector's fiction centered on character rather than plot, and it developed its characters through introspective or interior processes. In *The Passion...*, the author successfully blended poetic imagination with subtle and metaphysical experiences. *The Hour of the Star* (1977) was made into a film that received international recognition. French feminist critics, especially Hélène Cixous, use Lispector's writings as a model of *écriture féminine*—the inscription of the female body and female differences in language and writing.[3]

The importance of Clarice Lispector for modern Brazilian fiction has been established beyond dispute. She has been constantly hailed as a renovator of the national novel, both for steering it into the tradition represented by James Joyce and Virginia Woolf and for her concern with the poetic work, the aesthetic function of language.

After several years of fascination with the novels and tales of Lispector, I discovered one day that she was Jewish. I read that after her death, following a long battle with cancer, she was buried at the Cemitério Israelita do Caju, in Rio de Janeiro This multifaceted and innovative writer could now be incorporated into another tradition. The critic DiAntonio is of the opinion that, unlike the fiction of the Brazilian writer Moacyr Scliar and the American author Cynthia Ozick that "strongly expresses both traditional and mystical Jewish elements, Lispector's utilization of Jewish motifs or even a recognition of her Jewishness is less evident."[4] However, Di Antonio admits that in *The Hour of the Star* Lispector uses biblical and historical themes from her heritage.[5]

As a writer of Jewish origin, Clarice Lispector probably could not escape the past, the tradition that goes back to the bible. At the same time, she cannot be bound only to the past for she certainly belongs among the group of twentieth century experimental fiction writers characterized by their subversion of logic, closure, and authoritarian points of view. How do we reconcile these two apparently "contradictory" tendencies in Lispector's work? By focusing our reading at the crossroads of tradition

---

3. Marta Peixoto notes that before French feminist revisionist reading of Lispector, critics neglected to inquire into the specifically female dimension of Lispector's characters. Peixoto suggests that further critical readings from a feminist perspective will no doubt enrich Lispector's work with the discovery of previously unrecognized dimensions (188).

4. DiAntonio, "Aspects of Contemporary Judeo-Brazilian Writing," (118).

5. DiAntonio, 117.

and innovation—perhaps her new and original way of rethinking tradition—we can approach Lispector's texts with a better understanding of her singular worldview and unique narrative techniques.

Western thought has always attempted to thematize "the other." While in many cases the subject relationship to this "other" has appeared as an epistemological mode of interaction, it has also served as an instrument of mastery or domination. The creation and refining of speculation about "the other" have commanded the interest of the Hebrew imagination. Biblical form, the literary gesture by which the covenant is articulated— that is to say, the historical proceedings between Yahweh and his people— formulates the connection between subject and object or between knowledge and its object, expressing a sense of dependence. According to Robert Alter: "The biblical tale might usefully be regarded as a narrative experiment in the possibilities of moral, spiritual and historical knowledge, undertaken through a process of studied contrasts between the variously limited knowledge of the human characters and the divine omniscience quietly but firmly represented by the narrator."[6]

In the Judeo-Christian tradition, the story of symbolic knowledge is related to the Bible. God is the name of the law, the name of punishment by the masculine figure who cannot let himself act in a less powerful way because then there would be no society, no institutions.[7] Lispector's works are linked to the question of the subject; to speak in terms of the law is to identify with the law, with the "Other," with the rules governing languages, as a closed circular structure.

The texts of the Brazilian writer aim to establish a different relationship to the law; they explore sources of signification closer to a more innocent experience of living and writing, where there is no conflict between day and night or between good and evil. In her novel *Perto do coração selvagem* (Close to the Savage Heart), the main character, Joanna, is reprimanded by her aunt for shoplifting. Even though Joanna is a very young girl, she defiantly replies to the accusation, maintaining in essence that what she has done would be evil if she had stolen with a feeling of evil and fear. She has no fear and has taken the book willfully and consciously. (*Perto*, 51–52).

---

6. Robert Alter, 157.

7. Rosemary Radford Ruether argues that the feminist critique of sexism finds patriarchy not only in contemporary and historical Christian culture but also in the Bible. The Bible was shaped by males in a patriarchal culture that further canonized their patriarchal bias by eliminating traces of female experience. According to Radford, the Bible has become the authoritative source for the justification of patriarchy in Jewish and Christian society. See "Feminist Interpretation. . . ." 116.

At the heart of each of Lispector's fictions lies an epiphanic and metaphoric vision, images of "the Other" used to reverse or dismantle the hierarchial system of order and the law and to give presence and voice to what was denied or repressed. In *Close to the Savage Heart*, Lispector says that she continues to open and close circles of life. In *The Stream of Life* she achieves this. The question constantly raised is "Who lives? Who lives there?" *The Stream of Life* narrator states: "I write because I passionately want to speak. Even though writing is only giving me the great measure ot silence. And if I say 'I' it is because I don't dare say 'you' or 'we' or 'a person.' I am limited to the humble act of self-personalization through reducing myself, but I am the 'you are.' (*Stream*, 6).

Hélène Cixous has shown how an attentive reading of the biblical scene of "Eve in the Garden of Eden" highlights the functioning of the myth of an originary first term or logos (Western thinking is founded on this myth). The properties of the law become apparent. Not only is the law a word, but it is a word that has no meaning, since death does not exist in the paradisal state. The law also has a relationship to both knowlege and pleasure. Eve's response, her decision to follow her desire and refusal to grant the law its powers, inscribes not her submission but her defiance and subversion.[8]

In *The Stream of Life*, the question presented in the Garden of Eden cannot be resolved within the logic of prohibition and of permission. The hierarchical order of systems of knowledge and pleasures is introduced as an erotic subversion, as a poetic energy that agitates discourse by emotionally moving the reader: "First I gladly offer you the nectar, sweet juice that many flowers contain and insects avidly seek. . . Fertilization is the union of the two elements of generation—the masculine and the feminine—from which springs the fertile fruit. 'And the Lord God planted a garden in Eden, in the east; and there he put the man whom he had formed.' (Genesis 2:8) I want to paint a rose." (*Stream*, 45).

To write, keeping a dialogue between tradition and change, questioning the limits between self and other, masculine and feminine; these are Lispector's aims. In the texts of this Brazilian author, the biblical frame of reference takes many forms,[9] and while it is hard to establish a direct influence, the biblical references present the possibility of a dialectical

---

8. Hélène Cixous, "Extreme fidelity." 16.
9. The main character of *The Hour of the Star* fits Julia Kristeva's definitions of *l'abject*. Macabéa seems to reenact biblical abomination. The protagonist G.H. of *The Passion According to G.H.* holds a cockroach's white matter to her mouth and then vomits it with disgust. According to Kristeva, biblical abomination, with all the prohibitions and ritual purifying acts that is entails, has opened the way for the imposition of the logic that sets up the symbolic order. See Julia Kristeva, *Powers of Horror*.

encounter. In *The Stream of Life* the protagonist says: "Since God does not have a name, I'll give him the name of Simptar. It does not come from any language." (*Stream*, 35). In this process, the name of God has become a signifier, naming organizes the entire experience. It becomes a writing, a discourse that speaks by subversion and not according to the law.

Lispector's thinking takes place in the full stream of life, it is mostly poetic, immersed in its present context: "Now is an instant. And now, already is another one." (*Stream*, 21). "Is my theme the instant? My life theme," (*Stream*, 4). Like "The Song of Songs" in the Old Testament, Lispector's writings contain lyrical meaning in each of the parts of an unstructured whole. They trace a history of subjectivity, exploring, like in psychoanalysis, the multiple and possible identifications with the Other.

Hélène Cixous has said that in *The Stream of Life* one finds all the themes of *The Passion According to G.H.*[10] All the work on effacing the subject, the personal meditation on the writing process and language takes a new form in *The Passion. . .*, one of Lispector's most mystical works. This novel is a fictional work, a philosophical inquiry, and a mystical experience. The word *paixão* is the colloquial for love or lover, and it also refers to Christ's Passion.

In *The Passion According to G.H.*, Lispector also embarks upon a first-person narrative. The epistemological questions repeatedly raised in the earlier works are here explicated, though the crystal-clear syntax often has the deceptive simplicity of a Blake lyric. A tightly articulated network of images becomes the symbol of a woman's confrontation with an ultimate reality.

A seemingly trivial incident forms the basis of the plot of *A paixão segundo G.H.* The narrator and central character, named simply G.H., decides to clean up the room formerly occupied by her maid, a girl called Janair, who had left the previous day. G.H. has hardly entered the room when a cockroach emerges from a closet. G.H. tries to kill it but only manages to mangle it with the closet door. The cockroach, still alive, hangs there, turning legs and antennae and letting out a white mass. Hypnotized by the repulsive sight, G.H. falls into a kind of trance. A set of interlocked images, which have in common the suggestion of a many layered object (the layers of an onion, the geological layers of the earth, the several floors of the building), points to G.H.'s gradual plunge into her inner self. From the recapitulation of her relationship with the former maid, with her lover and with an aborted child, the narrator moves on to confront her own self, and her own existential anguish. We discover that G.H.'s whole life

---

10. Cixous, "Foreword," in *The Stream of Life*, XXXXIV.

has been a constant effort to arrange things around her, to frame reality according to traditional systems. She is also a sculptor, always trying to impose a shape on the material of life. She reminds us of Clarissa Dalloway,[11] Woolf's character who is also troubled by the compromises she has made in her life and is able to retain the "treasure" of a private self. Like Clarissa Dalloway, G.H. has almost become the social mask she has created for herself. Her full name is not known, only the initials are printed on elegant suitcases.

The general figure of *The Passion* is that of a quest: writing is experienced as an initiatory route across the topography of living, where G.H. goes forward in the light of questions. Her relation with the world is given by the writing of this book. But there is a great risk that in the quest of the other, the subject G.H. should lose the meeting with the other. The other, the one with whom it becomes a question of establishing a love relationship becomes a non-human subject.

"I swear that love is like that. I know, only because I was sitting there and I found out. Only because of the cockroach do I know that all that the two of us had before was already love. What had to happen was for the cockroach to hurt me like someone pulling out my fingernails—and then I couldn't stand the torture any longer and I confessed, and now I am telling it all...I am just in love with the cockroach. And it is hellish love," says G.H. (*Passion*, 106–107).

The texts of mysticism of the sixteenth and seventeenth century use the word "night" to describe their global situation, but they also apply it more particularly to ways of experiencing that situation as an existential question. Says the author in *The Passion*: "We are creatures who need to dive to the depths in order there to breathe, like fish dive in the water to breathe, only for me the depths are in the night air. The night is our latent state, night is my life, it grows late." (*Passion*, 121). The texts of mysticism are tales of "passions." The mystics' reinterpretation of the tradition is characterized by a set of procedures allowing a new treatment of language—of all contemporary language, not only the area delimited by theological knowledge or the corpus of patristic and scriptural works. Even when it is hard to postulate what constitutes a properly mystical text we can say that most mystical writings display a passion for what is, for the world as it exists, for the thing itself. Moreover, the experience by which mystic writings define themselves has as its essential elements the

---

11. The main character of Woolf's novel *Mrs. Dalloway* is convinced that there is a mystery at the heart of each person, even herself, and embarks in a voyage of discovery.

ego and the present. The spiritual labor cuts into the density of the world to make of it a dialogic discourse: I and thou seeking one another in the thickness of the same language: "¿A dónde te escondiste Amado y me dejaste con gemido?" (Where have You hidden Beloved, and left me moaning?), says St. John of the Cross.[12]

Clarice Lispector offers a modern day mysticism. Her plots are minimal, concentrating on the interior life of her characters, on "being in the world" and the problem of human existence.

G.H.'s main difficulty lies in her struggle to make herself small, to efface herself in order to perceive more clearly the things and events that surround her. Repressing her subjectivity prevents the protagonist from projecting already existing notions onto things in order to explain them. What is left is her own presence and the thing in itself, lying in front of her. Lispector dramatizes the difference between subject and object. In her narrative, the subject produces the "text" by giving the account of things. When G.H. arrives at the maid's room, she is surprised to discover figures drawn in black strokes on the white wall and she envisions that these figures are also traces opening up the first pages of the text of her life, an inscription that she is only beginning to decipher.

Who are you? Who or what says I? Is the "I" a fiction of the other, which offers itself in its place? Saint Teresa,[13] when discussing the "crystal-castle that is the soul," speaks of a disappearance (ecstasy) or death that constitutes the subject as pleasure (jouissance) in the other. "I is an other" is the secret told by the mystics long before the poetic experience of Rimbaud, Rilke, or Nietzsche. Writing as the giving of form to the other is the theme of *The Passion According to G.H.* G.H.'s writing gives form to G.H.'s experience, Clarice Lispector's attempt to understand, organize, and express G.H.'s story. It is the world and the self, the encounter and meeting of subject and object producing a new form. The writing "echoes" the experience of encountering the object to which it refers, making that existing intimacy more tangible, more poetic, more passionate, or as the narrator says: "To add infinitely to the entreaty born of lack." (*Passion*, 143). The use of the first person, Lispector's freedom to switch from the constant dialogue with herself to a more objective way of visualizing the events, the establishing of a space where change serves as a foundation, and expressing loss as "another beginning", these are some of the elements that make mysticism possible. After a long journey by the narrator of *The Passion*, we encounter this passage:

---

12. Saint John of the Cross, *Cántico espiritual*, in *Collected Works.* . . . , 416.
13. Saint Teresa de Jesus, *The Interior Castle*, 61.

Now I need your hand, not for me not to be afraid but for you not to be afraid. I know that believing in all this will, in the beginning, be a great solitude, for you, just like me, you will not be afraid to mingle in God's extreme energetic sweetness. Solitude is having only the human destiny.

And solitude is not needing.

Oh, my love, don't be afraid of that lacking: it is our greater destiny. Love is so much more fateful than I thought, love is as ingrained as is lack itself, and we are guaranteed by necessity that it is continually renewed. Love is now, is always. All that is missing is the coup-de-grace which is called passion. (*Passion*, 164).

Lispector's rethinking of biblical and mystical discourse brings to light the fact that certain concepts of analytic theory are inadequate to an understanding of how connections between body and language, between individual and socialized fantasy, between experience and desire and what is written between self and the world and between self and the Other are symbolized. Her texts question the validity of existing models and make impossible any reduction to a single form of meaning, to any hierarchical order or simple opposition. In her reading of *The Passion...*, Regina de Oliveira Machado emphasizes: "Perhaps here is where one can speak of a femininity in Clarice Lispector's texts: the writing is born of fissure and of loss and, to pursue the methaphor further, one could say that it is born of what is most maternal in construction and in language, a breach in the body of a construction, whether the wall of the maid's room or the construction of language and of the text. It is born of that point where language is opening, where it gives place, is a passage to something new."[14]

Lispector's novel modes of reading, thinking, and writing offer a new approach to tradition. Her originality and strength lie mostly in the way she deconstructs the concepts of the law and reveals its very working through metaphorical or poetic thinking. Her texts resist closure through a strategy that circumvents hegemonic exclusivities and oppositions. Rejecting the mechanisms of social control exerted by language, her discourse works against the reader's tendencies to stabilize meanings and consolidate textual power.

---

14. "Spinning Form," 108.

REFERENCES

Alter, Robert. *The Art of Biblical Narrative*. New York: Basic Books, 1981.

Cixous, Hélène. "Extreme Fidelity," in Susan Sellers ed. *Writing Differences: Readings from the Seminar of Hélène Cixous*, New York: Saint Martin's Press, 1988: 9–36.

De Certeau, Michel. *Heterologies. Discourse on the Other*. Trans. Brian Massumi. Minneapolis: University of Minnesota Press, 1986.

DiAntonio, Robert. *Brazilian Fiction. Aspects and Evolution of the Contemporary Narrative*. Fayetteville and London: The University of Arkansas Press, 1989.

Jakobson, Roman. *Selected Writings*. Vol. II. The Hague: Mouton, 1971.

Kristeva, Julia. *Powers of Horror. An Essay on Abjection*, trans. Leon S. Roudiez. New York: Columbia University Press, 1982.

Lispector, Clarice. *Perto do coração selvagem*. Rio de Janeiro: Vozes Ltda., 10th ed., 1984.

———. *The Hour of the Star*, trans. with an Afterword by Giovanni Pontiero. Manchester: Carcanet Press, 1986.

———. *The Passion According to G.H.* Trans. Ronald W. Sousa. Minneapolis: University of Minnesota Press, 1988.

———. *The Stream of Life*. Foreword by Hélène Cixous. Trans. Elizabeth Lowe and Earl Fitz. Minneapolis: University of Minnesota Press, 1989.

Oliveira Machado, Regina Helena de. "Spinning Form: Reading Clarice Lispector," *Writing Differences. Readings from the Seminar of Hélène Cixous*. Ed. Susan Sellers. New York: Saint Martin Press, 1988: 98–112.

Peixoto, Marta. "*Family Ties*, Female Development in Clarice Lispector," in *The Voyage in Fictions of Female Development*. Ed. Elizabeth Abel, Marianne Hirsh, and Elizabeth Langland. Hanover and London: New England University Press, 1983: 287–303.

Radford Rauther, Rosemary. "*Feminist Interpretation of the Bible*. Ed. Letty M. Russell. Philadelphia: The Westminster Press, 1985.

Sá, Olga da. *A escritura de Clarice Lispector*. Petrópolis: Voces, 1979.

Saint John of the Cross. *The Collected Works of Saint John of the Cross*. Washington: ICS Publications, 1979.

Saint Teresa of Jesus. *The Interior Castle*. Trans. by Kieran Kavanaugh and Otilio Rodríguez. New York: Paulist Press, 1979.

Woolf, Virginia. *Mrs. Dalloway*. London: Hogarth Press, 1947.

12

Aspects of the Jewish Presence in the Brazilian Narrative: The "Crypto-Jews"

REGINA IGEL

THE MANIFESTATION OF JEWISHNESS in the Brazilian narrative could be expected to be based on plots and characters of a Jewish nature, whether explicitly or implicitly embedded in the fictional discourse in Portuguese. One would think it would definitely imply the Jewish identity of its author, even if veiled. The Jewish authors of the Colonial Period on whom this study focuses were forced to hide their origins but nevertheless managed to imprint their fiction with their Jewish background, beliefs, and thoughts. In the course of almost five centuries of settlement in Brazil, the Jewish literary contribution was constant, except for certain involuntary lapses, as recorded by history.

The Jewish literary influence in Brazilian cultural life can be viewed in terms of the two extended periods into which the country's history is divided. Accordingly, they comprise the Colonial Period, which lasted from the European Discovery until the end of Portugal's control over Brazil (1500–1822), and the Independent Period, which spanned the Empire era (1822–1899), before the country was proclaimed a republic in 1899, and includes the twentieth century to the present day.

As far as the face of Jewish literature is concerned, each of these periods is distinguished by two different moods. One is characterized by a secret Judaic pulse, which can be perceived in the meager number of fictional writings that were conceived during the times of duress imposed by the Iberian Inquisition. The second, expressed through a liberated Judaic consciousness, reveals a sense of literary freedom of expression in contrast to the former.

Brazilian Jewish writings, rather scant during the nineteenth century and in the first quarter of the twentieth, gradually proliferated after the end of the Second World War. In spite of almost 500 years of Jewish establishment in the country, the last fifty proved to be the richest period of Judaic themes by Jewish writers. These are characterized by the authors' fondness for fiction over poetry or theater, recounting myriad experiences both within and beyond Brazilian frontiers. Already the focus of several critical studies are fictionists like Moacyr Scliar, Samuel Rawet, Clarice Lispector, Alberto Dines, and Zevi Ghivelder. This study covers the veiled side of those 500 years of Jewish contribution to Brazilian letters, dealing with writers who, as Jewish authors, remained invisible to their contemporaries: Bento Teixeira, Ambrósio Fernandes Brandão, and Antonio José da Silva, "The Jew."

The first Jews ever to set foot in Brazil, as far as documented history reveals, were of Sephardic origin. The fleet led by Pedro Alvares Cabral, whose voyage resulted in the "discovery of Brazil" on April 21, 1500, was a diverse company. From the admiral down to the last skipper, the seafarers were divided on religious matters as either Christians or Jews. While the former were proud to be recognized as "Old Christians," the latter were resigned to being dubbed "New Christians." These were, for the most part, former Jews forced into baptism at the prospect of being victimized by the Inquisition. It is assumed that a reasonable proportion continued to practice the forbidden Jewish faith in any way they could; if discovered by the inquisitors, they were branded "Judaizers" (*judaizantes*, in Portuguese) before paying the consequences for their "heresies."

Once settled in the new land, it was in such an atmosphere of secretiveness, camouflage, and persecution, that three literary pieces were authored by New Christians in Colonial Brazil. There is concealed in these works a Judaic vein, barely emerging through a few scarce innuendos to appear, respectively: in Bento Teixeira's poem *Prosopopéia* ("Eloquent Discourse"); in Ambrósio Fernandes Brandão's *Diálogo das grandezas do Brasil* ("Dialogue about the Greatness of Brazil"), an imaginary dialogue between two young men; and in Antonio José da Silva's *Obras do diabinho da mão furada* ("Tricks and Pranks of the Little Butterfingers Devil").

Bento Teixeira was born in Porto, Portugal, in 1561 and migrated with his family to Brazil at age five, where he was educated in Jesuit schools, practiced law, and taught Latin and mathematics. Teixeira is considered by some literary critics to be the first poet in Brazilian literature, chronologically. He led an adventurous life and was imprisoned several times, either under the suspicion of being a crypto-Jew or for other forms of civil disobedience. His ninety-four stanza epic poem "Eloquent Discourse" is an overwhelming exultation of the personal qualities and war victories of the then governor of the province of Pernambuco, where the poet was living at the time. Two of its verses seem to bear signals of Teixeira's alleged Judaizing activities: "May the grandiosity of your actions be sung / with sounds that will scare Air, Fire, Ocean and Earth!" ("Que a grandeza de vossos feitos cante / Com som, que Ar, Fogo, Mar e Terra espante!")[1] Historian Arnold Wiznitzer observed that the four elements linked in these verses were supposedly mentioned by Teixeira while talking to the priest who denounced him as a heretic to the Inquisition. In the conversation, Teixeira is said to have remarked that Adam must have died like any mortal, had he eaten the apple or not, for he was made of air, fire, water and earth, like the rest of the universe.[2] In the thirty-fifth stanza, Wiznitzer recognized "a continuous Jewish plaint, that the wicked prosper and the righteous endure pain and poverty," which appears in the Talmud (*Barachot* 7A) as "the righteous one suffers and the wicked one enjoys life." After denying the charges of being a "Judaizer" and being forced to abjure his heresies, Teixeira was sent as a prisoner to Lisbon, Portugal, where he died the year before his poem was published (1601).

Brazilian literary critics tend not to make an issue of the Judaic components of Teixeira's *Prosopopéia*. Actually, very few of them wrote about it, having devoted themselves to denigrating him as a copier of Camões' *The Lusiad*.[3] They found him rather mediocre, pointing out, for the benefit of novices in the history of Brazilian literature, some classic elements found in his verses. It is not at all surprising, therefore, that his "case" was taken by historians, who debated among themselves whether or not Bento Teixeira meant to imply his Judaic roots in these verses. The argument took a lively turn after Wiznitzer's conclusions on the poet's Jewish origin were refuted by the Brazilian bibliographer Rubens Borba de Moraes. In his article "Perguntas...,"[4] de Moraes discredits Wiznitzer by echoing historian Rodolfo Garcia, who implied that Teixeira wrote these verses as any cultivated man would, since he knew Christian and Judaic theologies, which for Teixeira would be a matter of quotation and not necessarily a crypto-message about his Judaic roots. The issue is still open, much to the discomfort of literary critics who had enough trouble trying to distinguish which among the works attributed to Bento Teixeira were really his and which were by another crypto-Jew, Ambrósio Fernandes Brandão.

1. These verses were transcribed in an article by Rubens Borba de Moraes, "Muitas Perguntas e Poucas Respostas sobre o Autor da 'Prosopopéia,'" *Comentário* V, 5, 17 (1964), 80.
2. Arnold Wiznitzer, *Jews in Colonial Brazil* (New York: Columbia University Press, 1960), 27.
3. Massaud Moisés, "Teixeira, Bento," *Pequeno Dicionário de Literatura Brasileira*, 2nd. ed. org. by Massaud Moisés and José Paulo Paes (São Paulo: Editora Cultrix, 1980), 418.
4. See Note 1.

A contemporary of Teixeira, Brandão is referred to in most volumes of Brazilian history as "a merchant and sugar planter who operated enterprises in Paraíba and Pernambuco... born in Portugal in 1555, Brandão arrived in Brazil in 1583 and settled in Olinda, Pernambuco."[5] Accounts of his contribution to Brazilian letters list a collection of six fictional dialogues between two men, Alviano and Brandônio, who supposedly represented opposing contemporary views on the incipient colonial Brazil. Brandão's cryptologic Jewish pulse was observed by Brazilian historian De Varhagen (quoted by Wiznitzer, note 2), in the disguise of a commentary by one of the two men on the possibility that Brazilian Indians were descendants from one of the legendary Ten Lost Tribes of Israel. The mere allusion to such a topic would have been enough for the condemnation of Brandão as a Judaizer, but the book was not published during his lifetime. Written in 1618, the *Dialogues* were unknown until a copy of the manuscript was discovered in Holland in 1848. It was 1930 before they were finally published in Brazil.

The topic of Brandão's Jewishness, however, has not yet been put to rest. Even when critics feel compelled to dismiss doubts about the author's origins, doubts still linger around them. The "Introduction" to the English version of the *Dialogues* states that they "provide little information about Brandão's religious faith. Almost pointedly, it seems, the author refrains from discussing religious matters.... But there is a notable scarcity of those references to the Virgin Mary and to Jesus that are so plentiful in many contemporary writings, and virtually all his scriptural allusions are to the Old Testament. The few points of doctrine that he mentions are common to the Jewish and the Christian faith (there was only one creation; all men are descended from Adam; God can do anything). These facts are, of course, too scanty to provide a conclusive answer to the questions of Brandão's religious beliefs."[6] Brandão's work has been read in part by generations of Brazilian students who are oriented toward its lyrical beauty and clarity of style, compared to the excesses of the Baroque atmosphere in which the author was immersed. The text is further enhanced by the information imparted in it about the inception of Brazilian society. No references are made, either in dictionaries or literary manuals, to the Judaic roots Wiznitzer pointed out as concealed in the exchange of ideas between the two Portuguese men.

---

5. "Introduction," *Dialogues of the Great Things of Brazil (Diálogos das grandezas do Brasil)*, *attributed to Ambrósio Fernandes Brandão*, translated and annotated by Frederick H. Hall, William F. Harrison, and Dorothy W. Welker (Albuquerque: University of New Mexico Press, 1986), 9.
6. *Ibid.*, 10.

As for a Judaic voice or its vestiges in the colonial period of Brazilian literature, these two authors are, as a matter of fact, seldom referred to as its representation by literary historians or critics. A third literary personality, however, arose about one hundred years after the death of Teixeira and Brandão, and his Jewish ancestry was brought up as if it were his only characteristic. José Antonio da Silva, lest his origin be forgotten, had a nickname appended to his full name, "O Judeu" ("The Jew"). Born in Rio de Janeiro in 1705, he died thirty-four years later in Lisbon, the victim of an *auto-da-fé*. At age eight, his parents were accused by the Inquisition of being Judaizers and forcibly removed from Brazil to Portugal, along with their children. The author spent the rest of his life in Lisbon, where he studied and practiced law, when not halted by imprisonment for the same suspicions that had earlier befallen his mother and father. Although he was a prolific playwright, he barely escaped total poverty by selling his plays, which were, even by contemporary standards, a great public success. As a playwright, da Silva combined the resources of Gil Vicente's popular theater and the Italian "opera buffa," thus creating a satirical text filled with a humorous view of his society set to instrumental music and voice.

Critics and literary historians agree that "The Jew's" plays are devoid of apparent Jewish vestiges or innuendos and that they bear no direct references to the author's Jewish origin. They are filled with ambiguities and veiled criticism of the Portuguese social and political affairs, enhanced on stage by *quid pro quos*, jokes, and other devices of the popular theater. These traits of da Silva's plays were overlooked by the Inquisition, which focused rather on the author's personal habits, such as wearing a clean shirt on Fridays, staying at home on Saturdays, or refusing to eat in the solitude of his cell during the many periods of incarceration he suffered. His individual choices were easily branded as actions typical of a Judaizer by his neighbors and servants who denounced him to the Inquisition.

Yet, da Silva's only literary work in which one can find allusions to his probable allegiance to the faith, and to a Judaic presence in Portugal and its social environment, is the short story "Obras do Diabinho da Mão Furada" ("The Tricks and Pranks of Little Butterfingers Devil"), where the author refers to the ever-present persecution of New Christians by the Inquisition. Literary critic José Carlos Bom Meihy, observing traces of Judaism in this work, comments that "to the historian of the Iberian society, of Judaism and of ideas, such a writing should not be unnoticed."[7] The

---

7. José Carlos Sebe Bom Meihy, "A literatura como defesa: O exemplo do teatro de Antônio José da Silva," *Boletim informativo, VII, 9* (São Paulo: Universidade de São Paulo, 1981), 13–19.

critic perceives that a parallel can be drawn between the hierarchy of the "Holy Inquisition" and the hell imagined by Antonio José da Silva in his story. He also proposes two levels of understanding for the plot: one, inconspicuous and metaphorical, was possibly directed towards the Jews of Portugal, as if subtly teaching them to avoid the pressures of the Inquisition by trickery like that of the little devil in the story; a second level, of course, would appeal directly to the masses attracted to amusing plays, such as the one exposing the little devil's pranks for the laughs. Moreover, the devil is a metaphor representing the alert Jew opposing the inquisitors, who are cunningly portrayed in the story as the "owners of Hell." Critic Meihy sees in the main character's physical clumsiness ("butterfingers") an allusion to the author's handicap. As a victim of the Inquisition, da Silva had been submitted to many sessions of physical torture, and as a result, according to the records, his hands became so useless for writing that he found difficult even the mere signing of the "confessions" extracted from him by his inquisitors. The Inquisition had da Silva eventually sent to his *auto-da-fé*, thus projecting the author for posterity as "the Jew," and so he is referred to by critics of literature and theater alike while recognizing him as an exceptional playwright.[8]

Between the self-effacing literary presence of Ambrósio Fernandes Brandão and the noticeably strong presence of Antonio José da Silva, there was a span of almost 150 years. During this period, as persecution by the Inquisition grew more severe, life became restless and increasingly dangerous for the New Christians. This explains the absence of literary works by New Christians, or crypto-Jews, either in Brazil or Portugal. The only pause in the phalangeal oppression conducted by the inquisitors was experienced when the Dutch invasion took place in the Brazilian northeastern region (1624). For the next thirty years, New Christians and Jews became acquainted with a parenthetical religious tolerance, though limited to the tiny area occupied by the Dutch, in what is now primarily the state of Pernambuco. During Dutch rule, many Portuguese Jews arrived from Holland, where they had first found refuge before settling in

---

8. The impact of the fate of "The Jew" in the histories of Brazil and Portugal reverberated in the literatures of both countries. Generations of writers succeeding the events that surrounded da Silva were touched by his tragedy, which became the source of several fictional works. Among the best known are: *Antonio José or the Poet and the Inquisition* (1839), a play by Brazilian romantic José Gonçalves de Magalhães; *The Jew*, a novel by Portuguese romantic fictionist Camilo Castelo Branco (1866); and a play bearing similar title, by Portuguese Bernardo Santareno (1924). For an encompassing bibliography see: Kathe Windmüller, *Antonio José ou Poeta da Inquisição* (São Paulo: Centro de Estudos Judaicos da FFLCH - USP, 1984).

Brazil.[9] For nearly the next 200 years, after the Portuguese recaptured the Pernambuco region from the Dutch, the Jewish presence in Portugal and its colonies became so scarce as to reach a zero population growth. Therefore, Jews were practically absent from Brazil when the country became independent from Portugal in 1822.[10] Even after the official banning of persecution of Jews, which was issued before the Independence, the shadows of the Inquisition were probably hovering vividly enough over the ex-colony as to become responsible for the self-curtailing of Jewish religious activities. Jews at large stayed a distance from the Brazilian shores until they felt somewhat assured that their religious rites would be tolerated in the newly independent country. Emperor Dom Pedro II (1831-1899) took the initiative to open the doors of his recently founded empire to immigrants, attracting them to Brazil to bolster its agricultural labor force.

The three colonial authors—Bento Teixeira, Ambrósio Fernandes Brandão and Antonio José da Silva—had been forced to refrain from exposing their Jewish faith, while subliminally evoking it. Proper recognition, however, is still due. Even today, Brazilian school manuals and teachers of history and literature still curb information on these authors. The pain of being born Jews, an "illegal act" during the Inquisition, was nevertheless woven into the authors' textual discourses, for which all of them paid with periods of humiliation (Brandão), imprisonment, and even their lives (Teixeira, da Silva).

---

9. Among the cultivated Jews arriving in Pernambuco was the Portuguese rabbi Isaac Aboab da Fonseca; upon disembarking in 1642, he found a synagogue that had had an organized congregation since 1637. While in Brazil, he authored many religious and related commentaries in Hebrew, whose examination exceeds the scope of the present study. Other than these works of specific range, no fictional or similar literary expression of Jewish content has reached the present day. The area where he settled along with Dutch and Portuguese Jews was eventually reconquered by the Christian Portuguese; as a result, fugitive Jews scattered through the Caribbean region, some of whom found their way to New Amsterdam, then a Dutch colony in the North American East Coast, later to become known as the Island of Manhattan.

10. Jayme Sapolnik, in A Contribuição Judaica à Independência do Brasil ("Jewish Contribution to Brazilian Independence," Bahia: Edições Convergência, Secretaria de Educação e Cultura do Estado da Bahia, 3rd ed., 1974) maintains that two prominent men of Jewish origin were of paramount importance in the political process of changing the country from a colony to an independent nation. They were Hipólito da Costa, born in Brazil in 1754, founder of "Correio Brasiliense," a liberal newspaper, during his exile in England; and Joaquim Gonçalves Ledo, also Brazilian, born in 1781, a freemason who vigorously fought in the press and elsewhere for the independence of his country. Apparently their individual Jewish origins were concealed. Da Costa's Jewish heritage was unveiled upon the Inquisition's accusation of his being a Jew, while Ledo's Jewish father is mentioned in several of his biographical notes (Sapolnik, 16–19).

13

Ethnic Identity in the Plays of Sabina Berman

SANDRA M. CYPESS

IF ONE WERE TO LOOK at the surname of Sabina Berman (1953), one might guess that she was of Jewish origin, yet most of her plays do not deal with particularly Jewish subjects or Jewish characters except for *Herejía* (1983, Heresy).[1] In that play, which was awarded the Premio Nacional de Teatro (National Theatre Prize) of 1983, she brings to the stage one of the important and painful episodes in Jewish and Hispanic history: the Inquisition's persecution of the Carbajal family in colonial Mexico. The important contributions of her play reflect the duality of her own identity as a Mexican and a writer of Jewish descent. Berman's exploration of the nature of ethnic identity is linked to its correlatives, recognition of difference and tolerance for cultural diversity. One of the recurrent themes in all her plays to date is the formation of identity, especially the idea of the definition of the self within a multicultural nation. Before analyzing the way *Herejía* conjoins her major preoccupations, I shall present a brief survey of how her other plays also insert the question of identity and difference into Mexican dramatic discourse.

From her first published play, *Bill* (1979), also known as *Yankee*, Berman has been concerned with the interrelationships between individual and national identities and the influences that impinge upon their formation.[2] The change in names of the play is a sign of the struggle she dramatizes: Bill is the name of the individuals while "Yankee" is the national category to which Bill belongs. Berman analyzes patterns of human experience that

---

1. In 1985 I first met Sabina Berman at her home in Mexico City. At a chance meeting with her father during that visit, he showed me a book that chronicled the lives of the Jews of Poland and their fate during the Holocaust. I bring up this anecdote to show that Jewish identity was not a hidden topic of the Berman family.
2. All references to her published plays refer to *Teatro de Sabina Berman* (Mexico: Editores Mexicanos Unidos, 1985). All translations from the Spanish are by me unless otherwise noted.

go beyond the initial context of Mexican-U.S. relations that the plot initially implicates. Although Bill may be a Yankee in Mexico, his individual struggle to understand himself and his interrelations with the Mexican family who takes him lifts him out of the stereotyped category of "enemy" or "Other." With this play Berman begins her deconstruction of official history and national myths that will be an essential subtext in *Herejía* as well. Whatever the official history or myths of national tradition may encourage us to think, Berman shows that human interactions on an individual level point out our commonalities, our shared human concerns.

Berman continues her investigation of identity and difference from a multinational perspective in *Rompecabezas* (1981, The Puzzle), also awarded the National Theater Prize given by INBA (Instituto Nacional de Bellas Artes). The play makes use of the techniques of documentary theater to present the assassination of Trotsky in Mexico in 1940.[3] Rather than clarify the historical event, however, the play directs the attention of the spectator to questions concerning the identity of both Trotsky and his assassin, the enigmatic Jacques Mornard. Since it is not my purpose here to analyze *Rompecabezas*, but to show how it relates to Berman's general project, I shall limit my comments to suggesting that "Trotsky"—both the man and the legend—represents an especially compelling figure for a Jewish Mexican writer interested in identity from both a national and ethnic perspective. Although Trotsky may have preferred to ignore his Jewish identity, and, indeed, favored assimilation, he could not escape being identified as of "Jewish background."[4] In Mexico, in particular, he stood out as a "Jewish type"; the Mexican writer Margo Glantz brings out this inability of Trotsky to avoid being identified as a Jew through an anecdote. She comments in her book of memories *Las genealogías* (1981, Genealogies) that when Trotsky was living in Mexico, her father was often identified as Trotsky and persecuted because of that confusion:

> La barba, el tipo de judío y quizá su parecido con Trotski hicieron de Jacobo Glantz el blanco perfecto para una especie de pogrom o linchamiento. (p. 122)

> (The beard, his look of a Jew, and perhaps his similarity to Trotsky, made Jacobo Glantz the perfect target for a pogrom or lynching).[5]

---

3. For helpful comments on documentary theater see Franz Haberl, "Peter Weiss: Documentary Theatre," *Books Abroad* 43 (1969), 359; Pedro Bravo Elizondo, "La realidad latinoamericana y el teatro documental," *Texto crítico* (1979): 200–10.
4. See Trotsky's biographical entry in *Encyclopedia Judaica* (Jerusalem: Keter, 1972) that refers to "Trotsky and the Jewish Question." vol. 15, 1404–06.
5. On the positive side, Diego Rivera used Glantz as a model for his portrayal of Trotsky (Glantz, *Las genealogías* 127).

Neither Jacobo Glantz nor Trotsky could escape being labelled as a Jew in Mexico because their physical appearance was markedly different from that of the majority of Mexicans—and from the stereotyped version of "Mexican." With regard to countering stereotyped reactions, Berman's play tries to strip away the superficial outer protective cover that encloses public personalities in order to *dis*cover the authentic aspects of the inner being.

Berman again uses the historical record to comment on national identity in another award-winning play, *Aguila o sol* (1984, Eagle or Sun).[6] Here she returns to the origins of Mexico and the clash of cultures that took place from the time the Aztecs first sighted the Spaniards until the death of Moctezuma. Berman states in the prologue to the published text that it was her clear intention to incorporate the point of view of those peoples who are generally excluded from the discursive enterprise in Mexico: "Se fundamenta en las crónicas indígenas de los sucesos, recopiladas por el maestro León Portilla en *La visión de los vencidos.*" (225). (The play is based on the indigenous chronicles of events as anthologized by Master León Portilla in *Broken Spears.*)

By going back to the conquest period, Berman questions the very formation of Mexican national identity and ethnicity. She shows that the official interpretation of the role of ethnic groups in Mexican history may not reflect the "true" situation, but represents only a version of events motivated by a particular ideology. By giving voice to different indigenous peoples, Berman reminds us that the ethnic differentiation among the various indigenous populations at the time of the conquest had been transformed by the Spanish conquistadors, so that all native people were considered part of a single ethnic category. In her satire, the Spaniards are demoted from their inscribed legendary position as gods or privileged people whose contributions to Mexican culture, as described from their perspective, should be singled out for special recognition. For example, one telling scene depicts the reactions of the Spaniards to the precious gold and jewel art objects made by the Indians. When the Spaniards express their desire to melt down the art objects to make gold bricks, even Moctezuma, who functions as their ally, is shocked at their philistine behavior. The scene in the treasure house, in which the group of Mexican Indians comments on the behavior of the Spaniards, points out the different cultural attitudes towards "art" and "precious objects." The Spaniards are labelled "monkeys" and "pigs" because they are unable to appreciate the true value of the precious objects:

---

6. For analyses of "Aquila o sol" see Sandra Messinger Cypess, "Dramaturgia femenina y transposición histórica," *Alba de América* 7, 12, & 13 (1989): 283–304; See also Cypess's "From Colonial Constucts to Feminist Figures: Re/visions by Mexican Women Dramatists," *Theatre Journal* 41.1 (1989): 492–504.

OTRO HOMBRE: Hicieron con todo un caldo de oro. . . .
UN HOMBRE: No pueden ser dioses. Y si son dioses, qué terror: son dioses ciegos, tienen el corazón de piedra. (258)

(*ANOTHER MAN*: They made a stew of gold out of our art of gold. . . .
A MAN: They can't be gods. And if they are gods, how awful! they are blind gods, they have hearts of stone.)

Similarly, Berman's presentation of Cortés serves as another brief illustration of her deft handling of revisionist history. She chooses to focus on linguistic signs as one way to recreate the real problems of communication attendant with the encounters between different ethnic groups. Cortés symbolizes the first speaker of Spanish on Mexican soil, although his language use distinguishes him from the indigenous characters on stage, ironically it is they who speak intelligible Spanish while Cortés speaks a humorous form of pidgin Spanish: "¿Gato por liebre, sucios negros trajinantes? ¿Mas cus-cus?io? nieve de orozuz" (234) (Cat for a hare, you dirty black traffickers? But 'fraid me-o? Licorice ice.) Cortés's language and actions on stage contradict the historical version of his behavior. The expectation is that he would speak in a manner understandable to the audience "since a concomitant feature of colonialism is the imposition of the language of the dominant culture on the colonized peoples."[7] The fact that Cortés cannot be understood without an interpreter is historically valid, yet the fact that his Spanish is so corrupted causes the audience to mock him and the imperialist enterprise for which he stands. Both in this play and in *Herejía*, Berman makes use of language difference as a technique to focus on a people's resistance to an oppressive culture. Berman's critique of the narrow Spanish perspective on ethnic identity is continued in *Herejía* with a special focus on religious identity. Just as *Aguila o sol* inserts into the national discourse a different perspective of the indigenous populations at the time of the conquest, *Herejía* presents on stage an ignored and painful aspect of Mexico's religious history.

Mexico is a nation with a restricted definition of nationality. The French cultural historian Jacques LaFaye defines Mexican nationality in terms of geography and religion: "Mexico is the combination of geographical zones and of ethnic communities which have in common the worship of the Virgin of Guadalupe and Mexico City as an urban force."[8] On the basis of such a definition, one must agree with Judith Laikin Elkin's comment:

---

7. Sandra Messinger Cypess, "From Colonial Constructs to Feminist Figures: Revisions by Mexican Women Dramatists," *Theatre Journal* 41.1 (1989), 501.

8. John Leddy Phelan, "Review of *Quetzalcóatl et Guadalupe, la formation de la conscience nationale au Mexique*" *Hispanic American Historial Review* 55.1 (1975), 105.

"The centrality of race to the concept of *Mexicanidad* and the impossibility of Jews being included in *la raza* raise impassable barriers for Mexican Jews."[9] By returning to the colonial period and dramatizing the particular experiences of the Carbajal family, Berman reminds her Mexican audience about the complexities of the Jewish presence in Mexico. Jews have been present since the inception of "Mexico" (that is, that nation formed from the union of indigenous and European races), but their minority status based on religious and ethnic distinctions has made them all but invisible in the official national history. In focusing on the experiences of the Jews in colonial Mexico as they face the terror of the Inquisition, Berman seems to be in agreement with the historian Anita Novinsky, when she remarks that "[i]t is impossible, to begin with, to speak of Jews in Latin America during the colonial period without mentioning the influence of the Inquisition. It was the reality of the Inquisition that oriented the destiny of the Jews..."[10] By electing to call her play *Herejía*, Berman recalls immediately the historical religious subtext: the Inquisition's persecution of those whose adherence to church dogma departed from established or accepted norms.[11] Because of the importance of the historical subtext, I believe it is useful to review some of the pertinent aspects of the history of Jews in colonial Mexico as a way to appreciate the play's impact and significance for contemporary Mexico.

Contrary to popular opinions, there is documented evidence that Jews arrived in New Spain from the very onset of the colonial period.[12] In *Los judíos en la Nueva España*, Alfonso Toro states:

> "fueron muchos los israelitas que pasaron al Nuevo Mundo, y que tuvieron parte en su conquista y descubrimiento, así como en la formación de la sociedad colonial, pues se le encontraron en todas las clases sociales, ejerciendo toda clase de profesiones y oficios." (there were many Israelites who went to the New World and who took part in its conquest and discovery as well as in the formation of colonial society; moreover, they

---

9. Judith Elkin Laikin, "The Evolution of the Latin American-Jewish Communities," in *The Jewish Presence*, ed. Judith Elkin Laikin and Gilbert W. Merkx (Boston: Allen & Unwin, 1987), 314.

10. Anita Novinsky, "Jewish Roots of Brazil," *The Jewish Presence in Latin America*, eds. Judith Laikin Elkin and Gilbert W. Merkx (Boston: Allen & Unwin, 1987), 34.

11. Some historians of the Inquisition believe that economic factors and political considerations as much as religious issues influenced the selection of victims. See Richard E. Greenleaf, *The Mexican Inquisition of the Sixteenth Century* (Albuquerque, NM: University of New Mexico Press, 1969), 5; Anita Novinsky, "Jewish Roots of Brazil," note 10.

12. See Seymour Liebman, *New World Jewry, 1493-1825: Requiem for the Forgotten* (New York: Ktav Publishing House, 1982).

could be found in all the social classes, performing all kinds of professions and occupations.)[13]

Despite this acknowledgement that Jews had arrived in the "New World" along with Columbus and had managed to persist in different colonies throughout the period of Spanish rule and into the era of national independence, the numbers and practices of the Jewish people intercalated among other peoples had received little attention in Latin American historiography until quite recently, as the investigations of Judith Elkin Laikin documents.[14] As one of the many marginalized "Others" in Latin America, they remained relatively hidden as a subject of discourse for reasons that may be labeled as much pragmatic as historical and cultural. According to Spanish beliefs in the colonial period, "the religious view of life was extremely powerful, [so] it was easy to believe that a religiously different group was inferior."[15] While it is well known that Spanish Jews were forced by law in 1492 either to leave Spain or to accept conversion to Catholicism, they were also prohibited by the edict of 1523 from officially emigrating to the "New World" as practicing Jews. Ever since the conquest religious issues and politics "have been linked closely. . ." and the Catholic church has long been identified with authoritarian power structures in Latin America to the detriment of any group with different beliefs."[16]

Subject to prejudice, discrimination, and segregation, members of the Jewish community often found it wise to avoid visibility that could lead to victimization by the officials in power. Many lived as crypto-Jews, or those who appeared on the surface to follow the beliefs and rituals of the Catholic church as New Christians but maintained their adherence to the Mosaic code of law in secret, in fear of the Inquisition. Because crypto-Jews only feigned formal assimilation and union with the majority, they were called "marranos" (a pejorative word derived from "pigs" that connotes a false profession of belief). Elkin observes that to this day, "Jewish marginality in Latin America expresses itself in a reluctance to

---

13. Alfonso Toro, *Los judíos en la Nueva España* (Mexico: Publicaciones del AGN, 1932), as quoted by Rafael Heliodoro Valle, "Judíos en México," *Revista Chilena de Historia y Geografía* 81, no. 89 (1936), 222.

14. See Laikin, "Latin America's Jews: A Review of Sources," *Latin American Research Review* 20.2 (1985), 124–41; also, Laikin and Merkx note in their Preface: "Scholarly research on Latin American Jewry has only recently come of age" (*The Jewish Presence in Latin America*, appears in note 9, ix.

15. George Eaton Simpson and J. Milton Yinger, *Racial and Cultural Minorities: An Analysis of Prejudice and Discrimination* 4th ed. (New York: Harper & Row, 1972), 107.

16. Daniel H. Levine, "Religion, Society and Politics: States of the Art," *Latin American Research Review* 16.3 (1981), 185.

submit to scholarly inquiry for fear that the results of any study will be misinterpreted and turned against Jews collectively."[17] She also adds that the Mexican Jewish community "has proved to be the most resistant" rather than the most accessible to North American (and I would add, Hispanic) scholars (137). Just as no new scholarship appeared on the Mexican Jewish community until the 1980s, relatively little has been written about their presence as writers or as literary figures: both Jewish Argentine writers and the presence of Jewish motifs in Argentine literature have been studied in far greater detail.[18] Although Berman is not the first Mexican writer to deal with Jewish motifs and experiences, she may well be the first to present *on stage* in Mexico both the Inquisition and its particular effects on a real family. She writes her play at a time in Mexican cultural history (post 1970s) when revisionist history has become the prevalent and acceptable perspective.[19] In the same manner that *Aguila o sol* questioned the myths and motifs of the conquest, *Herejía* challenges the doctrine of religious orthodoxy. She does not, however, repeat the same irreverent and cynical tone, but deals with the serious topic in a solemn and sober manner.

The Inquisition as a dramatic topic has rarely been treated. A comparison of *Herejía* with one of the more famous plays on the subject, *O santo inquérito* (1966), (The Holy Inquiry) by the Brazilian Alfredo Dias Gomes, shows that Berman's treatment is rooted in specific aspects of Jewish culture.[20] While it is not necessary that an author be of Jewish descent or background to deal with Jewish subjects, one notes that Dias Gomes uses Jewish characters in the universal tradition of the stage Jew, as studied by Ellen Schiff in *From Stereotype to Metaphor: The Jew in Contemporary Drama* (Albany: SUNY Press, 1982). Like Berman, Dias Gomes makes use of a recorded historical event. In the mid-1700s in Paraiba, Brazil, a secret Jewish community consisting of over forty-eight

17. Elkin, "Latin American Jews," 129.

18. See such works as Naomi Lindstrom, *Jewish Issues in Argentine Literature* (Columbia: University of Missouri Press, 1989); Saúl Sosnowski, "Contemporary Jewish-Argentine Writers: Tradition and Politics," *Latin American Literary Review* 6.12 (1978): 1–14; and in Spanish, Leonardo Senkman, *La identidad judía en la literatura argentina* (Buenos Aires: Editorial Pardés, 1983), and The Jewish Image in Brazilian and Argentine Literature, (unpublished dissertation) New York University, 1983.

19. See Thomas Benjamin, "The Leviathan on the Zócalo," *Latin American Research Review* 20.3 (1985), 217.

20. For critical articles on "O santo inquérito" written in English, see Sandra M. Cypess, "The Inquisition and the Jew in Latin American Drama," *New Horizons in Sephardic Studies* ed. Yedida Stillman and George Zucker (Albany: SUNY Press, 1991) in press: Leon F. Lyday, "The Theater of Alfredo Dias Gomes, *Dramatists in Revolt* Leon F. Lyday and George W. Woodyard, Eds. (Austin: University Texas Press, 1985) 221–242; George W. Woodyard, "A Metaphor for Repression; Two Portuguese Inquisition Plays," *Luso-Brazilian Review* 10.1 (1973): 68–75.

members was discovered and denounced to the Inquisition. According to Anita Novinsky, "One woman, Guiomar Nunes, was burned at the stake. She became the inspiration for a play by Dias Gomes, one of Brazil's greatest writers.[21] In Dias Gomes's play the Jewish woman, renamed Branca Dias, is accused and convicted of heresy, specifically of being a crypto-Jew, and burned at the stake for refusing to recant. Dias Gomes does not incorporate specific sociocultural behavioral elements that would distinguish the family as particularly Jewish in their actions. The play makes references to the general historical conditions that affected the Jews of Spain and Portugal as a result of the Edict of Expulsion of 1492, and to the practices of the Inquisition.[22]

The characterization of Branca and her father, however, fits the literary stereotype of the "belle Juive" and her repulsive father.[23] Dias Gomes changes the name of the historical character from "Guiomar Nunes" to "Branca" or "White" to show her purity and innocence: the use of the common surname Dias (not unintentionally, perhaps, an echo of part of the author's own name) raises her to a universal figure and encourages her identification not as "only a Jewess" but as "more than a Jew," for Dias Gomes considers her a symbol of all oppressed peoples and not the icon of Jewish persecution. Branca is described as the beautiful and innocent daughter of the crypto-Jew Samuel, who hides from his daughter her Jewish origins. Her relationship to the stereotype of the "belle Juive" is emphasized further when her innocent sensuality is used as the excuse for labeling her a heretic. Branca applies mouth-to-mouth resuscitation to Padre Bernardo to save him from drowning; when the priest realizes his own sexual attraction to her, he accuses her of heresy to mask his lustful feelings.

It is only after Branca is accused by Padre Bernardo of being a heretic that she is told the family secret: her grandfather had left Lisbon as a New Christian but had practiced Judaism in secret, as did her father. According to Branca, she was raised a Christian and so identifies herself as Christian:

Mas que querem? Que eu me considero uma herege, sem ser?...Não fui convertida, nasci cristão e como cristão tenho vivido até hoje." (100, 102)

(But what do you want: Should I consider myself a heretic although I am not?....I was not a convert, I was born a Christian and as a Christian I have lived to this day.)

---

21. Novinsky, 42, note 10.
22. For an informative review of the Inquisition's role in Brazil, in addition to Novinsky's work, see Patricia Aufderheide, "True Confessions: The Inquisition and Social Attitudes in Brazil at the Turn of the XVII Century," *Luso-Brazilian Review* 10, 2 (1973): 203–240.
23. Ellen Schiff, *From Stereotype to Metaphor: The Jewish Contemporary Drama.* Albany, NY, SUNY Press, (1982)

Despite her definition of religious identity, as the daughter of a Jew she is considered Jewish by her accusers. However, no mention is made of her mother, whose Jewishness would be required for Branca to be considered a Jew by Mosaic law. Dias Gomes does not take into consideration the Jewish need for maternal identity to be established in order for ethnic identity to be affirmed; the point is ignored in the development of the play's actions, since the concern is not for religious accuracy but for symbolic efficacy. Branca is meant to be a symbol of all those who are persecuted by a totalitarian system. Dias Gomes uses the Holy Office to symbolize any dictatorial power structure that brooks no opposition. Because of Brazil's repressive political system at the time of the play's production, the playwright was able to avoid censorship and at the same time present his critique of oppression by using the practices of the Inquisition as an allegory for his contemporary situation.

Despite the polarity set up between the Inquisition and the Jew by the nature of the topic, in the actual enactment of the play no specific Judaic practices are presented on stage that would identify them semiotically through gestures or through the use of Hebrew, a direct linguistic sign that Berman employs. The spectator must accept each character's word or definition of religious affiliation, since only by linguistic labeling are they identifiable as Jews. It is ironic that Dias Gomes falls into the trap of repeating a stereotyped view of the Jew in a play that is meant to glorify religious freedom and question "whether or not the church has the right to legislate beliefs, restrict liberty or demand conformity to a particular set of religious principles."[24] Branca, the daughter of a Jewish father, is treated as a heroine, a strong and steadfast figure who is willing to die for her beliefs—not for any abiding faith in Judaism, but for her belief in religious freedom. Her refusal to submit to torture, to acquiesce to persecution, is contrasted with the behavior of her father. Although he admits to his daughter that he is a crypto-Jew, he readily recants his faith under the threat of torture. He is derived from the same stereotype noted by Schiff for English drama, as "the repulsive father...a creature accursed and apart."[25] The portrayal of Samuel, the professing Jew, as a despicable character, while the true heroes are the martyred Branca and her Christian fiancé Augusto, certainly continues a negative characterization of Jews that deconstructs the playwright's ostensibly tolerant perspective and plea for religious freedom.

---

24. George W. Woodyard, "A Metaphor for Repression: Two Portuguese Inquisition Plays," *Luso-Brazilian Review* 10.1 (1973): 70–71.
25. Schiff, 4, 5.

In contrast to Dias Gomes's stereotyped account of Jews and his metaphorical use of the Inquisition, Berman defies stereotyping by emphasizing particular Jewish experiences.[26] She emphasizes the Jewish identity of her characters by including not only the Hebrew language, but also the enactment of important events in the Jewish life cycle from birth to death. It is not just that a casual reference is made to circumcision, a wedding, a funeral, or the weekly Sabbath observances, but that the appropriate linguistic and kinesic signs are included on stage as verification of the Jewish nature of her characters. She documents the *religious* practices in the same way that she makes use of the ample primary sources in the archives of the Inquisition and the historical documents that relate to the lives of the Carbajal family; Berman uses the techniques of documentary theatre to validate the somewhat controversial material, and to suggest her own dispassionate perspective and the explosive topic of the Carbajals' persecution and torture. Although the author provides a note to the play's script that cites the specific texts she used in the forming of the play, she does not use a realistic form of presentation nor a chronological order, but instead offers a theatricalized, or Brechtian, version of the information contained in documents: that is, she has selected key events that serve as synecdoches for the entire historical record of the Carbajal family. Instead of following a chronological development of events, she organizes the episodes to stress thematic developments. The first and last scenes, for example, portray acts of torture so there is no way the audience can forget the role of the Inquisition. She encourages the audience to witness events and maintain at all times the perspective of the judge, for the impartial judge was the participant missing from the drama of the Inquisition at the time its rites were performed.

A careful reading of the play text reveals that Berman was conscious that she was presenting material that would not be familiar to the general non-Jewish Mexican audience, to whom her play was addressed as much as it was to a Jewish audience. For example, it is important that Luis de Carbajal, el Mozo (the Younger, as he is called to distinguish him from his uncle the conquistador) reveal his decision to become circumcised as a sign of his firm adherence to Mosaic laws. In the scene that depicts his circumcision, he and his sister Viviana are alone in the countryside, and Viviana is translating into Spanish the Hebrew words of the Bible,

---

26. Compare what Simpson and Yinger observe, note 15, about the relationship between stereotyping and the denial of individuality and difference: "One of the functions of stereotypes is shown by. . . [its] failure to adjust to individual differences—to do so would be to destroy the discriminatory value of the stereotype" (154).

an expository technique that fits in well with the plot's trajectory as well as with the audience's need to understand the action in Spanish. As Viviana reads the biblical injunction that commands Abraham to submit to circumcision as a sign of his acceptance of God, Luis goes through the actions himself. The stage directions indicate that he is behind a palm tree as he performs the circumcision, and Viviana and the audience hear him groan as a verification of the act. This sacred Jewish rite is not portrayed as a barbaric bloodletting, as the tortures of the Inquisition will be presented, but as a positive and joyous sign of consent, a confirmation of his Jewish identity. Berman's dramatic technique stresses the Jewish perspective, for Luis cries and laughs at the same time (Llora y ríe, 185), and his own perspective is immediately verified when a chorus of people shout "*Mazal Tov*. Buena suerte. Felicidades." (185); ("*Mazal Tov*. Good luck. Congratulations.") The light dims on the scene of the circumcision and it is replaced by a wedding scene. As the light on stage grows stronger, the voices of acclamation grow mute, but clearly the clamor of congratulations applies both to the act of circumcision and to the wedding, a universally extolled act. Although weddings are common in both the Jewish and Christian worlds, the marriage ceremony presented on stage incorporates specific signs that mark it as a Jewish wedding: a "hupá" is brought out, a rabbi performs the ceremony in front of witnesses, and the groom breaks a glass as the final gesture that the service is completed. It is significant that in the published play script Berman offers an explanatory note for the reader about the nature of the "hupá" (186) that the members of the theatrical audience would not need since they would be witnessing the use of the actual object on stage.

Berman makes frequent use of the blending technique noted above, in which the action of one scene leads into the stage business of the next scene. The two scenes need not be related chronologically but are juxtaposed because of thematic relevance. Another good example is found in the linkage of scenes eight and nine. The wife of the conquistador Luis de Carbajal, Doña Guiomar, is reviewing aspects of Judaic rituals with her niece Doña Isabel. The religious song they chant at the end of their scene is picked up in the following scene in which Luis de Carbajal, el Mozo is shown to be imprisoned for his judaizing practices. The stage directions describe him in the Jewish stance of prayer so distinct from the traditional Catholic kneeling position:

> Calabozo. Luis de Carbajal, el Mozo, agacha y levanta y agacha el torso, en el movimiento usual de los judíos cuando rezan. Con voz baja continúa la oración que doña Isabel y doña Guiomar entonaban en la escena anterior. (164–165)

(Prison. Luis de Carbajal the Younger bends and raises and bends his body again, repeating the movements associated with Jewish prayer. In a low voice he continues the prayer that Donã Isabel and Doña Guiomar sang in the preceding scene.)

Luis notes that the light of the stars have entered his cell, signalling that the Sabbath has begun: his memory of his mother's prayers are recreated on stage when in a corner of the cell Doña Francisca appears and lights the Sabbath candles. The audience hears her recite the blessing in Hebrew, just as later in the scene another member of the family will intone the Kiddush, or the sanctification of the wine, and the blessing over the challah (165–66). Each character reproduces authentic aspects of Jewish ritual that are still performed today. By means of such a technique, the spectators witness not only the continuity of certain Jewish practices on stage, but the documentary context encourages them to think of the continuity of the actions beyond the stage, into real life. By presenting on stage a vivid reenactment of the particularities of Jewish life for both the men and women of the Carbajal family, Berman rescues them from their status of stereotypes. When she brings this marginalized group out of the wings into the spotlight, making visible their oppression, she also helps to defeat the objective of the Inquisition to silence and eliminate religious differences from the definition of Hispanic identity.

Berman's revisionist enterprise encompasses more than the decentering of Mexican national identity. She deconstructs some of the popular myths about Jews in Mexico and the true motives of the orthodoxy required by the Inquisition. She includes information that confirms some contemporary revisionist perspectives on the motives of the Inquisition, exposing its representatives not only as a vengeful "thought-police corps" as Dias Gomes also argues, but as a covetous economic power.[27] Although there is evidence that the conquistador himself was a sincere convert to Catholicism, and he is presented in that way in *Herejía*, the play action shows that the motivations for the persecution of the family include interest in their wealth and extensive land holdings, as well as personal jealousies and animosities.

In *Herejía* Berman has created a text that exhibits her dual cultural and national identity and that strives to be true to both facets. She rereads the past to integrate into the official national record episodes that many would prefer to ignore or forget. *Herejía*, like *Aguila o sol*, exposes the lie

---

27. Liebman, p. 21; I follow the research of Greenleaf, Liebman, and Novinsky concerning the ulterior motives of the Inquisition. With regard to *Herejía*, this point is elaborated in greater detail in my article "The Inquisition. . ."

inherent in the concept that Mexican cultural identity is a single, monotone hegemonic voice. Moreover, in the clash between orthodoxy and individual differences, Berman offers multiple centers of audience identification.

Herejía is a work of resurrection, a play that reverses the official record by turning legends and icons back into living human beings. The historical victory of the repressive Inquisition is proven ephemeral not only by the presence of the play text that gives voice to a people who were meant to be silenced, but also by the presence of an author whose identity is both Mexican and Jewish.

14

Angelina Muñiz's *Tierra adentro*: (Re)creating the Subject

EDWARD H. FRIEDMAN

ANGELINA MUÑIZ, THE WRITER, is indebted to predecessors who self-consciously acknowledge the authors and texts that promote and energize their individual literary enterprise. Born in 1937 in France to Spanish parents, she currently teaches Spanish and comparative literature at the Universidad Autónoma de México in Mexico City, contributes to a number of journals, and writes prose fiction and poetry. In an age of intertextuality, Muñiz resorts to other times, other places, and other modes of composition for inspiration, for starting points. Like Borges, an implied presence in her works, Muñiz creates by recreating, invents stories anew by retelling them in her own way. *Morada interior* (Internal Abode, 1972) is informed by *Las moradas*, Saint Teresa of Avila's narrative of the soul's journey toward union with God. The allegorical *La guerra del unicornio* (The War of the Unicorn, 1983) converts combatants in the Spanish Civil War into medieval knights. In the short story collection *Huerto cerrado, huerto sellado* (1985), translated by Lois Parkinson Zamora as *Enclosed Garden* (Pittsburgh: Latin American Literary Review Press, 1988), such "sources" as Sophocles, Sem Tob de Carrión, Garcilaso de la Vega, Luis de Góngora, San Juan de la Cruz, Sor Juana Inés de la Cruz, Fray Bartolomé de las Casas, Azorín, the Bible, and the Spanish ballad frame the selections. Muñiz unites reading and writing by using the rewritten story as her primary conceit. External reality makes its way into the texts in an indirect manner, through other texts. Her second novel, *Tierra adentro* (From the Interior, 1977), pays homage to the picaresque tradition and to the plight of the Jewish people in Inquisitorial Spain.

Picaresque narrative occupies a problematical place in literary history. The picaresque variously has been defined in terms of genres, mode, point of view, characterization and social status of the protagonist, and satire of idealistic literature.[1] One critic asks "Does the Picaresque Novel Exist?" and responds in the negative.[2] Questions of judgment tend to confuse *a prior* with *a posteriori* scrutiny. The matter bears analogy to the chronological dispute regarding the chicken and the egg, for in many cases novels are judged to be, or not to be, picaresque according to criteria derived from examination of works deemed to fit the category. From the end of the sixteenth century, there seems to be a certain cognizance of a picaresque model. The galley slave and autobiographer Ginés de Pasamonte of *Don Quixote* notes, for example, that his own "life" will surpass *Lazarillo de Tormes* (1554) and "all others of that kind [*género*] (I, 22). Generic self-consciousness of this type suggests not only that texts display variations on picaresque themes, but that novels from Mateo Alemán's *Guzmán de Alfarache* (1599) to contemporary works offer implied commentary on the picaresque through readings of the intertext. Each writer begins, in a manner of speaking, by confronting previous texts, by dealing with what Harold Bloom has called "the anxiety of influence."[3] The interplay of similitude and difference has fostered and enriched picaresque tradition, despite the fact that the abundance of texts and criticism does not make definition *per se* less elusive. In *Terra adentro*, the picaresque model is only part of the story, a major element of a hybrid text.

If there is a common ground for consideration of the picaresque, the general features probably would include a first-person narrator/protagonist, an outsider in the social hierarchy, and rites of passage, as well as a series of episodes in diverse locales and including figures from all strata of society.[4] One also may discover in picaresque texts an ironic manipulation

---

1. General studies of the picaresque include Robert Alter, *Rogue's Progress* (Cambridge: Harvard University Press, 1964); Alexander A. Parker, *Literature and the Delinquent* (Edinburgh: The University Press, 1967); Stuart Miller, *The Picaresque Novel* (Cleveland: The Press of Case Western Reserve University, 1967); Richard Bjornson, *The Picaresque Hero in European Fiction* (Madison: The University of Wisconsin Press, 1977); Harry Sieber, *The Picaresque* (London: Methuen, 1977); Alexander Blackburn, *The Myth of the Picaro* (Chapel Hill: The University of North Carolina Press, 1979); Peter N. Dunn, *The Spanish Picaresque Novel* (Boston: Twayne, 1979); Walter L. Read, *An Exemplary History of the Novel: The Quixotic Versus the Picaresque* (Chicago: University of Chicago Press, 1981); Helen H. Reed, *The Reader in the Picaresque Novel* (London: Tamesis, 1984); Francisco Rico, *The Spanish Picaresque Novel and the Point of View*, trans. Charles Davis, with Harry Sieber (Cambridge: Cambridge University Press, 1984); José Antonio Maravall, *La picaresca desde la historia social* (Madrid: Taurus, 1988); and Ulrich Wicks, *Picaresque Narrative, Picaresque Fictions* (New York: Greenwood Press, 1989).
2. Daniel Eisenberg, "Does the Picaresque Novel Exist?," *Kentucky Romance Quarterly* 26 (1979): 203–19.
3. Harold Bloom, *The Anxiety of Influence* (Oxford and New York: Oxford University Press, 1973).
4. Among the most influential generic treatments of the picaresque are three essays by Claudio Guillén ("Toward a Definition of the Picaresque," "On the Uses of Literary Genre,"

of discourse. The narrator, whose "voice" seems to be unmediated, is apparently the controlling agent of the story, and yet the picaresque speakers rarely assume full authority over the events they describe, over the words which they supposedly choose. In the process of explaining his "case" to the narratee addressed as Your Worship (Vuestra Merced), Lázaro de Tormes concludes that at the moment his narrative ends he is "at the height of all good fortune."[5] The story itself shows a man who has come full circle, as the discourse repeats the images and motifs of the opening chapter. Prosperity is relative, at best, and hardly free of irony. Similarly, Guzmán de Alfarache tells a story of sin and conversion, but his post-conversional discourse is never without bitterness or resentment toward his fellow men. When Juan Martí, under the pseudonym of Mateo Luján, publishes an unauthorized sequel to *Guzmán de Alfarache*, Mateo Alemán adds his own vengeance, and an ironically negative pattern of discourse, to the penitential stance of his narrator/protagonist. In *El Buscón* (1626), Francisco de Quevedo intrudes on the discourse of the protagonist Pablos by counterposing narrative situations and their representation. The text seems to say what Pablos may be attempting to avoid saying and to avoid showing: that he is greatly affected by the humiliations he has suffered, that he is filled with shame, that his life is a continuous mortification. The Baroque diolect through which he conveys his story is another sign of the presence of a voice-over, of an additional authorial presence in the text.

The concept of the "implied author," introduced by Wayne Booth in *The Rhetoric of Fiction*, may serve to illustrate the dynamics of picaresque discourse. The first-person narrator enjoys, arguably, only the illusion of authority, while ironies of language and circumstance mark changes in the direction of the text. The implied author, as distinguished from the real author, operates within the text to make the message system accessible to the (implied) reader. There is no reason for the mature Lázaro, for example, to underscore the similarities between his life and the lives of his ill-fated parents, or to provide linguistic and thematic links between the chapters of his account. Much of what Lázaro says emphasizes his failures rather than his successes; he is the object of a discourse which

---

"Genre and Countergenre: The Discovery of the Picaresque"), published in *Literature as System* (Princeton: Princeton University Press, 1971), 71–158. See also Ulrich Wicks, "The Nature of Picaresque Narrative: A Modal Approach," *PMLA* 89 (1974): 240–49.

5. Lázaro says at the end of the novel, "...en este tiempo estaba en mi prosperidad y en la cumbre de toda buena fortuna" (*La novela picaresca española*, I, ed. Francisco Rico [Barcelona: Planeta, 1967], 80).

belittles or demeans him and his social aspirations. His discursive style, in short, is not always to his advantage, and this would suggest the intervention of the author as representative of the dominant social order. Pablos of *El Buscón* goes to great lengths to insert himself into a hierarchical society in which upward mobility is not a viable option. The novel sets forth an acceptable standard of behavior, essentially the opposite of the codes and motives to which Pablos ascribes. Heredity both predetermines how one will be treated and precludes radical change. Pablos wants to be a gentleman, but society aims for stability, conformity, complacence. Within the text, the implied author becomes a standard bearer of sorts for institutionalized thought, yet another nemesis for the social upstart.[6]

The anonymous author of *Lazarillo de Tormes* opens the text by concealing a portion of its contextual associations. Of what social class is the author? Is he a New Christian or an enemy of New Christians, a conservative or a reformer, a satirist or a moralist? To what extent does he associate with his creation?[7] Because the identity of the author is unknown, the text itself gains increased authority. In contrast, what is known about Quevedo generally leads critics to view him as the polar opposite of Pablos. It seems unlikely that Pablos would be the alter-ego, rather than the antithesis, of his creator, and this point may strengthen the case for reading *El Buscón* as a type of double discourse that juxtaposes the narrator's commentary with the implied author's ironic countercommentary. In his collective writings, Quevedo shows himself to be an advocate of the class-conscious, ultra-conservative social establishment. When he controls the discourse of the lowborn, socially ambitious *pícaro*, as well as the events recounted in the discourse, he is free to mock the speaker, to conspire against him, as it were.[8] The discursive

---

6. For definition and discussion of the construct of the implied author, see Wayne C. Booth, *The Rhetoric of Fiction* (Chicago and London: The University of Chicago Press, 1961); Seymour Chatman, *Story and Discourse* (Ithaca and London: Cornell University Press, 1978); and Susan Sniader Lanser, *The Narrative Act* (Princeton: Princeton University Press, 1981); and, for an application of this construct to the picaresque see Edward H. Friedman, *The Antiheroine's Voice: Narrative Discourse and Transformations of the Picaresque* (Columbia: University of Missouri Press, 1987).

7. For general considerations of *Lazarillo de Tormes*, including the authorship issue, see R. O. Jones, Introduction, *Lazarillo de Tormes* (Manchester: Manchester University Press, 1963); A. D. Deyermond, *Lazarillo de Tormes: A Critical Guide* (London: Grant and Cutler, 1975); and Robert L. Fiore, *Lazarillo de Tormes*, (Boston: Twayne, 1984). Other critics, including Marcel Bataillon, Francisco Rico, Donald McGrady, and Thomas Hanrahan, have presented challenging perspectives on the question of authorship. See, for example, McGrady's "Social Irony in *Lazarillo de Tormes* and Its Implications for Authorship," *Romance Philology* 23 (1969–70): 557–67; and Hanrahan's "Lazarillo de Tormes: Erasmian Satire or Protestant Reform?," *Hispania* 66.3 (1983): 333–39.

8. See Edwin Williamson, "The Conflict between Author and Protagonist in Quevedo's *Buscón*," *Journal of Hispanic Philolgy* 2 (1977): 45–60.

scheme replicates the social order by subordinating the individual to the ruling temper. After Pablos describes his father and mother—a thief and a witch who wish to have their son follow their career choices—in the first chapter of the *Buscón* he thanks God for blessing him with parents so concerned for his well-being.[9] When he nearly succeeds in duping a gentlewoman, a fall from a horse puts him in his place toward the end of the narrative, as had an earlier fall during his youth.[10] And Pablos concludes, as he reaches the moment in which he will take off for America, that things cannot get better for one who changes locale but not life and customs.[11] The moralizing voice here may lack a certain freedom of expression.

In one of the most devastating episodes of *El Buscón*, Pablos is tormented by students and others in the university town of Alcalá de Henares. After having been insulted and spat upon, he fears his Moorish landlord is about to do the same and cries out, "Tened, huésped, que no soy *Ecce-Homo*"[12], thus denying that he is Jesus Christ, and, perhaps, by metonymy, that he is a Christian. If the Old Christian Quevedo punishes his narrator/protagonist for being unlike him, the New Christian Mateo Alemán must try harder to separate himself from Guzmán de Alfarache. Guzmán hopes to deny his bloodlines," but finds that all paths lead to rejection."[13] There is irony in the fact that while Guzmán is unsuccessful at distancing himself, literally and figuratively, from his father, so too is Alemán unable to keep his personal anguish out of the discourse of the narrative persona. The intervention of the author is especially evident when Guzmán is forced to react to the spurious sequel, to the detriment of the story of his conversion. Whether consciously or not, Alemán foregrounds on a subjective level precisely what his character seeks to conceal. A message of picaresque narrative seems to be that social determinism is a major factor in the way that one is perceived, and received, by others. When Pablos and his master Don Diego Coronel, travel to Alcalá, for example, they both suffer abuse on the road. After they reach

---

9. Chapter 1 of the *Buscón* ends, "Y yo me quedé solo, dando gracias a Dios porque me hizo hijo de padres tan hábiles y celosos de mi bien" (Francisco de Quevedo, *Vida del buscón llamado don Pablos*, ed. Fernando Lázaro Carreter, notes by Juan Alcina Franch [Barcelona: Juventud, 1968] 48).

10. See Book I, Chapter 2, and Book III, Chapter 7, of the *Buscón*.

11. Pablos observes at the end of the *Buscón* that "nunca mejora su estado quien muda solamente de lugar, y no de vida y costumbres" (254).

12. Quevedo, 83.

13. Guzmán wavers between distancing strategies, specifically a negative description of his father, and a desire to get to know his "noble" relatives in Italy. See Edward Nagy, "El anhelo de Guzmán de 'conocer su sangre': Una posibilidad interpretativa," *Kentucky Romance Quarterly* 16 (1970): 75–95.

the university, Don Diego is protected by those who fall under his father's influence while Pablos is scorned. It is not the inner self but the external projection of the self which determines one's social destiny, that is to say, one's identity.

Each of the archetypal picaresque narratives deals with the issue of lineage. The society in which the protagonists live and the texts which they inhabit establish restrictions for behavior and boundaries for self-improvement. The individual citizen and the narrator cede authority, respectively, to the State and to an implied author intent upon validating the hierarchical structure rejected by the protagonists. Pablos of *El Buscón* is the most presumptuous of the *pícaros*, in his endeavor to marry far above his social caste by inventing a new identity, but the past comes back to haunt him. Guzmán de Alfarache likewise attempts to eradicate his family history ("negar la sangre") as a means of escaping the negative associations and connotations of his Semitic background. Both characters—and, one might add, Mateo Alemán—address their feelings of inadequacy by overcompensating. Denying their blood, they embrace an extreme form of assimilation whereby they fight to inscribe themelves into Christian history. (This is the central conceit of Mario Szichman's *A las 20:25, la señora entró en la inmortalidad* [*At 8:25 Evita Became Immortal*, 1981].[14] Picaresque narratives are, for the most part, success stories gone awry, failed attempts at revisionist history. These stories demonstrate that there is no existence without context, no self without circumstance. In varying degrees, the question of purity of blood affects plot and resolution in the picaresque. In the Inquisitorial period, the marginated character who strives for integration into society has few opportunities to improve his lot. The world in which he lives limits his potential for growth and censors the authors who grant him narrative space, with or without their complicity.

If picaresque narrative concerns itself with what may be termed a negative identity, a fundamental element of the inverted perspective would be Jewish blood. The New Christian is always suspect, publicly ostracized not for what he is but for who he is. Such factors as delinquency and immorality, among those traits cited as "picaresque," are causes rather than effects of social treatment. The narratives themselves seem to bear the message that a system of poetic justice is at work in the texts, that the protagonists get what they deserve, but this would only be viable if there were alternatives to negative actions, if some form of upward mobility or social acceptability were possible. The picaresque presents instead a series

---

14. Szichman's novel was published in Spanish and in English (trans. Roberto Picciotto, 1983) by Ediciones del Norte.

of blind alleys; these are not lessons in how to triumph but in the preposterousness of a will to triumph.

The relation of *Tierra adentro* to picaresque narrative is noteworthy for points of contact and differences. Like the picaresque and the later *Bildungsroman*, the novel traces an education in the ways of the world. The narrator/protagonist undergoes a series of trials on a journey that brings him into contact with a wide range of social types. The background is a recognizable Spain, the Spain of the Inquisition, of social and religious wars. The status of the main character—an example of environment as a function of heredity—plays a crucial role in the story and in the discourse of the narrative. There is a clear disjunction between the individual and his society, an urgent need for him to defend himself against the obstacles that confront him at every stage of the story. Ostracism, solitude, and rejection are constants in his life, but he is never truly defenseless or completely alone. Muñiz borrows from romance a love interest, separation, and a final reunion (and happy ending) following what in idealistic fiction is a testing or probationary period. *Tierra adentro* nonetheless operates in a realistic mode dependent on its picaresque precedents. Here, the implied author becomes an advocate of the oppressed figure. The conspiratorial alliance of author and society is transformed, as in many of the twentieth-century variations of the picaresque, into a union of the (implied) author and the narrator/protagonist.[15] As part of the ironic reversal, the very element which in the earlier texts would have prescribed the condemnation of the marginated figure—his Jewish ancestry—is the unifying thread and the heart of the narrative. Muñiz rewrites the intertext by redefining margins, by decentering the images of the past. She takes a genre that, as a rule, undermines the aspirations of its protagonists, and, in the process, performs an undermining of her own, by presenting a heroic portrait and a discourse that is ironic only in its deviation from the norm.

The narrator/protagonist of *Tierra adentro* is Rafael, born in Toledo in 1547, a place and time in which a Jewish identity could only mean a lack of security. Those who give up their faith are never fully safe because they are never fully trusted. Those who practice Judaism in secret are always in danger of exposure. Rafael's father, a doctor, seeks whatever solace assimilation can provide. His maternal grandfather teaches the boy Hebrew and instills in him an awareness of tradition. Rafael begins his narrative around the year 1560, near the point, under other conditions, at which he would have celebrated his Bar Mitzvah. The father is not a coward,

---

15. The use of the individual/society dichotomy in picaresque fiction and its modification in the twentieth century form a central thesis of Friedman, *The Antiheroine's Voice*.

but a pragmatist. He reminds his son that in another setting or in periods of religious coexistence one could openly recite his Haftorah in a synagogue, but now the Jewish people are society's scapegoats, labeled as deicides, heretics, blasphemers, poisoners of wells, drinkers of blood, usurers, childkillers, enchanters.[16] The best path, he determines, is that of least resistance; before the public, one must be as inconspicuous as possible. Inspired by his elementary religious training, Rafael cannot accept his father's position. He refuses to give up his faith, whatever the consequences. He vows to accept the suffering that is certain to come his way in order to maintain his identity. He leaves Toledo in secret and sets out for Madrid, where he will seek a rabbi to teach him and to preside over his Bar Mitzvah.

The departure from home, the journey to unknown places, and the testing of survival instincts relate Rafael's story to the picaresque tradition. The events that occur on the road and the movement toward a particular goal reflect the earlier models, but the nature of the undertaking and the attitude of the protagonist are strikingly different. In a text such as *Guzmán de Alfarache*, the motivation is a burning desire on Guzmán's part to escape his Jewish roots, and the unifying element of the story is the theme of conversion, in a multiple sense. The *pícaro* rejects a family heritage in an attempt to make his way in the world. He wants life to be easier, more bearable, less defined by an identity over which he has no control. The classic picaresque narratives show that control in society and in the conventions of discourse is an illusion, that authority operates at a level beyond that which the protagonist can attain. *Lazarillo de Tormes, Guzmán de Alfarache*, and *El Buscón* are about, among other things, a sense of decorum, which to a large extent may be understood as social acceptability. Individual freedom is mediated by the greater good of the collectivity, and in this atmosphere it is rarely difficult to distinguish between what is sanctioned and what is condemned. In the drama of Golden Age Spain, one may find an exaltation of sorts of the common man (always an Old Christian), but the authority of noble blood—most notably, royal blood—is never in question.[17] The overreaching commoner threatens to destroy the hierarchical balance, and he must be thwarted at every step. The underlying premise of *Tierra adentro* bespeaks an attitude of tolerance and

---

16. "Estamos oprimidos, perseguidos, se nos acusa de deicidas, de usureros, de envenenadores de pozos, de bebedores de sangre, de infanticidas, de profanadores, de blasfemos, de hechiceros, de herejes" (Angelina Muñiz, *Tierra adentro* [Mexico City: Joaquín Mortiz, 1977] 13).

17. See Frank P. Casa, "Affirmation and Retraction in Golden Age Drama," *Neophilologus* 61 (1977): 551–64.

an historical distance from the events recounted. Not only does Muñiz use authorial control toward contrasting ends from those of her predecessors, but her work reflects a modified sensibility, determined in part by a lack of concern over censorship. She is no less the controlling agent of the protagonist's destiny, but he may enjoy her sympathy and her power of invention.

Rafael's commitment to his faith, despite the risks involved, establishes the direction of his journey and of his story. As he sees his people terrorized and killed, he affirms his identity. He recognizes that only his survival can assure the survival of the religion and can lead to a day when he can live in Spain in freedom.[18] As in the archetypal picaresque, the first adventure on the road takes place at an inn. The muleteer who has led Rafael to the inn disappears before he awakens, but turns up in Madrid and proves to be a type of guardian angel. While the danger is most grave, the protagonist is not without protection. Stoned at the entrance to Madrid, he is aided by a girl named Almudena, and in the Jewish quarter another young girl, Míriam, guides him to the house of the rabbi, Josef el Cohen. Welcomed into the rabbi's home, Rafael pursues biblical studies amid the sounds of torture and death. When his own death seems imminent, the rabbi refuses to flee, noting that a part of him, and of his faith, will survive in his student. Rafael responds in a defiant manner. He is more adamant than before about self- preservation. He will do anything to avoid being killed by those who would annihilate his people. After the rabbi's death, the muleteer leads him from the city. He returns to the inn, where he chastely spends the night with a girl whom he had met on his first visit there. On the way to Toledo, he reflects on his fate. His love for Spain conflicts with his love for Judaism, and the two seem irreconcilable. As it happens, destiny will make the choice for him.

The journey to Madrid gives Rafael the opportunity to test his independence. He cannot celebrate the Bar Mitzvah, but the experience corroborates his faith, brings him into manhood. On the road and in the city, he meets people who will play crucial roles in his life. Experience, substituting for the official religious ceremony, offers the rites of passage that will serve him in the future. The journey becomes life-sustaining in an ironic way, for when Rafael arrives in Toledo, he finds that his parents are prisoners of the Inquisition and that he is being hunted. He sees his grandfather, who, disoriented, wanders the streets praying in Hebrew. He

---

18. "...en el fondo seré yo, y sobreviviré por los siglos de los siglos y llegará el día en que ya no tenga ni que huir, ni que esconderme, ni que engañar, ni que mentir. Llegará el día en que regrese a mi tierra y ahí me quede" (Muñiz, 45).

learns that his mother and father will be burned in an *auto-da-fé* on the following day. It is at this moment when Rafael feels abandoned, totally alone. A woman named Helena gives him comfort and a sexual initiation, and he departs Toledo with the help of the muleteer, as the smoke from the *auto* rises toward the heavens. This is the definitive break from childhood: "Cruzamos la puerta. Me siento libre. Voy mirando el cielo, el último pedazo de cielo que verán mis padres" (We pass through the gate. I feel free. I look up at the sky, the last piece of sky that my parents will ever see).[19] The journey now will be toward the Holy Land.

Muñiz's decision to divide the protagonist's journey into two parts, with recourse to repetition of themes and events, may suggest the circular structure of picaresque narrative. One may note also an analogy with *Don Quixote*, Part I, in which Cervantes includes two sallies undertaken by the knight errant, the second intensifying a pattern established in the first. (Cervantes, like Rafael, was born in 1547.) Rafael's first journey takes him from Toledo to Madrid, the second through Spain and ultimately to Jerusalem. He will have the chance to observe the world, to reflect, to make choices regarding the future. The sympathetic reader—hardly the implied reader of picaresque fiction—probably will be inclined to respect the options he selects and the utter lack of fear with which he approaches the hardships on the road. Like his picaresque antecedents, he is without family and without a home, and yet he struggles to reach the Promised Land, the land of his people. In the picaresque tradition, coming full circle involves an ironic deconstruction of the protagonist's illusions of grandeur; in *Tierra adentro* it is a bittersweet fulfillment, a return to one's origins.

Rafael spends a full year with an alchemist devoted to the study of the philosopher's stone. This is a year for meditation, for dedication to a mystical science, and for further reading of the Bible. The silence and the otherworldliness of the alchemist give Rafael an increased sense of solitude. When he meets the muleteer at the end of the year, he feels depleted, empty. He rejects the battle to which he has devoted himself, claiming a loss of faith. In his helplessness, he will change course to live with the poor, to become one of them, and to emulate their suffering.[20] Disheartened by Rafael's position, the muleteer refuses to deliver a letter sent by Míriam. Rafael befriends an old beggar by giving him his cape, and he learns much about the underside of society and its peculiar rituals. Once again, he becomes an outsider, this time among outsiders, for the

---

19. Muñiz, 59.
20. "Me iré con los pobres, con los mendigos, con los que sufren de verdad, y aprenderé de ellos, me volveré como ellos" (Muñiz, 84).

group of beggars suspects that he is a heretic. When the old man dies, Rafael plans an escape. Certain that God has reserved a special destiny for him, he goes in search of the muleteer and the letter he bears.[21]

In this part of the narrative, Muñiz replaces action with contemplation, observation. This section has ties with the fifth chapter of *Lazarillo de Tormes*, in which Lázaro describes rather than participates in the plot events.[22] In *Tierra adentro*, as in the earlier text, the passage of time is significant in its own right, in order for the character to develop in accordance with his experience and reflection. Rafael is affected by his year with the alchemist. He loses faith and the aggressive stance toward survival. Ironically, perhaps, his degrading existence among the beggars renews his faith and his aggression. When he finds his guide and reads the optimistic letter from Míriam, he becomes more determined than ever to reach the Holy Land. The muleteer informs him that it is his special duty to aid those who, like Rafael and Míriam, desire to return to the Promised Land. The muleteer devises a strategy whereby Rafael will mix with the company of a dancer named Rodolfo in order to reenter Madrid. At the gates of the city he encounters Almudena, who "chastely" offers her body to him. Shortly thereafter, he is reunited with Míriam, seated at the same place in the Jewish quarter and dressed in the white dress that she was wearing at their first meeting. They join a diverse assemblage, including other disguised Jews, headed for the Holy Land. As the company makes its way out of Madrid, Rafael feels as if he were leaving a part of himself. Fearing that forgetfulness will temper his thoughts, he pledges to keep alive as many memories as possible.[23]

The travelers pass through France and Germany. They observe misery, war, plague. They are concerned for their own safety and bewildered by a world with no peace. Entering Italy, they find "a clear sky and a new sun,"[24] and a clock in the town square on which is written *Post tenebras lux* [After darkness, light] the phrase used in the title-page emblem of the 1605 and the 1615 *Don Quixote*. They spend time in a monastery before

---

21. "Estoy decidido a escapar de nuevo. Este mi constante huir debe tener algún sentido. Seguro Dios me guarda algún destino especial y me deja sobrevivir. Iré a buscar al arriero, esta vez no le pediré que me salve, pero sí que me dé la carta de Míriam que aún tiene consigo" (Muñiz, 101).
22. See Raymond S. Willis, "Lazarillo and the Pardoner: The Artistic Necessity of the Fifth *Tractado*" *Hispanic Review* 27 (1959): 267–79.
23. "Al llegar a la última puerta de Madrid, siento que se me desgarran las entrañas. De ahora en adelante, toda cosa que pase ante mis ojos estará marcada con la certeza del olvido, y me esfuerzo en que éste no llegue a ser, y en que la memoria sea tan poderosa que fije en cuadros todo lo que ya no habré de volver a ver" (Muñiz, 119).
24. "Entramos en tierras de Italia con un cielo limpio y un sol nuevo" (Muñiz, 153).

Rafael, Míriam, the nobleman Don Alvaro, and his page, in pilgrims' garb, board a ship bound for Turkey. Rafael sees a monk waving in the distance and realizes that it is the muleteer who has been his protector and guide. He spends his days on the ship studying the Bible and reflecting on the rabbi's teachings and on his family life. When the ship lands, the four travelers are pulled over by guards of a sultan, who make Don Alvaro pay for their "rescue" from the slave market, and they continue their journey toward Damascus. They reach the desert, and Rafael feels a strong need to be alone, to put his thoughts in order. He separates from Míriam, who will wait for him before entering Jerusalem. He celebrates the Sabbath in the home of a Jewish family and in a synagogue. He later joins Míriam and kisses a piece of the earth, wet with his tears. He considers himself at home in the land of his people.[25] Don Alvaro dies, entrusting his son, Gabriel, who had posed as his page, to Rafael and Míriam. The boy's mother was Jewish and had died at the hands of the Inquisition. Rafael and Míriam leave Gabriel with a rabbi in Jerusalem, and they make their way toward Safed (Safad), where Rafael will look for a friend of his father, a companion from the time of their medical studies. He succeeds in finding *Lázaro ben Israel* (italics mine), who helps the couple adapt to the new land. Rafael notes that he awakens each day to a different light, that he wakes up amazed, as if he were another, as if he had just been born.[26] And he closes the narrative with an allusion to the journey that continues within Spain: "A lo lejos, contra el horizonte, pasa el arriero con su carreta. Tierra adentro" (In the distance, against the horizon, the muleteer passes with his cart. Going inland.)[27]

Tierra adentro takes the solitary figure—the outsider—of picaresque fiction and engages him in a heroic struggle. The structural motifs remain constant, but the conceptual base of the narrative moves from the undoing of the narrator/protagonist to his elevation. Muñiz converts the picaresque plot into a success story, while she portrays the tragic existence—and the tragic demise—of the New Christians in Spain. Rafael's journeys show a world in chaos, a world of cruelty, in contrast to the land of milk and honey. It is an effective and wise stroke to end the work, together with the happy ending, with a reference to the ongoing persecution in Spain. The muleteer has a subtle role in the novel. He is as inconspicuous, yet as omnipresent, in the discourse as in the story. Rafael is never alone,

---

25. "He llegado. He tomado un punado de tierra y la he besado, y la tierra se ha humedecido con mis lágrimas. Es tierra mía, de mi pueblo. . ." (Muñiz, 170).

26. "Cada día abro los ojos a una luz diferente. Cada día despierto asombrado, como si fuera otro, como si hubiera nacido" (Muñiz, 177).

27. Muñiz, 177.

it would seem. God and this humble man are on his side, as is an implied author, who underscores the ironies of history but not of the narrating subject. Muñiz combines the intense realism of Inquisitorial times with a strong dose of idealism (the repeated return of the muleteer, set pieces such as the image of Míriam—in her white dress—awaiting Rafael, for example). The creative energy of the author supports her protagonists, just as the picaresque authors conspire to do their characters in. Rafael is a man of action and a scholar, decisive yet reflective. He is loyal to his people and, at the same time, patriotic. He dislikes having to leave Spain, and his homeland remains in his thoughts. He undergoes a number of trials which lead him to maturity. The theme of denying one's blood, as seen in *Guzmán de Alfarche*, is overturned here in favor of affirmation at all costs. The figure of Míriam offers a female counterpart of the protagonist. Their union assures that their children will be not only Jewish, but Spanish, and thus a positive, sustaining, alternative to the New Christians. Somewhat paradoxically, *Tierra adentro* follows its precedents with respect to the emphasis on identity.

Because of the age of the protagonist and the relatively short period covered in the narrative, the discourse of *Tierra adentro* does not carry the chronological force of the picaresque texts, which place a mature narrator against a more youthful protagonist, the voice of experience against the moment of experience. In *Tierra adentro* one might argue that distance is geographical rather than psychological, or that distance in this case relates to the juxtaposition of a sixteenth-century story with contemporary readers. The modern history of the Jewish people and the State of Israel are factors in the process of reader response. The intertext, including picaresque narrative, encompasses developments in literature and events in world history up to the present, and it is in this diachronic field that the irony of the novel is most pronounced. Muñiz transforms the shame felt by Guzmán and Pablos into pride and converts their incriminatory discourse into a rhetoric of liberation. The implied author, who controls story and discourse, has a counterpart in the text in the figure of the muleteer, who works behind the scenes, so to speak, to guide and direct Rafael.

One may applaud Muñiz's achievement in *Tierra adentro*, yet point to details which seem problematical. There are several anachronisms. In his reflections on the life of a *converso*—or Jew converted to Catholicism—during the journey from Madrid to Toledo, for example, Rafael alludes to El Greco (b. 1541), who settled in Toledo at around the age of forty, and to Velázquez (b. 1599).[28] In the section relating to the alchemist, there

---

28. Muñiz, 50.

is a "prophecy for future centuries," dated 1938, a consciously inserted anachronism which seems to have little bearing on the content or the context of Rafael's story.[29] Given the age and inexperience of the protagonist, the sexual attraction he seems to possess, as well as his self-confidence in the matter, may be overstated. On his second entry into Madrid, he goes to bed with Almudena who then calmly directs him to Míriam, an act which may puzzle the reader. True to their historical moment, the women of *Tierra adentro* serve men in one way or another; brave, patient, and self-sacrificing, they have learned to subordinate their needs to those of the men in their lives. Míriam is an obvious example of the idealized female image, a beautiful object dressed in white, full of optimism in spite of the violence which surrounds her, willing to wait as long as necessary for her beloved to appear. In the Holy Land, she will become a type of earth mother, love object, and procreator.

A key issue in terms of verisimilitude is Muñiz's skill in creating a voice for the narrator. Because the story is moving and unique in perspective, and because the discourse does not impact negatively upon the presentation of character or event, one might be reluctant to criticize the author's decision not to attempt a recreation of sixteenth-century discourse. (A recent example of this technique is Erica Jong's *Fanny, Being the True History of the Adventures of Fanny Hackabout-Jones* published in 1980, an exercise which combines eighteenth-century linguistic practice with a contemporary feminist sensibility.) Muñiz's choice affects specific linguistic aspects of discourse analysis, but the distinction between voice and voice-over, narrator and implied author, remains. The picaresque tradition parodies the noble quest of chivalric fiction. *Tierra adentro* tells of a noble quest that occupies the margins of Spanish history. The shared identity of author and protagonist is cause for pride, as well as the source of a shared perspective in which the enemy is the social norm. In rewriting her models, Muñiz seems more intent on recapturing a spirit than on defining a narrative voice. Appropriating a form and a topic from Golden Age Spain, she elevates her subject, in the double sense. She looks inward, "inland," to the interplay of literary and social history, of homeland and Diaspora.

---

29. Muñiz, 73.

15

Visions of Esther Seligson

ILAN STAVANS

> Again, could anything be more miraculous than an actual
> authentic Ghost? The English Johnson longed, all his life, to
> see one; but could not, though he went to Cock Lane, and
> thence to the church-vaults, and tapped on coffins. Foolish
> Doctor! Did he never, with the mind's eye as well as with
> the body's, look around him into that full tide of human life
> he so loved; did he never so much as look into Himself?
>
> Thomas Carlyle, "Sartor Resartus"

A WRITER WITHOUT A CRITIC is like a beauty without a mirror—
unreflected, unchallenged, uncelebrated. Esther Seligson is one such
writer. Beyond a handful of volatile book reviews and scattered articles,
little has been written on her. She has neither successors nor an echo;
she's out there, silent, an unheard voice. Readers who consult *A Dictionary
of Contemporary Latin American Authors*, 1975, edited by David William
Foster, will find that between Schinca, Milton and Shelley, Jaime Augusto,
her name is absent. Neither does it appear in *Mexico in Its Novel* by John
S. Brushwood, nor in the anthologies of Hispanic American women writers
by Alberto Manguel and Evelyn Picon Garfield. More recent is the 1989
study by Jean Franco, *Plotting Women*, concerning the feminine contribution
to Mexican art (i.e., photography, painting, films) and literature. Here one
comes across comments on Castellanos, María Antonieta Rivas Mercado,
María Luisa Puga, Sor Juana Inés de la Cruz, Ana de Aramburu, even
on Luis Buñuel and Anthony Quinn, but there is no trace of Seligson.

In 1930 Borges prophesized that Evaristo Carriego would soon become
part of the *ecclessia visibilis* of Argentine letters. The opposite applies for
Seligson: I believe she'll remain, perhaps forever, part of the *eclessia
invisibilis* of Mexican literature. The hard esoteric content of her art, so

unpopular and obscure, perpetuates her low profile and elitist appeal. No doubt she belongs to the firmament of female post World War II Mexican luminaries, alongside Inés Arredondo, Angeles Mastretta, Angelina Muñiz, Rosario Castellanos and the two Elenas: Garro and Poniatowska. Yet she's a phantom. Her best books have been published by minor publishing houses, in very limited editions. Add to this the fact that for years she was reluctant to grant interviews, appear at public events, and seemed content, almost pleased, to flaunt her recalcitrant, antisocial behavior.

But here's the clue: Such isolation, such nonpresence, is part of her creative being; Seligson wants to be invisible, unattached, concealed, unnamed—like her characters. It would be puerile of me to think I could remedy such reclusiveness in this all-too-brief evaluation. Besides, why bring light to an oeuvre the author herself has kept in obscurity? Of course, one could think of an anti-model, Kafka, who before dying indicated to his friend Max Brod that he wanted all his manuscripts burned. Yet thanks to Brod's stubborn disobedience we have more than just *The Metamorphosis* and a few stories published before 1924, the year Kafka died. Because of him, Kafka's art emerges in the encounter with others and his memory is honored today.

My objective here is not to antagonize Seligson by playing the redeeming Brod role; instead, I would like to point out a few intriguing elements in her work. Two reasons: in doing so, I will be leaving traces of the joyful, arresting moments when I first read her narratives; and, most of all, I'll be able to suggest what others are missing.

To begin, some biographical background. Since no dictionary is willing to include her, I have recoursed to inventing the *González-Wipper Encyclopedia of Mexican Appellations*. The following entry appears on pages 586–87 of the 1988 edition:

SELIGSON, Esther (Mexico, 1941). One of the key figures of feminine writing in Mexico. She possesses a keen eye for spirituality. Novelist as well as short-story teller, she has remained reluctant to accept the rules of realism.

Born in Mexico City on 25 October, her oeuvre, because of its Jewish content, belongs to the heterogeneos group of Latin American Jewish authors which includes Mario Szichman, Victor Perera, Luis Reznik, Alberto Gerchunoff, Moacyr Scliar, Isaac Goldemberg, Isaac Chocrón and Alicia Steimberg. Ironically, she shares no affinities with them: her topics are kabbalistic and introspective, her narrative style abstract. Perhaps she could be equated only with Angelina Muñiz, author of *Forbidden Garden*, as both women produce stories about medieval heretics, have akin interests in Jewish legends, the supernatural, scholarly codes, and employ the life of philosophers and mystics as sources of inspiration.

S. studied in Yavneh, a semi-orthodox Hebrew School in Mexico City. Early on in her career she contributed to *Plural,* under the editorship of Octavio Paz, and was one of the founding members of *Vuelta* and a short-lived Jewish magazine (1977–1978). Former wife of filmmaker Alfredo Joskowitch, with whom she has two sons, she was raised in a family with suicidal tendencies. A fellow of the Centro Mexicano de Escritores in 1970–71, in 1973 S. won the prestigious Xavier Villaurrutia Literary Prize for *Otros son los sueños* (Other Dreams). Using narrative devices she would elaborate upon in later works, characters in this book are not named as they are allegorical, metaphors or simply exist as sensations. The central figure is a female narrator, trapped in the triangle wife/mother/lover, from which she decides to escape in order to achieve a better understanding of herself.

Her most celebrated book, highly influenced by E. M. Cioran, the Rumanian-born thinker, is *La morada en el tiempo* (A Home in Time). It has been compared to Carlos Fuentes' *Terra Nostra* and Fernando del Paso's *Palinuro en Mexico,* although without the historiographical aspect.

S. has never been translated into other languages. She is presently a professor of literature and theater at Universidad Nacional Autónoma de Mexico and often lectures extensively on Kabbalah, Jewish esoterics and theater. Innovative, at times obtuse, her work is considered in the same vein as Edmund Jabés, Virginia Woolf, Clarice Lispector and Marguerite Yourcenar.

Although the entry is frugal, limited in scope, it's helpful in contextualizing Seligson. It offers a few scattered bibliographical references (quoted in the addenda at the end of this essay) so that curious readers pursue their own research.

To fulfill my next two intentions—examining some of her most accomplished titles and talking about some of her favorite themes—what follows is a list of her publications. There are nine books in total, published in Mexico unless otherwise noted. One novella: *Sed de mar* (Ocean Thirst), Artífice 1987. Two novels: *Otros son los sueños,* Editorial Novaro 1973, and *La morada en el tiempo,* Artífice 1987. Five collections of stories: *Tras la ventana un árbol* (Behind the Window a Tree), Editorial Bogavante 1969; *Tránsito del cuerpo* (Voyage Through the Body), La máquina de escribir 1977, later expanded in *Diálogos con el cuerpo* (Dialogues with the Body), Artífice 1981; *Luz de dos* (Light for Two), Joaquín Mortiz 1978; *De sueños, presagios y otras voces* (Dreams, Prophecies and Other Voices), UNAM 1978; and *Indicios y quimeras* (Intuitions and Fantasies), UAM 1988. And a book of essays:

La fugacidad como método de escritura (Fastness as a Writing Method), Plaza y Valdés 1988. She also translated, from French to Spanish, three books by Cioran: *Contra la historia* (Against History), Barcelona, Tusquets 1976; *La caída en el tiempo* (Man's Fall From Time), Caracas, Monte Avila 1977; *Del inconveniente de haber nacido* (The Inconvenience of Being Born), Madrid, Taurus 1980; and *Historia y utopía* (History and Utopia), Artífice 1981.

Elena Poniatowska once argued that women's literature belongs *sine qua non* to the literature of the oppressed. False! Marauding Seligson's oeuvre, one is likely to find references to passionate relationships, dependencies, and human attractions but never stories of political oppression, abuse, or incarceration, not even metaphorically. A partial list of her subjects includes emotional pilgrimage, personal reminscences, sexual and sensorial knowledge, love and the Western sense of responsibility. Her work is an ensemble of anonymous and iridescent characters, generalizations, ideas, and abstract thoughts. Take the Other, for example: appearing in numerous narrations, she's always an alter ego, a bisexual lover, a farewell sign, a companion in the voyage of the soul, a dream, an uncertainty and an undefeatable reminder of time—a shadow, never a definite person. Or take the clock, which, similar to Borges' story "The Secret Miracle" and Ambose Bierce's "An Occurrence at Owl Creek Bridge," in some texts stops to interrupt the continuum of life and bring insight, in others preludes eternity. Seligson is concerned with the aging of the human body, with our inescapable limitations, with cosmic mysteries. Her creatures are often aesthetes in search of metaphysical truth, most of them Jews in various diasporas, from Spain to Eastern Europe. Her plots are never set in Mexico, as if that would be too immediate.

No doubt *Indicios y quimeras*, a collection of amorphous narrations, can be taken as an introduction to her craft. Three of its pieces are outstanding. The first is "La invisible hora" (The Invisible Hour), containing echoes of Bruno Schulz and the Eastern European literary legacy best protrayed by Danilo Kiš, deals with a broken quartz watch taken to a specialist for repair. The description of the clock workshop underscores the agelessness of the place, locating it beyond terrennial ephimerality. Hence, the hero visits his afterdeath but only momentarily. What he sees is a brilliant landscape where jewels are shining and bodies are decomposing—a frightening, masterfully described sight! "Borrando huellas" (Erasing Fingerprints), the second story, like Jean Paul Sartre's *Nausea*, tells of a protagonist suddenly discovering he is molecularly, cellularly real—a revelation leading to an existential crisis. The third story, "Oscuro y olvidado" (Dark and Forgotten), is less an introspective narration than an exercise in the fantastic, one recalling Julio Cortázar's "House Possessed," Maupassant's *Le Horla* and Felipe Alfau's segment "A Romance of Dogs," from *Locos: A Comedy of Gestures*. With a powerful first-person voice, it depicts the adventure of someone overtaken by an awesome, inexplicable, transcendental force, one controlling all acts and limiting freedom. The reader gets no more than an overview of the difficult battle and eventual defeat of the protagonist. It begins in the character's big toe of the left foot, and ends with a bewildering suicide, succeeded by a monologue about the unknown.

Seligson's essays, most of them occasional pieces published in Mexican magazines and newspapers between 1967 and 1986 and collected in *La fugacidad como método de escritura*, throw light on her preferences, dislikes, and influences. They lack the precision of, for example, an Annie Dillard; instead, they indiscretely follow the fashion of French discursive evasion, so popular in Mexico in the pen of Octavio Paz. All of them are segmented, subjective, inconclusive; their hidden agenda is not to debate but to confess and self-explain, not to instruct but to find subtle chords that ring like music in the reader's ears. She deals with Greek myths and biblical images, the poet as citizen of a Platonic republic, the theology of Judaism, Christendom and Buddhism, the female character as androgynous—these are some of the subjects that confront and intrigue the author, the fountain from which her fiction flows.

As themes, myths appear mixed with images of love and separation in *Sed de mar*. This perhaps-too-short epistolary novella, reminiscent of Yourcenar's *Memoirs of Hadrian*, describes the anger, resentment and nostalgia experienced by Ulysses, who, at his return from Ithaca, discovers that his wife Penelope has left him for good. The language used is precious, the style exact and harmonious (Seymour Menton has called the book a small literary gem). As in *Otros son los sueños*, the female protagonist explains—in diary form, here—why she has decided to flee from her family life, to break away. While the scenario is Homeric, the characters acquire a human dimension through the writer's inner psychological inquisitiveness. The book would have become a favorite of Alfonso Reyes.

Yet I prefer *La morada en el tiempo*, more beautiful and engaging. Reading it is like penetrating a Renaissance document of the *spirito peregrino*. It's similar to Sor Juana Inés de la Cruz's *First Dream*, a text in which the soul travels to search for clues to the mysteries of the universe but ends disappointed, defeated, and empty. Although Seligson's novel is also a part of this *corpus hermeticum*, it doesn't present the soul as protagonist. The Spirit, a Hegelian ghost in constant mutation, travels through time. This very spirit comes to symbolize Israel, the Jewish people from the biblical period to our modern time, embarking on a pilgrimage to resolve enigmas but, also, to find a homeland, a permanent place to settle. Israel is personified in various archtypes: an Old Lady, perhaps the *shejinah* or female presence of God in the universe; Jacob and Rachel, the male and female symbols, an *Adam Kadmon* of sort divided into two parts, male and female, symbolizing all the Jews; the Craftman, a rebellious Neoplatonist creature (loosely based on Baruch Spinoza) with pantheistic views, who trusts that God appears even in the vulgar, futile element of nature; the Prophet, Israel's only future-teller; and the Citizen, a witness of history, a metaphor for all gentiles.

The narrative, abstract and amorphous, intertwines references to historical events with quotes from important documents such as the 1492 Edict of Expulsion of the Jews from Spain, a paragraph from the Talmud, an anecdote concerning the Maharal of Prague and his Golem, the modern Spanish poet Leon Felipe, the pseudo-messiah Sabbatai Zevi, the Baal Shem Tov, and the angels Metatron and Gabriel. Far from being a novel in the strict, romantic sense, this is an attempt to rewrite the Bible using the *Sefer ha-Zohar* and some other Kabbalistic and rabbinic sources. The book's origin reaches back to 1979, when Seligson translated one of Cioran's books and sent it to Spain, where it was lost. She, Seligson, used this as an excuse to travel to Europe. She stayed in Toledo, Prague, and later in Jerusalem, where she registered as a student at an orthodox *yeshiva* until expelled (her defiant presence wasn't a model for young seminarians). The three cities appear as temporary "homes" for the Jews: Toledo, scene of Spanish intellectual battles; Prague, house of melancholia, Kafka, and Ashkenazic Judaism; and Jerusalem, considered in the novel a temporary asylum for the nomadic, diasporic Jews.

Drafted at the end of 1974, but interrupted in 1975, *La morada en el tiempo* got its final shape (still considered unfinished by Seligson) between October 1979 and April 1980 and was published only a year later. It doesn't have a clearly defined development. And perhaps because both the author and Sor Juana are skeptics, in the end no spiritual fulfillment is achieved; but most of all, the discovery of the Absolute remains unreachable, beyond human strength, as does a permanent home for Israel. The moral, of course, is pessimistic: the several Jewish exiles are the essential mechanism that sets in motion the entire universe, which means that Israel's sorrow is an inherent need of nature. As claimed in the *González-Wipper Encyclopedia of Mexican Appellations*, this book is unquestionably the writer's best.

Seligson, like Nathaniel Hawthorne, nurtures herself from allegories, her fantasies possessed by archetypes of hell, earth, and eternity. One could claim that in her literary visions she describes the naked anonymity of man and tries to make art the least imperfect of our offerings to God. Ludwig Wittgenstein once forcefully argued that the aspects of life that are most important for us are hidden because of their simplicity and familiarity. In her texts, Seligson inquires as to what those aspects are and even when she is unable to find an answer, the inquiry is a pleasurable literary experience. She is a lonesome, ethereal wanderer with a desire to be outside the canon of Mexican letters—a ghost, a Jew without a territory, a mirage.

* * *

Addenda: Some of the ideas in this evaluation were first developed in a series of lectures at The Jewish Theological Seminary of America in New York City (7, 14, and 21 September 1986); later on, they were published in Mexico City in *Siempre!* (no. 1866, 29 March 1989), the literary supplement of *Uno más uno* (no. 472, 25 October 1986) and *Revista de la UNAM* (no. 443, December 1987). Additional sources on Seligson include an interview by E. Aguilar (*El universal*, 31 August 1981) and the notes by Angelina Muñiz on *La morada en el tiempo* (*Uno más uno*, 23 January 1982). See also the useful piece by J. Ann Duncan in *Ibero-Amerikanisches Archiv* (no. 10, 1983: 23–43) and the panoramic study by Seymour Menton *Hispania* no. 73, 2 May 1990: 366–70) on stories by Mexican women writers between 1970 and 1989, in which one of Seligson's titles is included.

I would like to finish with a personal confession: After reading all of the above, I realized, unhappily, that the true essence of Seligson's psyche had eluded me. A bizarre Oriental tale by Herbert A. Giles, part of *The Book of Fantasy* edited by Borges, Silvina Ocampo, and A. Bioy Casares, suddenly took over my mind. Chu Fu Tze, who didn't believe in miracles, died, claims Giles, while his son-in-law was watching over him. At dawn the coffin rose up of its own accord and hung noiselessly in the air, two feet from the ground. The pious son-in-law was terrified. "Oh venerable father-in-law," he begged. "Don't destroy my faith that miracles are possible." At this point the coffin descended slowly and the son-in-law regained his faith.

A deep and unexplainable story.

16

The Family, the World: The Poetry of José Kozer

JACOBO SEFAMÍ

JOSÉ KOZER WAS BORN IN Havana in 1940. He left Cuba in 1960 and has been teaching literature at Queens College since 1965. Kozer started his literary career in New York. He does not belong to any group, nor can his poetry be located in a particular movement within Latin American literature. His peculiarities have, as far as one can tell, no possible association.[1] Even though he has worked in other literary genres, such as essay and translation, Kozer is primarily a poet, in the most absolute possible sense. For him, poetic activity is a vital necessity; writing a poem is as important as breathing, eating, or sleeping. Therefore, the poet has written almost three thousand poems (only a small number have been published) in spite of being only fifty years old.

Kozer's poetry portrays the multiplicity and complexity of the world through a detailed account of daily events. Anything can be the subject of his poems. Kozer's work comprehends an enormous variety of themes that could be reduced to a single one: his search for totality is an obsession that leads to the ultimate consequences—the poet's family is the whole world and he sees in everything a key to understanding himself. Although Kozer respects tradition, his work reflects a voracious need for

---

1. Eduardo Milán relates the poetry of José Kozer to the work of some poets from Rio de la Plata: Osvaldo Lamborghini, Néstor Perlongher, Arturo Carrera, Roberto Echavarren, Emeterio Cerro and others (Rodolfo Hinostroza, David Huerta and Raúl Zurita, from Peru, Mexico and Chile respectively, are usually included in the list). Milán speaks of this group as the "neo-barroso", that is, a Neo-Baroque that comes from the "barro" (mud) of the Rio de la Plata. In general terms, the link of these poets is through language and form; their poetry uses irony, hyperbole, devices as a way of putting into question all models to make poetry. Although Kozer's work shares some of these basic assumptions, his poetry is unique in its long and complex verses; the poet's obsession with heterogeneity, totality, and oblivion has almost no relation to the above mentioned writers. See Eduardo Milán, *Una cierta mirada* (Mexico: Juan Pablos Editor, Universidad Autónoma Metropolitana, 1989).

experimentation, and experimentation not only means the search for new forms in language, but also a variety of aesthetic and philosophical attitudes towards art, life, ethics, spirituality, history, etc.

Kozer is the author of ten books and two anthologies. In chronological order, the books are: *Padres y otras profesiones* (Ancestors and Other Trades, 1972), *De Chepén a La Habana* (From Chepén to Havana, in collaboration with Isaac Goldemberg, 1973), *Este judío de números y letras* (This Jew of Numbers and Letters, 1975), *Y así tomaron posesión en las ciudades* (And Thus They Took Possession in the Cities, 1978), *La rueca de los semblantes* (The Winding of the Semblances, 1980), *Jarrón de las abreviaturas* (Abbreviations on an Urn, 1980), *La garza sin sombras* (The Heron without a Shadow, 1985), *El carillón de los muertos* (The Carillon of the Dead, 1987), *Carece de causa* (Lacking Cause, 1988) and *De donde oscilan los seres en sus proporciones* (On How Beings Oscillate in Harmony, 1990). The volume that has circulated most and has attained a wider audience for his poetry is an anthology published by the Fondo de Cultura Económica of Mexico in 1983, titled *Bajo este cien* (Under this Hundred).[2]

An assessment of Kozer's complete poetry would be difficult and perhaps unattainable. This brief essay deals mainly with his immediate family as a way of establishing a point of departure for the analysis and description of his poetry. Some of the basic assumptions in Kozer's poetry come after his revision of family conflicts and heritage. This is the first and most intimate circle: understanding this allows us to extend our critical observations to other areas of interest.

A genealogical tree of Kozar's work comprehends four generations: grandparents (mainly maternal), parents, sister, and daughters. The family shows a pattern of emigration. Kozer's father moved from Poland to Cuba;

---

2. In chronological order, Kozer's volumes of poetry are (he has also published five chapbooks):

Padres y otras profesiones, (New York: Ediciones Villamiseria, 1972).

De Chepén a la Habana, In collaboration with Isaac Goldemberg. (New York: Bayú Menorah, 1973).

Este judío de números y letras, (Tenerife: Nuestro Arte, 1975).

Y así tomaron posesión en las ciudades, (Barcelona: Ambito Literario, 1978). 2nd. ed., (Mexico: Universidad Nacional Autónoma de México, 1979).

La rueca de los semblantes, (León, Spain: Provincia, 1980).

Jarrón de las abreviaturas, (Mexico: Premiá Editora, 1980).

Antología breve, (Santo Domingo, Dominican Republic: Luna Cabeza Caliente, 1981).

Bajo este cien, (Mexico: Fondo de Cultura Económica, 1983).

La garza sin sombras, (Barcelona: Llibres del Mall, 1985).

El carillón de los muertos, (Buenos Aires: Ultimo Reino, 1987).

Carece de causa, (Buenos Aires: Ultimo Reino, 1988).

De donde oscilan los seres en sus proporciones, (La Laguna, Tenerife, Canary Islands: H. A. Editor, 1990).

earlier, his mother and her family came from Czechoslovakia to Havana. José Kozer considers himself the first and last generation born in Cuba, since he left in 1960 and settled in New York. This is why one cannot properly discern where this poet is from. Kozer is Cuban in terms of language, an Eastern European Jew in his tradition, and an American in his daily experience.[3]

There are many poems dedicated to the family. In the anthology *Bajo este cien*, one of the three sections uses family as the unifying theme. It is titled "Album de familia" ("Family Album") and is precisely an overview and submersion into his genealogical roots. Usually, the texts start with a reflection of an image, an evocation of the past, or a remembrance of a particular detail in an event. Kozer's deep analysis is not general and abstract, but more microscopic and liminal. His poetry is an elaboration of the circumstance: an insignificant act becomes a major quest for thought and knowledge.

In an interview with Miguel Angel Zapata, Kozer establishes a double and contradictory consciousness in understanding the world through his family. He explains his heritage in the following terms:

> The maternal heritage, where I evoke my grandfather, an orthodox Jew, believer, honest, dedicated with exclusivity to the idea of God....On the other hand, there is my father, the rebel, the one who isolates himself from his own father, from tradition and orthodoxy,...my father is a Marxist....He later will be disappointed, Stalin is going to disappoint him and in him there is nothing solved: he can not go back to God, nor to Marxism....I am in the middle, I am the intermediary; that is, the canal, the poet.[4] (Zapata, 172)

This double movement is going to be represented in Kozer's writing: there is an important sense of sacredness and respect for tradition, but also there is irreverence, nihilism, deception.[5] Although religious faith comes (from Kozer's maternal geneaology) in terms of Jewish orothodoxy as a way of life and also as the need to find God, spirituality does not appear only in those conditions. In Kozer's books, besides Kabbalah or rabbinical liturgy, there are other religious practices: Christian imagery and oriental philosophy.[6] Again, the search for the other is a form of

---

3. As we will see in "Gaudeamus," the poet finds pleasure identifying himself with many nationalities, races, religions, etc.

4. The original is in Spanish. This is my translation.

5. In many poems there is a pessimistic perception of reality. "Tierras de promisión" ("Promised Lands," from *La garza sin sombras*), for example, returns to the story of Moses and Mount Sinai, but to predict a future erected by scrap iron.

6. Interest in oriental philosophy started with four poems grouped in a section titled "Interludio" ("Interlude") in *Y así tomaron posesión en las ciudades*. In later books, oriental themes

discovering oneself. Attraction to forms of faith and totality is indicated, for example, in the structure of his books. *Bajo este cien* consists of three sections of thirty-three poems each and a final poem where everything culminates. Dante's model shows number three as the key cipher of unity and multiplicity of the divine. *Carece de causa* follows the parts of the Catholic mass: Introitus, Dies Irae, Offertorium, Miserere, Graduale, and Communio. Perhaps this perfect religious order counterpoises the chaotic implications of exile, extermination, war, and death.

Even though spirituality is associated with religion, in Kozer's poetry daily activities are also dealt with in a sacred manner. Domestic work, for example, is seen as a ritual that could lead to the secrets of splendor. Memories about the grandmother go to the space where she works; the kitchen becomes a sacred place because in it the basis of life is revealed. In "Evocación de abuela en casa" ("Evocation of Grandmother at Home"), we read:

> al atardecer la Pascua nos entregaste la forma del arenque en sus cremas,
>   alburas de una sopa de acelgas y tu hado
> nos embriagó
> con su olor a frambuesas y fue tu púlpito para nosotros tu horno con
>   su flan nuevo que olió a glorieta y nos agasajabas, vieja
> figura de Israel en su cítara. (Bajo este cien, 29.)

> (at dusk on Pesach you handed us the herring in its cream, egg whites
>   in a spinach soup and your destiny
> intoxicated us
> with its raspberry smell and your pulpit for us was your oven with its
>   fresh custard smelling of bowers and you paid us homage, old
> figure of Israel on your zither.) [Translated by Gregory Rabbasa.]

In the same way, the father's trade implies other connotations: being a tailor has an ulterior meaning in which the son will find divine designs. All seven poems in the section "Miserere" in *Carece de causa* are dedicated to exploring the relationship with the father. Very complex texts develop the idea of a double presence: that is, one is the texture, the weave, that in the terms of the son becomes text, language, literature; the other is the disenchantment, helplessness, loss, which prevail as a philosophical background for this poetry. It is important to indicate that all of the father's family (with the exception of one uncle) died in concentration camps during the Second World War. Kozer's poetry establishes itself as the

---

are frequent. See in particular *Jarrón de las abreviaturas* and the fourth section of *La garza sin sombras*.

communicative link, it is the expression of those who are unable to speak: his ancestors.[7] The last verse of "Requiem del sastre" ("Requiem of the Tailor") says:

> Nada: el constructor es otro. Mi padre es otro vástago suyo que ocupara la profesión de sastre (abejorro) cotidiano: urdió (y) urdió telas completas de miope vivo sentado con el pie sobre un escabel el filo de su pupila horadando la carne (alzando) un hilo al cielo (pobre) abejorro: a mí me vistió (países) vistió: reparia (enfebrecido) al final, sus hilos; (vástagos) truncos de lino (campos) azules, de algodón: hemos quedado (truncos) ambos muy de la mano viendo nevar (aquí) fuera (de la mano) mirando hilos al bies la nieve en alto (tú, traje de casimir que pareces un hidalgo pese a los puños de vegetal deshecho del saco; yo, pez que sube a mamar la fibra que se desprendió de tus borras). [*Carece de causa*, 81.]

> [Nothing: the maker is another. My father is one more of his off shoots taking up the mundane trade (bumblebee) of the tailor: he stitched (and) stitched entire rolls of fabric short-sighted sitting quick with a foot on the stool the ridge of his pupil piercing the skin (lifting) a thread to the sky (poor devil) bumblebee: he dressed me (countries) he dressed: handing out (feverish) at the end, his thread; truncated flax (fields) of blue, of cotton: we stayed (cut off) both clustering at the sight of snow (here) outside (of the hold) watching the warp snow on high (you, cashmere suit that makes you look like an *hidalgo* despite the cuffs vegetal jacket decomposed; I, a fish that alights to suckle the fiber that unraveled from your lining).] [Translated by Amiel Alcalay.]

In an earlier text ("Mi padre, que está vivo todavia", "My Father, Who is Still Alive"), Kozer explores deception and despair as ways of seeing reality in the world. Here, the link from father to son is visualized through a wider image: the tailor stitches suits that dress large populations, entire countries: nevertheless, the complete suit is still unfinished, with the material loose and the cuffs faintly marked for the initial fitting. The father's figure in this sense, acquires a quixotic dignity, but the son remains unprotected. The image of Christ looking again for his Father, God, seems to allow this assumption: "[F]ish that alights to suckle the fiber that unraveled from your lining."

The vision of simple stories that becomes major sources of revelations reaches its culmination in the last poems of *Bajo este cien* and *La garza sin sombras*. Both texts are seen as the final path of this poetry. One of them

---

7. A poem like "Holocausto" ("Holocaust", from *El carillón de los muertos*) ends with an incomplete word: "quieb", instead of "quiebra". The word itself, to break, shows the mutilation and annihilation within language.

is dedicated to Saint Francis of Assisi, the other (more radical, perhaps) to a cow.[8] In these two poems, the wonders of the world are found in their most natural, elemental, and superficial appearance. Religiosity is transformed into the simple acts of life. Francis of Assisi is the emblem of universal confraternity; everything reveals perfection:

> Desde sus ojos, ama las cosas del mundo: las muchachas en los fondos del estanque, los peces maravillados sobre la superficie del milagro de los mares, la propia escena de la crucifixión.
> Y como un riachuelo ama la incorrupta concatenación de las flores en la fértil horizontalidad de la bienaventuranza.
> Los lagartos reflejan al asno en la aparente divinidad de los rostros. (Bajo este cien, 136.)

> (From his eyes, love for the things of the world: maidens at the bottom of a pond, astonished fish on the face of the miraculous sea, the very scene of crucifixion.
> And like a little creek he loves the incorruptible link of, flowers on the fertile horizon of bliss.
> An ass reflects the lizards in the apparent divinity of their visage.)
> [Translated by Amiel Alcalay.]

Within this brief panorama of the family album, it is important to emphasize the presence of Guadalupe, the poet's wife. In *Bajo este cien*, the third part of the second section consists of eight texts about her. In these poems, Guadalupe is sensual evocation, but also tranquility. She gives light and nourishment; she is the purpose of life. In the face of wars and exterminations, Guadalupe is joy, peacefulness, jubilation:

> Lupe cantando en la cocina,
> toda la tierra adobada por Lupe,
> Lupe es el azúcar a montones en los muelles de La Habana,
> y yo vuelvo a emigrar por el salitre,
> y yo vuelvo a emigrar por la tierra cuajada de las ristras de ajo checoeslovaco,
> Lupe por el cantábrico católico como una colegiala...[*Bajo este cien*, 87.]

> (Lupe sings in the kitchen,
> the whole earth dressed by Lupe,
> Lupe is the mountains of sugar in the piers of Havana,
> and I am going to immigrate for the cane,

---

8. The last text of *La garza sin sombras* is titled "Margen" ("Margin") and represents the tranquility and peacefulness of a cow. The vision of the cow in a sacred manner reinforces the idea of basic and elemental things in life as a form to reach spirituality and perfection.

and I am going to immigrate for a land decked in strings of Czech garlic,
Lupe by the Catholic Cantabrian like a school girl...)
[Translated by Amiel Alcalay.]

In these lines, it is easy to determine how her being diversifies and contributes to the cultural idiosyncrasies of the poet. Through her, Kozer will find other ways of knowing more about himself. In an unpublished interview, the poet explains:

> I discover true softness and true tenderness through Guadalupe; my soft and tender roots, that are Cuban and maternal, are discovered through her. There is a confluence of materials that allow us to relate authentically and that softens daily life. Lupe becomes, not this specific woman, but a sign of something higher (not her, not me): the capacity, in a state of justice and freedom, to accede to equality.[9] (Sefamí, 208–209.)

In each member of his family (and in everything in the world), Kozer recognizes parts of him. Thus, when he has to define his own person, the poet identifies himself as a hybrid: a mixture of languages, cultures, origin, substances, etc. In "Gaudeamus" (in Latin, "Let's enjoy ourselves"), we read:

...(me privan) los mestizajes
(peruanismos) (mexicanismos)
de la dicción y los vocablos: ni soy uno (ni otro) ni soy recto ni ambiguo,
    bárbaramente
romo
y narigudo (barbas) asirias (ojos) oblicuos y vengo del otro lado
del río: cubano
y postalita (judío) y tabernáculo (shofar y taled) violín de la Aragón o
    primer corneta
de la Sonora Matancera: qué
más quisiera uno que no haber sido ibis migratorio (ludibrio) o corazón
esporádico...
soy así, él
y yo, cisterna y limbo (miríadas) las manos que trepan por la escala,
    contaminan
el pensamiento
de tiña y verdin (aguas) imperturbables: sin nación, quieto futuro
y jolgorio de marmitas redondas (mis manos) son mi raza que hurgan
    en la crepitación
de la materia. [*Bajo este cien*, 44]

---

9. The original is in Spanish. This is my translation.

(. . .mestizo
[Peruvian] [Mexican]
diction and vocabulary [overcomes me]: I'm neither one [nor the other]
   neither in line nor ambiguous,
barbaric nose
blunt and wide [beards] Assyrian [eyes] oblique I come from the other side
   of the river: Cuban
and stuck up [a Jew] tabernacle [shofar and *tallith*] violin of Aragon or
   lead trumpet in the Matancera Sound: what
more could you want than to be a migratory ibis [mockery] or sporadic
   heart. . .
That's how I am, me
and him, cistern and limbo [myriads] the hands that scale the steps,
   contaminate
thought
ringworm and verdigris [water] imperturbable: nationless, a quiet future
and the buzz of ringing cauldrons [my hands] are my race poking at the
   crackling
material.) [Translated by Ammiel Alcalay.]

Identity is to be found in the blend: to know how to speak like the people from Spain, Cuba, Mexico or Peru; to have an expression or physical figure that combines all races; to be able to play popular or classical music; to be Jewish, Catholic or Buddhist; to have hands and heart ready to receive everything, or better, to look for the center of things.

The family album could be extended to many other matters. Kozer's illuminations start with a reflection of a banal and common object and finish as spiritual inquiries that come close to the mystical. Language also acts with the same necessity as the absolute. Although Kozer's first books were formulated with a strong resemblance to the poetry of César Vallejo and Nicanor Parra,[10] the last ones have created a voice in a continued experimentation that goes far beyond the initial tone of satire in search of spiritually deeper expressions. This gradual change can be seen in the extension of the verse. In *Carece de causa*, there are some cases where a single verse spans two pages. This is especially unusual in Latin American poetry, where poets of the last decades have had the tendency to be less innovative in that sense.[11] Although long verses do not explain by themselves the spirituality, it seems that Kozer's respiration and language

---

10. I am referring, in particular, to *Padres y otras profesiones* and *De Chepén a La Habana*.
11. See note 1. Kozer's poetry is unique in terms of extension of verse and syntaxis. There are other poets, however who also experiment with form and language. Zurita, Huerta, and Perlongher, are some of them.

construction have to be close to the point of asphyxia: the need to fill in all the spaces, to say all the phrases, is an aspiration for totality. Kozer has indicated as one of his goals to exhaust the dictionary (his language is very rich in this sense). There is also a new and unique syntax, morphology and rhythm. The page is, as the world, the space where the poet works to fabricate his own face. The poetic experience of Kozer considers agglutination of words, experimentation with the syntactic structures, half-cut narrations, an intense breathing mechanism, as ways to represent plurality.

The sum of heterogeneity, the ultimate texture that this poetry tries to weave is the impossible meaning to reach and express: unity, absolute. Kozer has posed this search as his final and mysterious achievement, because he knows that only in doing so will he finally discover his origin, his family, and the world.

REFERENCES

Kozer, José. *Bajo este cien*. México: Fondo de Cultura Económica, 1983.
————. *Carece de causa*. Buenos Aires: Ultimo Reino, 1988.
Sefamí, Jacobo. "La devoción en busca del poema," in his *Tríptico de la imaginación poética. Entrevistas con Gonzalo Rojas, Alvaro Mutis y José Kozer*. Unpublished manuscript.
Zapata, Miguel Angel. "José Kozer y la poesía como testimonio de la cotidianedad." *Coloquios del oficio mayor. Inti* 26–27 (1987–1988): 171–186.

17

Samuel Rovinski and the Dual Identity

MARIO A. ROJAS
Translated by Clare M. Aris

SAMUEL ROVINSKI IS A WELL-KNOWN Costa Rican dramatist. In addition to plays, he has written short stories, novels and essays.[1] This essay examines two of his works that deal with Jewish issues: the play, *La víspera del Sábado* (The Eve of the Sabbath) and his collection of short stories, *Cuentos judíos de mi tierra* (Jewish Short Stories from my Land).[2] In these works, from the intertext of his country, Rovinski weaves motifs, themes, and images related to the Diaspora that have recurred in Jewish literature. In the short story, "Con el pie derecho" (With the Right Foot), the narrator describes the protagonist, Frida, as follows:

> Frida era la tradicional intérprete del pueblo judío y le encargaban siempre el trabajo de fondo para la discusión de los temas fundamentales sobre identidad, asimilación, integración, doble lealtad, emigración a Israel y Diáspora. (30)
>
> (Frida was the traditional interpreter of the Jewish people and was always asked to be in charge of the discussion of fundamental themes of identity, assimilation, integration, dual loyalties, emigration to Israel and the Diaspora.)

As will be shown later, precisely these themes reflect the interests of the author himself, who addresses in these works the typical problems

---

1. Among the numerous works of the author, the plays *Las Fisgonas de Paso Ancho, Gulliver dormido, El martirio del Pastor* and the novel *Ceremonia de Casta* deserve special mention.
2. For this work the following editions were used: *Cuentos judíos de mi tierra.* (San José: Editorial Costa Rica, 1982). "La víspera del Sábado" in *Tres obras de teatro.* Editorial Costa Rica, 1985. This play made its début at the National Theatre in March, 1984 under the direction of Daniel Gallegos.

211

encountered by the Jew who arrives in a strange territory, and whose optimistic image is always blurred by the fear of rejection, even if the new country is originally anticipated as a land of promise. Rovinski's characters, without renouncing their traditional Jewish values, try to find their way into a host society that is not always willing to accept and integrate them completely.

According to Gershon Shaken, Jewish literature written in languages other than Hebrew is always permeated either explicitly or implicitly by the crisis of dual identity.[3] Some Jewish writers approach and openly thematicize the nature of their hidden identity, while others, though they try to avoid mentioning it, cannot avoid implying it in their writing. Consequently, Jewish literature can be characterized as "a highly complex embodiment of both identities" (58). The problems of Jewish identity are derived principally from two sources: the Jew's desire to integrate in a new world, and his faithfulness to the Jewish tradition. The Jewish social status is very similar to that of other minority groups which also experience marginalization. At the same time that these people struggle to maintain their bonds and the protection of their group, they strive to integrate with the majority who, though well-intentioned and receptive, are often full of prejudices that could easily lead to discrimination. But the Jewish identity crisis is even more complex than that of other immigrant groups because, besides retaining the value system of the country they left behind (Poland, Germany, Russia, etc.), they also retain the religious/social values of the Jewish tradition. Both of these sets of values need to be reconciled with the cultural system of the society they are joining. Thus, a fictional world emerges that is structured by a web of intermingled motifs, such as persecution, exile, integration with a new world, all of them having as thematic focus or dominant motif the crisis of identity.

La víspera del Sábado, as well as several of the stories in *Cuentos judíos de mi tierra* (from now on *Cuentos judíos*), fictionalizes the personal experience of Rovinski, whose parents, Polish Jews, emigrated to Costa Rica after the First World War. The play, which was published later than the short stories, shares intertextual ties while reusing many of the same motifs, but the hypotext[4] to which it is more directly linked is "El miedo a los telegramas" ("Fear of Telegrams"), which becomes the pretext from which the *fabula*, the set of events that will mold the fictional world of the play, stems.

---

3. See Gershon Shaked, *The Shadow Within*, (Philadelphia: The Jewish Publication Society, 1987).
4. Here I am referring to hypotext as defined by Genette in *Palimpsestes* (Seuil: Paris, 1982).

In "Fear of Telegrams" there is a narrator/protagonist who recalls the first years of his life up to the moment when reality loses the innocent charm of a child's point of view. The narrative is arranged around a single motif: a telegram with bad news, which appears at the beginning and at the end of the story. The first telegram announces the serious illness of the father, who must abandon a recently bought farm to recuperate from tuberculosis in a sanitarium. The second telegram, from Poland, brings news of the death of the maternal grandmother who had provided moral and material support to the family. She dies just before the German invasion of Poland. In the story there is a double focalization or point of view: that of the mature narrator who remembers his childhood, and that of the boy protagonist; the vision of the latter is the predominant one. The intimate world of the family is unveiled from the ingenuous and wondering perspective of the child who witnesses the vicissitudes of his family threatened by conflicts arising from his father's constant failure in business ventures, from contextual hostile forces that obstruct the family's integration into the Costa Rican milieu, and from the persecution and extermination of the Jews in Europe, the psychological and social impact of which is being felt not only in the family circle but also in Costa Rica and Latin America. The child's degree of assimilation is different from that of his parents, who live with one foot in Costa Rica and the other in Europe: he thinks, feels and acts like a Costa Rican. If his well being is affected by the bad news of the first telegram, he is affected more by the fact that he cannot enjoy with his friends the fascination of an environment in which he feels completely integrated. The story has an open ending. It concludes at the point after which he will become aware of his double identity, of being a 'Costa Rican Jew'.

In *La víspera del Sábado* (from now on *Víspera*), the problems of the Diaspora are fully unfolded. The individual and family conflicts are rendered in a more profound way and mingled with the repercussions in Costa Rica of the Second World War and of the Jewish extermination in Europe.

The play is divided into three acts through which the development of two conflicts is interwoven: one gravitates around the figure of the father Berlinski who reveals from within the intimacy of the family; and the other springs from the family's striving to adapt themselves to their new surroundings. The first act opens with scenes from the daily life of the Berlinskis. The stage directions carefully describe the interior of the Berlinskis's home. The scenographic codes call for a modest but neat space shared by a living and a dining room. The rooms are decorated with objects that function as signs representing the social status of the family, their immigrant status, and their Jewish identity: "Es la víspera del sábado. La mesa está puesta para cinco personas y, en uno de los extremos, hay dos candelabros con sus velas...[en la pared] hay un viejo tapiz de Polonia con algunas escenas bíblicas." (65) ("It is the Eve of the Sabbath. The table is set for five people and at one end of it there are two candelabra...[on the wall] hangs an old tapestry from Poland with some biblical scenes.") This stage setting will remain relatively unchanged for all three acts. The modest condition of the family is underscored in the dialogue between Moisés (Moishe) and his mother. She tenderly but firmly advises him to eat an orange or a banana, which are local fruits, instead of an apple, which is an imported and expensive fruit. The first indications of the problems the family has with the outside world are revealed through the dialogue between Jaya and Regina, characters who are contrasted in juxtaposition as sisters. While Jaya, the elder, listens to romantic Latin American ballads and has no interest in matters related to Israel, Regina reads poems by Bialik[5] and sees the creation of Israel as the possibility of a land where people would not discriminate: "¿No crees que sería lindo vivir en una tierra donde no te discriminan, donde no te digan polaca ni te hagan a un lado?" (70) ("Don't you think it would be nice to live in a land where they don't discriminate against you, where they don't call you a Polack or push you aside?") In their dialogue they allude to the father's lack of business acumen "Con esa facilidad de papá para los malos negocios (se ríen) (72) (...With that tendency of Papa's for getting involved in bad business deals [they laugh...]) This proleptic dialogue is important because it anticipates the two main conflicts of the play. The first conflict appears clearly outlined when the father, embarrassed, is obliged to confirm what Mrs. Berlinski has learned from a friend: that he is in the process of buying a farm. Mrs. Berlinski, knowing her husband well, opposes this project emphatically. Towards the end of the first act, despite everyone's anxiety—with the exception of Moises, for whom it would be the ideal holiday place—Mr. Berlinski affirms that the business deal has already been closed. The family conflict is this: Will Mr. Berlinski triumph this time with his business dealings, or will he cause the ruination of his family? The second conflict is structured around the family's problems with its integration in the Costa Rican environment. The difficulty arises not so much from rejection by the host country as from the effects of the Second World War already manifest in Latin America. The news of the "Jewish Agency" is alarming: "los alemanes están juntando a todos los judíos polacos en guetos" (81) ("the Germans are amassing all the Polish

---

5. Ben-Zion Eisenstadt (1883–1951). See the interesting essay by Shaked (note 3) "Bialik here and now" (124–132).

Jews in ghettos"). Mr. Berlinski consoles his wife, assuring her that "Todo saldrá bien, ¡ya lo verás!. . .y los polacos volverán a ser libres." ("All will turn out well, you will see!. . .and the Polish people will again be free"). Mrs. Berlinski asks ¿Y los judíos? ("And the Jews?"). With a tone that attempts to be persuasive, but is not very convincing, Mr. Berlinski replies "¿Los judíos. . .,acaso no son polacos también? (82) ("The Jews. . .are they not Polish also?") At the end of Act I, a loudspeaker can be heard on the street proclaiming that the government of Costa Rica has declared war on Germany. Everyone is happy except Mrs. Berlinski, who murmurs while the scene darkens "¿Eso es bueno o malo para los judíos? (101) ("Is that good or bad for the Jews?") At the conclusion of Act I the two conflicts have been defined clearly and tension and suspense have been created, leaving the reader/spectator with four projected possibilities, two for each conflict: Will Mr. Berlinski succeed in his enterprise or not, and how will his success or failure affect his family's well being? Will the problems of Jews in Europe affect the efforts of the Berlinski family to integrate and live peacefully in Costa Rica, or not?

In Act II, seven months later, Mrs. Berlinski hastily finishes sewing a suit: she has had to take up sewing in order to support her family while they wait for the farm to start to produce some incomes. Right after Mrs. Berlinski has experienced a rough time with doña Bolcha, a rich and parsimonious customer, Mr. Berlinski makes a surprise appearance. He is very ill, and he is returning from the countryside to see a doctor. According to him, all is going well with the farm and soon they will begin to receive some profits from their investment. But nobody is quite sure that this is the case. Doña Bolcha has brought the news that the Costa Ricans, in a public demonstration, have asked the government for the expulsion of all Germans and Italians from the country. On the other hand, Jaim H., a good friend of the family, delivers the alarming news that in Europe "están sacando a los judíos de los guetos y los meten en campos de concentración" (125) ("they are pulling the Jews out of the ghettos and putting them in concentration camps"). The situation of the Jewish Costa Ricans is surrounded with uncertainty and insecurity. The conversation is interrupted by shouts from the street, where slogans against the Germans and Italians are heard: "¡Mueran los boches! ¡Abajo los túteles!" (135) ("Death to the Boches! Down with the *Túteles!*") After Jaim and his wife quickly say good-bye, a young Italian tailor, Luigi, asks Mr. Berlinski to protect him from the mob that wants to lynch him. Risking their own safety, the family provides protection for him. With courage, Mr. Berlinski faces the crowd and saves Luigi. The act ends with a dialogue between Regina and Jaya:

REGINA: ¡Crees que podamos vivir en paz?
JAYA: Sí, claro...Cuando termine la guerra
REGINA: Tengo miedo, Jaya. Siento como si todo fuera a acabar para
        nosotros...
JAYA: ¡Qué tontería...!
REGINA: ¿Sabés qué...? Creo que el mundo es injusto. (145–146)

(REGINA: Do you believe that we can live in peace?
JAYA: Yes, of course...When the war ends.
REGINA: I'm afraid, Jaya. I feel as if everything is about to end for us.
JAYA: What foolishness...!
REGINA: Do you know what...? I think the world is unfair.)

Both conflicts have reached a climax. The family situation worsens with the illness of Mr. Berlinski and it is probable that he will not be able to return to the farm for a long time. The threats and attacks against the Germans and Italians—innocent victims of what is happening in Europe—endanger the safety of the family who at any moment, on account of their being immigrants and Jewish, could also become the targets of an attack.

In Act III, two weeks later, the doctor diagnoses Mr. Berlinski with tuberculosis, due to the unhealthy living conditions in the countryside and malnourishment. He will have to be placed in a sanitarium. This news produces great consternation in the family. With the help of their good friends Jaim y Gueña and with the earnings of Mrs. Berlinski, they should be able to support themselves. Even if this should prove to be the case, the farm could be sold to pay for the medical treatment and the medicine. The act ends with alarming news about the war: the penetration of von Paulus's troops in Russia and the death of thousands of Jews in the Nazi concentration camps. In the face of his mother's anguish, Moses tries to console her by saying that when he is grown up, he will become a soldier and kill all the Germans. His mother replies: "¡Moishele, usted no va a matar a nadie! (le acaricia el pelo). Es pecado matar. La Torá lo prohíbe. Es malo matar...¡Nosotros no debemos matar! ("Moses, you are not going to kill anyone! [she strokes his hair]. It is wrong to kill..., We should not kill! The Torah forbids it. It is a sin to kill.") In the last scene, the mother "enciende las velas y dice la oración del Shabat..." (188) ("lights the candles and says the prayer of the Sabbath...")

The conflicts can be synthesized in the following schemes:

Conflict A

Sender: Mr. Berlinski's desire to better his family's situation
Receiver: Mr. Berlinski's family

Subject: Mr. Berlinski
Object: He buys a farm that produces dairy products
Helper: The knowledge that Mr. Berlinski has of this type of business
Opponent: The lack of ability Mr. Berlinski has for business
            Mrs. Berlinski, Regina, Jaya
            Unhealthiness of the countryside
            Lack of sufficient capital
            Illness of Mr. Berlinski
            Cost of medical treatment for Mr. Berlinski

Conflict B

Destinator: The Berlinski family's desire to integrate with the Costa Rican
            environment
Destineé: The Berlinski family
Subject: The Berlinski family
Object: Integration with the Costa Rican environment. To be accepted
            as Costa Rican. Not to be discriminated against.
Assistant: Moisés, Jaya, Mr. Berlinski, the Costa Ricans who are willing
            to accept the Jews
Opponent: The discrimination against the Jews by some Costa Ricans
            The particular experience of the family in Poland
            The persecution and extermination of the Jews by the Nazis
            The repercussions of the war in Costa Rica: expulsion of the
            Germans and the Italians and the fear of what this could bring
            to the Jews

The resolutions of both conflicts hang in suspense. All the clues given to the reader/spectator indicate that the farm will be sold. Those who have read the short story "Fear of Telegrams" (internal intertextuality) know that in effect the farm will be sold and that after other failures, the family will finally improve their economic situation.

In the second conflict, different from the first in that the direction and development of the conflict depend solely on the family, the forces that control the resolution of the conflict are external. The family's uncertainty and insecurity grow, because at any moment the Jewish community could be treated in the same manner as the German and the Italian residents of the country. Within the family nucleus the most positive force for integration is Moisés, who acts like a Costa Rican child and—as generally happens in immigrant families in which the integration takes place via the children—who will play a fundamental role in the process of the acculturation of the Berlinskis. Jaya performs a similar role, though with less intensity. The drive, idealism, and honesty of Mr. Berlinski similarly helps the integration. Mrs. Berlinski appears to be more of a force that obstructs the integration. Overprotective of her children and not bold enough to face the outside world, her environment is always the home. She prefers to earn less doing work at home rather than using her skills in a job that would expose her to outside forces. Regina is the shadow of her mother. For the sake of security she feels more comfortable at home and close to the Jewish tradition, and her perception of the outside world is always negative. On the other hand, the German advance through Europe and the extermination of the Jews keeps the family burning with the fear that despite the fact that Costa Rica has united with the Allies and has declared war on Germany, the universal situation of the Jews might worsen and they might have to emigrate once more. The story of the Diaspora reminds them that the Jew can easily become a scapegoat who pays for another's sins. Just like the family conflict, this one also is left hanging in suspense.

As illustrated, *Cuentos judíos* shares with *Víspera* many themes and motifs. One of these, the theme of marriages arranged by the parents, alluded to but not developed in *Víspera*, is central in "Con el pie derecho." Here, Frida, an intelligent girl, surprisingly receives from her parents "como regalo de bachillerato un shidaj de primer orden" ("a first rate *shidaj* as a graduation gift"). Her reaction is perplexed". . .lloró mucho. . .se sentía como objeto manipulable en las manos de los mayores" (31) ("she cried a lot. . .she felt like an manipulable object in the hands of her elders"). However, when she finds out that the bridegroom is one of the young men most sought after by the ladies, she accepts the marriage with pleasure. The ironic tone of the narrator becomes almost farcical when relating how, in order to get the bridegroom to appear at the wedding, the parents of the bride have to add something more to the already considerable dowry agreed upon: "Al son de una melodía hebrea, inició la marcha el novio del brazo de sus padres, muy satisfecho porque esa noche habían logrado agregar una hermosa residencia a la dote convenida." (35) ("At the sound of the Hebrew melody the bridegroom began the march arm in arm with his parents, very satisfied, because that night they had been able to add a beautiful residence to the arranged dowry").

In "Las naranjas de Pascua" ("Passover Oranges"), a narrative voice speaks with a narratee, who does not answer and whose replies can only be inferred. Obsessively, the whole speech of the enunciator revolves around finances. As Mr. H. maintains in *Víspera*, money is the only thing that gives the Jew security and permits him to be prepared for any eventuality. Around this thematic nucleus appears a series of motifs related to the Jewish tradition and the Diaspora, such as persecution: "Los judíos somos chivos expiatorios..." (22) ("The Jews are scapegoats..."); the nostalgia for the homeland and the discrimination suffered there: "Claro que era muy bonito nuestro pueblo en Polonia. ¿Puedo yo negarlo? El bosque, el río, los trigales. Todo muy lindo, si no fuera por los patanes antisemitas. Y no hay peor antisemita que el polaco..." (24) ("Of course, our town was pretty in Poland. Could I deny it? The forest, the river, the wheat fields. All very pretty, if it weren't for the anti-Semitic louts. And there is no anti-Semite worse than a Polish one..."); the land of promise that receives them: "Este es el paraíso, Janche..." (26) ("This country is Paradise, Janche"), gratitude and prayer of protection: "Hay que dar gracias a Dios todos los días, Janche, y pedirle que no cambie las cosas para mal de Costa Rica." (26) ("We must thank God every day, Janche, and ask him not to change things for the worse in Costa Rica.")

One of the best short stories in the collection is "El fantasma pardo" ("The Dark Ghost"). Herman, a survivor of the Holocaust who had lost his memory from being tortured, surprisingly recaptures it while sitting in a synagogue upon hearing shouts outside which are threatening foreigners, among whom Jews are named: "Blandían pancartas con lemas como 'El comercio es para los costarricenses.' '¡Fuera extranjeros indeseables!' y 'polacos, a sembrar papas!' " (50) ("They brandished signs with slogans like 'Trade is for the Costa Ricans,' 'Out, undesirable aliens,' and 'Polacks, go plant potatoes!' ") Herman remembers the time years before when he was in a synagogue that was attacked—its glass windows were broken and it was then set on fire. While trying to escape from the temple to save his family, he was separated from his wife and son whom he never saw again. That time, neither Herman nor anyone else had opposed the attack. Now he reproaches his previous "pasividad ante los asesinos pardos" (53) ("passivity before the dark murderers"). While he recalls those ominous fragments from the past, excited by the memories and by the great guilt that he feels, he interprets the murmuring in the street and the passage of a light reflected in the colored glass to be history repeating itself. The past becomes the present (the number 135878 marked on his arm acquires full meaning) and this time he will act: "La gigantesca sombra del vengador se lanzó sobre el fantasma pardo que blandía la antorcha" (54) ("The gigantic shadow of the avenger leaped upon the dark ghost who brandished the torch"). In the story the narrator limits his point of view to that of the character and it is from this viewpoint that the world is shaped. The end of the story is ambiguous: Will history repeat itself, or is the scene recreated by the disturbed mind of the character?

"Cambio de identidad" ("Change of identity"), also narrated in the second person like "Las naranjas de Pascua," tells the story of a Jew who enlists in the military to fight against the followers of Figueres. When he becomes separated from his unit, his capturers want revenge by hanging him, the only Jew. With the help of his parents he takes refuge in Nicaragua, and from there flees to Venezuela, always hiding his identity, before finally arriving in the United States. At the end of the story, the narrator—whose narratee is a friend to whom he has told his story regarding the resistance of the hippies who refuse to go to war—is asked:

¿Quién soy? ¿Cuál es mi verdadera identidad? ¿Podrías darme una luz sobre lo que yo debo ser? Cuando mis hijos deseen rastrear mi pasado, se encontrarán con una maraña....Aprendí a estar en cualquier sitio, adoptando una conducta necesaria para sobrevivir. He huido varias veces de una personalidad para crearme otra. (90)

(Who am I? What is my true identity? Could you shed some light on what I should be? When my children want to trace my past, they will find a tangled web. . . . I learned how to exist in any situation, adopting behavior necessary to survive. I fled several times from one personality to create another.)

This segment is a metaphorical icon that synthesizes the story of the Diaspora.

In conclusion, the two works of Rovinski describe the vicissitudes of Jewish families transplanted from Eastern Europe to Costa Rica. All of them trace individual identity problems and the Jews' relation to the non-Jewish world. In his texts, the inferred intention of the speaker of these works is clear. The Jews in Costa Rica should integrate into this new society, but without renouncing the traditional fundamental values of Jewish culture. On the other hand, Jews should question some aspects of their social behavior, for example, the institution of marriage contracts. Rovinski seems to recognize and accept a dual identity for the Jews, which is signaled textually in the title of the collection of his stories *Cuentos judíos*; (which can be paraphrased as 'stories of the Costa Rican Jews') and is also explicitly verbalized in the words of Mr. Berlinski: "Somos judíos costarricenses" (97) ("We are Costa Rican Jews"). Although his characters are at the first stage of the immigration process (nationalization)—Costa Rican Jews/Jewish Costa Ricans—their gradual integration is anticipated by the presence of the child, detached in the story as focalizer and in the play as the character who serves as a bridge between the family circle and the outside world.

Contributors

Edna Aizenberg is associate professor of Spanish at Marymount Manhattan College. She is author of *The Aleph Weaver: Biblical, Kabbalistic and Judaic Elements in Borges*, which was published in Spanish translation in 1986, and of numerous articles on Latin American and comparative literature. Her book *Borges and His Successors*, 1990, deals with, among other aspects of his writing, the "Hebraism" in his work. Aizenberg is a frequent contributor to Judaic journals in this country and abroad.

Lois Barr has taught language and literature at Northwestern University since 1975. She has published articles and reviews on Benito Pérez Galdós, Ramón Sender, Osvaldo Soriano, Gerardo Mario Goloboff, Victor Perera, and Teresa Porzecanski. She is currently writing a book entitled *Latin American Jewish Novelists and the Patriarchal Code*.

Murray Baumgarten is a professor at the University of California at Santa Cruz. He heads the Dickens Project at Kresge College where he has published numerous books and articles both in the field of English literature and Judaic studies.

Sandra M. Cypess first became acquainted with Sephardic studies at Brooklyn College as a student of Mair José Benardete. She received her doctorate from the University of Illinois-Urbana, working with Luis Leal on the dead narrator in Latin American prose fiction. Her publications have focused on Latin American drama (with emphasis on work from Argentina, Mexico, and the Caribbean) and women's writing. She is collaborating on a series of critical bibliographies, the first of which, *Women Authors of Modern Hispanic South America: A Bibliography of Literary Criticism and Interpretation* (Scarecrow Press), appeared in 1989. Her book *La Malinche in Mexican Literature* (University of Texas Press) studies the representation of La Malinche in all genres from a diachronic perspective. She is a professor of Spanish and Comparative Literatures at SUNY-Binghamton, where she was also director of the Latin American and Caribbean Area Studies Program.

Robert DiAntonio attended the University of Massachusetts at Boston (BA), the University of Iowa (M.A.), and St. Louis University (Ph.D.). He was a Fulbright Scholar at the University of Buenos Aires and studied at the Universidade Federal do Pernambuco in Recife, Brazil. He has taught at the University of Manitoba, Wisconsin State University, and Southern Illinois University. The author of *The Admissions Essay*, 1987, and *Brazilian Fiction*, 1989, he is a regular contributor to the *Jerusalem Post*, *Jewish Spectator*, *Hadassah Magazine*, the *Denver Post*, *Kansas City Star*, and the *St. Louis Post-Dispatch*. He has also received three National Endowment for the Humanities fellowships.

An article on the Holocaust in Brazilian fiction appeared in *Hispania* in 1991 and a study on Jewish writing in Brazil appeared in 1989 in the *Latin American Literary Review*. Other studies have appeared in *World Literature Today*, *Modern Fiction Studies*, *Chasqui*, *Judaism*, *International Fiction Review*, *Judaica Book News*, *Confluencia*, the *Luso-Brazilian Review*, *Annali Sezione Romanza*, *Mester*, *Romance Quarterly*, *Quaderni Ibero-americani*, *Romance Notes*, *Rivista di letteratura moderne e comparate*, and in several Brazilian and Argentine journals.

David William Foster (Ph.D., University of Washington, 1964) is regents' professor of Spanish at Arizona State University, where he serves as director of Spanish graduate studies and directs the publications program of the Center for Latin American Studies. Although he has written on a wide range of topics in the field of Hispanic literature, the majority of his research has focused on Argentine cultural history, with an emphasis on the narrative and theater. Foster has served as a Fulbright Professor in Argentina, in Brazil, and in Uruguay, and he has been an Inter-American Development Bank professor in Chile.

Edward H. Friedman is a professor of Spanish at Indiana University. His major field of research is Golden Age literature. He is the author of *The Unifying Concept: Approaches to the Structure of Cervantes' Comedias* (Spanish Literature Publications, 1981) and *The Antiheroine's Voice: Narrative Discourse and Transformations of the Picaresque* (University of Missouri Press, 1987), and co-author of *Aproximaciones al estudio de la literatura hispánica* (Random House, 1982).

Nora Glickman was born in La Pampa, Argentina. She studied in Israel, England, and the United States and received her graduate degrees from Columbia University (M.A.) and New York University (Ph.D.). She began her research on Jewish characters and themes in Latin American literature as part of her doctoral dissertation, "The Jewish Image in Brazilian and Argentine Literature," and has since published numerous articles and has lectured and organized conferences on this topic, focusing mainly on the work of dramatists and novelists from Argentina.

Her book of short stories *Uno de sus Juanes* was published in Buenos Aires (Ediciones de La Flor, 1983). Some of her works have been translated into Hebrew, English, and Portuguese. Her second volume of short stories, *Mujeres, mensajes, malogros* appeared in Buenos Aires in 1991. Glickman's critical study on the white slave trade includes a Yiddish translation with Rosalía Rosembuj of Leib Malach's play *Regeneración* (Buenos Aires: Pardés, 1984).

Nora Glickman is a professor of Spanish at Queens College (The City University of New York) where she specializes in Latin American literature. She is a member of the editorial board of *Modern Jewish Studies* and *Letters*.

Florinda Goldberg was born in Argentina in 1943 and has lived in Israel since 1977. She has published articles in collective books and literary reviews (among them *Sur, Cuadernos del Sur, Nueva Crítica, Hispamérica,* and *Noaj*), as well as special editions of D.F. Sarmiento and A. Carpentier. In 1988 she published with I. Rozen *Los latinoamericanos en Israel-Antología de una aliá.* She founded and edited the review *Rumbos,* on contemporary Jewish issues, and is presently assistant editor of *Noaj,* the literary review of the International Association of Jewish Writers in Spanish and Portuguese. She is affiliated with the International Center for University Teaching of Jewish Civilization in Jerusalem.

Regina Igel Associate Professor, Coordinator of Portuguese, Department of Spanish and Portuguese, University of Maryland at College Park. Born in São Paulo, Brazil. B.A. in Romance Languages, University of São Paulo, Brazil; M.A. in Hispanic Language and Literatures, University of Iowa; Ph.D. in Portuguese Language and Luso-Brazilian Literatures, University of New Mexico, USA. Book: *Biografía Literária de Osman Lins* (1987). Selected articles: "O Tema do Holocausto na Literatura Brasileira" (1990, *Noaj,* Israel), "Surcos Literarios e Ideológicos en la obra de Adão Voloch" (1991, SHALOM, Buenos Aires). "Imigrantes na Ficção Brasileira Contemporânea" (1992, *Revista Interamericana de Bibliografía,* USA), "Avaliação sobre Estudos sobre os Negros no Brasil" (1993. *Iberamericana* Hamburg), "Nélida Piñon" (1993, *Anthology of Latin American Writers*, USA) "The Sugarcane Plantation in the Poetry of João Cabral de Melo Neto" (1992, *World Literature Today*, USA).

Naomi Lindstrom is a professor of Spanish and Portuguese at the University of Texas at Austin, where she is also affiliated with the Institute of Latin American Studies. Her recent publications include *Women's Voice in Latin American Literature* (Washington, D.C.: Three Continents Press, 1989) and *Jewish Issues in Argentine Literature: From Gerchunoff to Szichman* (Columbia: University of Missouri Press, 1989).

Mario A. Rojas, Associate Professor at The Catholic University of America, Washington, D.C., is a member of the Executive Council of the *Instituto Internacional de Teoría y Crítica de Teatro Latinoamericano* and a member of the editorial board of *La Escena Latinoamericana*. He has published several articles on the semiotics of theater and Latin American drama, as well as on narratology as applied to Latin American texts. He has recently served as the guest editor of a special volume of *Dispositio* (University of Michigan) on semiotics of theater.

Flora Schiminovich teaches Spanish and Latin American literature at Barnard College, Columbia University. She is the author of *La obra de Macedonio Fernández, una lectura surrealista*, (Madrid: Pliegos, 1986) as well as many articles on Latin American literature. She has contributed a chapter for the book *Gender and Genre: Redefining Women's Autobiographies*, Edited by Colette Hall and Janice Morgan, New York: Garland Press, 1990). She is currently working on a book about Latin American women writers and preparing an anthology of contemporary Latin American female playwrights.

Judith Morganroth Schneider teaches Spanish and French at the University of Maryland, Baltimore County. She edited a special issue of *Folio*, 17 (1987) on Latin American Jewish writers and has published articles on French Jewish writing in the *Romantic Review* (January 1989), the *French Review* (October 1989), and *Symposium* (Winter 1990), as well as many articles on Latin American literature.

Jacobo Sefamí received his licenciatura in letras hispánicas from the UNAM and his Ph.D. from the University of Texas at Austin. He is currently an assistant professor at New York University. He has published a book, *El destierro apacible y otros ensayos*. *Xavier Villaurrutia, Alí Chumacero, Fernando Pessoa, Francicso Cervantes, Haroldo de Campos* (Mexico: Preliá, 1987), and several articles on Latin American literature. He has two books forthcoming: a bibliography of contemporary Spanish American poets and a study on the Chilean poet Gonzalo Rojas.

Leonardo Senkman is a professor at the Hebrew University of Jerusalem. He has published in many fields, but is best known for his book *La identidad judía en la literatura argentina*. He is also the editor of *Noaj*, a literary journal.

Ilan Stavans is a Mexican novelist and critic. His books include *Imagining Columbus: The Literary Voyage* (Twayne, 1992) and *Growing up Latino: Memoirs and Stories* (Houghton Mifflin, 1993). His book *Talia y el cielo* (Plaza and Valdes, 1992) won the Latino Literature Prize. Stavans is the editor of *Tropical Synagogues: An Anthology of Jewish Latin American Short Stories* (Houghton & Meier, 1993). He is presently a professor of Spanish at Amherst College.